Field Guide
to the
Cascades
&Olympics

SECOND EDITION

Field Guide is special. Handy color tabs provide easy access to a variety of topics . . . The comprehensive field guide is amazingly specific.
> —*Klamath Falls (OR) Herald & News*

Clearly organized . . . Beside the illustrations are brief descriptions of each item. You won't be able to tell a meadow vole from a northern bog lemming without it.
> —*Olympian*

This book is clearly organized and a pleasure to thumb through.
> —*Tacoma News-Tribune*

A good, all-purpose field guide is something to treasure. *Field Guide to the Cascades & Olympics* is such a book.
> —*Bend (OR) Bulletin*

A volume steeped in pure love of the area it describes . . . . Arguably the best book of its type for non-professionals. The paintings are in true color and the information is precise and concise.
> —*Salem (OR) Statesman–Journal*

Take [a copy of this book] on your brief excursions into the mountains. You'll be surprised how often you refer to it and what satisfaction it brings.
> —*Centralia Chronicle*

An ideal backpack companion for people who want to know about the plants and animals they encounter on hikes.
> —*Eugene Register–Guard*

For those people who can't decide whether to pack a bird, plant, mushroom, rock, or insect book on hikes, here is a field guide to everything.
> —*Bellingham Herald*

Field Guide
to the
Cascades
&Olympics

SECOND EDITION

Stephen R. Whitney
& Rob Sandelin

Illustrated by Stephen R. Whitney with contributions from Elizabeth Briars

THE MOUNTAINEERS BOOKS

To my wife and companion, Vandana Whitney,
who has stayed with me through both editions.
—Stephen R. Whitney

THE MOUNTAINEERS BOOKS
*is the nonprofit publishing arm of The Mountaineers Club,
an organization founded in 1906 and dedicated to the exploration,
preservation, and enjoyment of outdoor and wilderness areas.*

1001 SW Klickitat Way, Suite 201, Seattle, WA 98134

First edition 1983. Second edition: first printing 2003, second printing 2005,
third printing 2007, fourth printing 2008, fifth printing 2010

Distributed in the United Kingdom by Cordee, www.cordee.co.uk

Manufactured in China

Project Editor: Christine Hosler; Copy Editor: Kris Fulsaas; Cover Design: Helen Cherullo;
Book Design and Layout: Mayumi Thompson; Cartographer: Brian Metz
Cover illustrations: Stephen R. Whitney and Elizabeth Briars
Frontispiece: *Grizzly bear*

The illustration of the mountain goat on Plate 100 was derived from the photograph
Mountain Goat, Enchantments, Washington State by Jay Potts, American Focus Photography
(The Castaways, Inc.). The photograph was used courtesy of the photographer.

Library of Congress Cataloging-in-Publication Data
Whitney, Stephen, 1942-
  Field guide to the Cascades and Olympics / Stephen R. Whitney and Rob Sandelin ;
illustrated by Stephen R. Whitney with contributions from Elizabeth Briars.— 2nd ed.
   p. cm.
Includes bibliographical references (p.   ).
  ISBN 0-89886-808-4 (pbk.)
  1. Natural history—Washington (State)—Olympic Mountains. 2. Natural history—Cascade
Range. I. Title: Cascades and Olympics. II. Sandelin, Rob. III. Title.
  QH105.W2W47 2004
  508.795—dc22

                    2003022134

contents

acknowledgments

In the same way an ecological community is the sum of many parts, a book of this nature has many people who in one way or another have helped it along.

Rob Sandelin thanks Stephen Whitney both for the opportunity to collaborate on this revision and for sage advice in the art of book writing. The mushroom text was improved by Igor Malcevski's generous input, and Dr. Thom Odell and Bill Clifford helped me sort through the many mushroom species to pick just the right ones. Sharon Coleman provided invaluable assistance in sifting through the mysteries of insects, and James R. Labonte helped with beetles and other entomological advice. Scott Babcock taught me much about the rocks and their arrangements in the North Cascades. Alan Bauer and Bob Carson provided excellent photographic support. Special thanks to Helen and Stan Engle for their enthusiastic support and to all those Mountaineers who gave me suggestions on how to improve the book. And finally, my loving gratitude to my life partner, Heidi Engle, who for twenty years has been my companion on many a mountain trail throughout the Cascades and Olympics, and to my daughters, Kara and Helen, who have endured frogs and mice in the freezer, innumerable containers of bugs, and all the trials and trails of growing up with naturalists for parents.

Stephen Whitney thanks coauthor Rob Sandelin for his splendid work bringing the text of this book up to date. Thanks also to Elizabeth Briars for her fine illustrations of the fish, amphibians, reptiles, and trees, and to wildlife photographer Jay Potts for permission to use one of his photos as the source for the illustration of the mountain goat. Finally, the support of William Kemsley Jr. brought the first edition of this book into being more than twenty years ago.

The authors would like to thank our editor, Kris Fulsaas, and the staff at The Mountaineers Books, especially Deb Easter and Kathleen Cubley, who helped make a good old book into a better new book.

introduction

The Pacific Northwest is home to spectacular mountain scenery. A couple hours' drive out of urban centers such as Seattle, Vancouver, Portland, and Salem give travelers easy access to several types of habitats: forests, wildflower meadows, alpine parklands, volcanoes, and jeweled mountain lakes. Dozens of parks provide camping, hiking, fishing, and other outdoor recreation. Mountain trail systems consisting of thousands of miles yield hiking trips ranging from a few minutes to several weeks. For those seeking solitude amid primal conditions, many wilderness areas offer a taste of nature that is both raw and refreshing to the spirit.

This book is intended to provide hikers, campers, and lovers of the outdoors with a handy guidebook to the common plants and animals of the Cascade Range and Olympic Mountains. Learning the names of the life forms around us is the first step in becoming acquainted with nature. As we become familiar with the locals, we begin to notice them in new places, like old friends at a dinner party. As we begin to recognize them as individuals, we start to wonder why, how, and where. Thus we begin to broaden our perspective and understanding of the natural world around us.

The sections and chapters of this book illustrate and describe the plants and animals most commonly seen by travelers, campers, and hikers. Part I gives an overview of the mountain environment: its commonly encountered communities of plants and animals and an overview of the region's geology, including a field guide to the common rocks. Part II contains field guides to mushrooms, ferns, trees, shrubs, and wildflowers. Part III provides field guides to insects, butterflies, trout and salmon, amphibians, reptiles, birds, and mammals. So this field guide is essentially more than a dozen field guides rolled into one volume, allowing the mountain traveler to identify a wide variety of plants and animals in the Cascades and Olympics.

WHAT'S NEW IN THIS EDITION

The original edition has been extensively updated. The species descriptions have been revised according to the latest taxonomic changes, and the introductory material is now focused on ecology. Expanded coverage now includes rocks, mushrooms, and insects, which combine with existing species descriptions to create fourteen field guides in one book. The geology chapter has been revised to include the latest findings and now features a pictorial guide to identifying the more common rocks in the region.

The illustrations, including photographs of major habitats, are all in color. The field guide sections are color tabbed, and a quick reference index added to the front cover makes it easy to speedily find each section.

THE GEOGRAPHIC SCOPE
The Cascade Range

The Cascade Range is part of a long line of mountain ranges that run parallel to the Pacific coast and stretch for more than 2,000 miles. The portion of the Cascades covered in this book starts in southern British Columbia at the Fraser River and follows the mountain range, running south by southwest, approximately 600 miles to the Willamette/Umpqua divide, around Crater Lake National Park in Oregon (see figure 1). As one travels south from Crater Lake, the vegetation changes and merges into that of the Sierra Nevada, and while many plants and animals in this book can be found in the southernmost Cascade Range, as far south as Lassen Peak, there are many Sierran species not covered here. The book is also useful in the forested lowlands and Coast Ranges of southwestern Washington and Oregon, southwestern British Columbia, and Vancouver Island.

The Cascade Range can be divided into three large general provinces, based roughly on temperature and precipitation gradients, with the coldest and wettest environment in the north and gradual warming and drying to the south. The North Cascades stretch from the Fraser River south to Snoqualmie Pass at Interstate 90. The middle Cascades extend from Snoqualmie Pass south to Mount Hood and the southern Cascades continue from Mount Hood south to Crater Lake and beyond.

The Cascade Range creates a rain-shadow effect, with much higher precipitation levels falling on the western slopes than on the eastern side of the range. The difference in rainfall creates an obvious and noticeable difference in the vegetation and associated wildlife between the east and west sides of the range.

Lofty, snowcapped volcanoes are characteristic of the Cascade Range, as are lesser volcanic features such as cinder cones, lava flows, and ash deposits. The tallest volcanoes tower above the surrounding ridges and host permanent snowfields and glaciers. From the Three Sisters in central Oregon northward, all the major Cascades volcanoes but Mount St. Helens have alpine glaciers on their flanks. The dominant volcano in this chain is Mount Rainier, which rises 14,410 feet and commands the landscape of the Puget Sound area. With twenty-six named glaciers, Mount Rainier is a reminder of the powerful forces of volcanic fire and glacial ice that shaped and created the magnificent mountain landscapes we enjoy today. Other notable volcanoes include, from north to south, Mount Garibaldi, Mount Baker, Mount Adams, Mount St. Helens, Mount Hood, Mount Jefferson, the Three Sisters, Mount Bachelor, Mount Thielsen, Mount Mazama (Crater Lake), Mount McLoughlin, Mount Shasta, and Lassen Peak. (For more information about volcanoes, see chapter 2, The Geologic Story.)

The Olympic Mountains

The Olympic Mountains form a roughly circular range, in the heart of the Olympic Peninsula in the northwestern corner of Washington State (see figure 1). The mountains rise up in such close proximity to the Pacific Ocean that no peak is more than 30 miles from the ocean, and the range forms a barrier to the moisture-laden Pacific

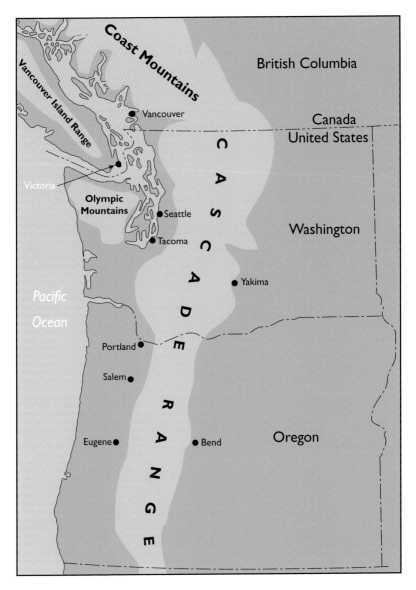

Figure 1. *Map of mountain ranges covered in this book*

winds. As the damp ocean air rises and cools, it releases moisture as snow and rain. The western side of the range receives a wet blanket of rainfall and snow exceeding 140 inches per year in places. As the moisture is wrung out of the clouds passing over these mountains, it creates a rain shadow, so that the northeastern corner of the Olympic Peninsula receives only a scant 15 to 18 inches of rain per year, the lowest rainfall anywhere along the coast north of central California. The southwest-facing river valleys of the Olympics are famed for their mossy, dripping, temperate rain forests. Record-sized and near-record specimens of several species of trees are found along the river drainages and ridges.

The tallest of this jumble of mountains is 7,965-foot Mount Olympus, which rises more than 6,000 feet above the adjacent valleys. Several other peaks exceed 7,000 feet, and the topography tends toward steep ridges cut with river valleys. Unlike the Cascade Range, which has a clear east-west drainage pattern, the rivers and ridges of the Olympics run in all cardinal directions, forming a roughly circular pattern of drainages.

HOW TO USE THIS BOOK

The core of this book is the species descriptions and their corresponding illustrations. Each species description includes a common name, scientific name, description of important features, habitat and geographic range, and, in some cases, brief accounts of similar species. Each chapter has an introduction to the organisms described, which includes pertinent information regarding their ecology and identification.

In some cases brief descriptions of similar species have been included in the text but not illustrated. Also in a few cases, accounts may describe one organism that is more or less typical of a whole group. Insects in particular, because of the huge numbers of species and very minute and technical details that differentiate species, lend themselves to this treatment. For example, there are dozens of species of butterfly commonly called "blues," each so similar that attempting to identify individual species is difficult or nearly impossible for anyone but an expert.

Species are organized by family and then listed by common name and scientific name, which includes genus and species. If the reader chooses to search for further information on the species listed, the scientific name may yield more accurate results since common names are local and variable.

ON BEHALF OF THE MOUNTAINS

Those of us who love and frequent the mountains of our region should always leave an area and its inhabitants as little disturbed by our passage as possible so that what attracted us to the place will remain intact for others to enjoy. The natural wonders of our mountains draw millions of visitors annually, with peak visitation from May through September. As many as 50,000 people might walk the same popular alpine trail during the summer season. In many fragile communities, plants cling precariously to existence and regrowth is a long and difficult prospect, especially in high elevations where short growing seasons make life very difficult. Some communities can take decades to fully recover from a thoughtless action resulting in crushing or damage just from walking off the trail. It is important not only to not cut across switchbacks and take shortcuts, but also to extend our sensitivity by educating those who do.

This book was designed to enable outdoor enthusiasts to identify species without having to collect specimens. Collecting plants and animals should be left to scientists. To destroy a plant or animal simply to learn its name is inexcusable under most conditions and against the law in many parks and preserves.

By picking up any litter we encounter, we set an example for others and also help discourage future littering. Research has shown that a lack of litter inhibits those who are inclined to toss their trash. By pitching in and picking up, we take an active role in the management of our public lands.

It cannot be overstressed that we should not feed wildlife. When we encourage campground animals to take handouts, the animal ignores its primary natural foods in season and replaces them with human-provided foods that often are empty of the nutrients on which the animal's survival depends. Once campers are gone in the fall, it is often too late for the hapless handout-conditioned animal to gather its winter food supply that meets its dietary needs. To protect ourselves and the wildlife, be sure to secure food properly: Use a bear canister (required in some places) or hang food 4 feet from tree trunks and 10 feet off the ground. When a large animal such as a bear becomes conditioned to cruise campgrounds for food, it may be killed by rangers who want to protect the very campers who created the food problem in the first place. Be proactive for wildlife, and help your outdoor neighbors be good campers too.

One of the largest impacts on wildlife is free-roaming dogs. Wildlife often lives on a thin margin of energy expenditure, and even the simple presence of a pet can affect a wild animal's ability to forage or travel. Consider leaving pets at home. If you do take your dog hiking with you, make sure that this is allowed in the area you are visiting (national parks do not allow dogs, for instance), and keep your dog leashed and on the trail with you. Many pets are inclined to give chase, and such actions drive animals away from areas, depriving other hikers of a future chance of wildlife observation. If you encounter a wild animal and it appears stressed or agitated, move your pet back and move away from the animal.

Those who love our region's mountains have an increased responsibility to educate and correct the actions of those who by their thoughtless and unknowing actions destroy the very thing they come to see. By taking an active conservation role, you are creating a lasting connection to the places you love and making the world a better place for all the creatures we share it with.

ABBREVIATIONS

To keep all species descriptions on the page facing their corresponding illustrations requires the extensive use of abbreviations. Most should be self-evident. In any case, all are listed below. In addition, when the name of a genus occurs more than once in a single paragraph, it is first written out completely, then indicated in subsequent citations by only its initial letter. For example:

Grand Fir, *Abies grandis;* Red Fir, *A. magnifica (Abies magnifica);* Shasta Fir, *A. m.* var *shastensis (Abies magnifica variety shastensis).*

'	foot/feet	ea	each
"	inch(es)	E Cas	eastern Cascades
+	more	E CMtns	eastern Coast Mountains
±	more or less	el	elevation
%	percent	esp	especially
abdm	abdomen	F	female
abun	abundant	Feb	February
Alas	Alaska	flr(s)	flower(s)
Albta	Alberta	flt	flight
alp	alpine, alpine zone	FW	forewing (butterflies)
alt	alternate		
Amer	America	gen	generally
Apr	April	grnd	ground
Ariz	Arizona		
Atl	Atlantic	H/B	head and body length
att	attached		(mammals)
Aug	August	ht	height
		HW	hindwing (butterflies)
Baja	Baja California		
BC	British Columbia	inflor	inflorescence
blk	black	irreg	irregular
ca	approximately	Jan	January
Cal	California		
Can	Canada	L	length
Cas	Cascade Range	lb(s)	pound(s)
cen	central	lf	leaf
Cen Amer	Central America	lfless	leafless
cf	refer to	lflet	leaflet
CMtns	Coast Mountains of	lowl	lowland(s)
	British Columbia	lvd	leaved
Colo	Colorado	lvs	leaves
com	common		
conif	conifer(ous)	M	male
CRGorge	Columbia River Gorge	Mar	March
		mdw(s)	meadow(s)
Dec	December	Mich	Michigan
decid	deciduous	mid	middle
diam	diameter	midsum	midsummer
dk	dark	migr	migrant (or migration)
		Minn	Minnesota
e (or E)	east (or eastern, eastward)	Mont	Montana

mont	montane	segm	segment(s)
Mt	Mount	Sept	September
mtn(s)	mountain(s)	SNev	Sierra Nevada
		sp	species (singular)
n (or N)	north (or northern, northward)	spp	species (plural)
		spr	spring
N Amer	North America	subalp	subalpine, subalpine zone
NCas	North Cascades	sum	summer
NDak	North Dakota	sum res	summer resident; bird that nests in our region in summer, absent in winter
ne	northeast (or northeastern, northeastward)		
NEng	New England		
Nev	Nevada	sw	southwest (or southwestern, southwestward)
NMex	New Mexico		
n Mex	northern Mexico		
Nov	November	T	tail length (mammals)
occas	occasionally	uncom	uncommon
Oct	October	US	United States exclusive of Alaska and Hawaii
oft	often		
OMtns	Olympic Mountains	usu	usually
OPen	Olympic Peninsula		
opp	opposite	Vanc I	Vancouver Island
Ore	Oregon	var	variety
		vis	visitor
Pac	Pacific	Vt	Vermont
perst	persistent		
		w (or W)	west (or western, westward)
r, R	river		
reg	regular	W Cas	western Cascades
res	resident; present year-round (birds)	W CMtns	western Coast Mountains
		win	winter(s)
RM	Rocky Mountains	Wn	Washington
		WS	wingspan (butterflies)
s (or S)	south (or southern, southward)	wt	weight
		W Vir	West Virginia
S Amer	South America	Wyo	Wyoming
sbsp(p)	subspecies		
SDak	South Dakota	×	times, as in 2× (two times)
se	southeast (or southeastern, southeastward)		

PART I
The Mountain Environment

communities

If we were to examine a careful log of the species of plants and animals we encountered over the course of our travels in our mountains, patterns would begin to emerge. As the observer changes locations in the Cascade Range from north to south, associations of certain kinds of plants and animals reappear more or less consistently in similar types of places. For example, the vegetation around a stream or in a nonforested meadow at higher altitudes would show considerable likeness in either the North Cascade Range, on Mount Rainier, on Mount Hood, or in the Olympics. Of course each place has its differences, but many plant and animal associations are consistent enough that we are able to recognize them.

Plant associations exist in similar places because the environmental conditions that affect them are similar in those places. To understand what plant life to expect, we need to examine the environmental conditions that create the boundaries for what plants can live in any particular place. Environmental factors include elevation, which defines temperatures and the length of the growing season, precipitation and availability of water, snow cover, the aspect (for example, north- or south-facing), the slope (steep or shallow), the amount of cover (which determines how much sunlight is available), and the chemical characteristics of the soils.

Biological factors, such as relationships to other plants, soil organisms, competition from other plants, and the impact of herbivory by insects and mammals, also impact plant distribution. The combination of these environmental and biological factors determines what plants and, ultimately, which animals survive in a given area.

Animals associate in a particular place in response to their needs for food, water, shelter, space to raise young, and competition from others of their own species. Since animals can move from place to place, they can take advantage of cover or seasonal food variations. Some animals are found only in particular areas, while others may be found throughout many types of places. Pikas, for example, tend to be found above 2,000 feet in rock piles with associated meadows, while an elk may forage in a meadow in the morning but bed down several miles away in a dense stand of timber to avoid a chilling wind.

Plants and animals interact with and affect each other. Through photosynthesis, plants use energy obtained from sunlight to manufacture carbohydrates. Herbivores obtain nourishment (their share of the sun) by consuming the carbohydrates bound up in plants and converting these to proteins. Carnivores receive their share by eating the herbivores. In return, carnivores keep populations of herbivores under control through predation and thereby help maintain the stands of vegetation upon which both herbivores and, indirectly, carnivores depend.

Animals also perform other functions that are beneficial to plants. Pollination of flowers by butterflies, bees, and other insects is perhaps the best-known example. Another is the dispersal of seeds, which may ride along in a mammal's fur or a bird's feathers or pass through an herbivore's digestive tract into feces that are then deposited in a potential growing site. Burrowing animals, such as moles, gophers, and earthworms, aerate the soil, and all animals enrich it through the contribution of feces and, ultimately, their remains. Microogranisms and mushrooms break down the remains of both plants and animals into humus from which new plants will spring. They also interact with the roots of plants in ways that allow the latter to utilize otherwise unavailable nutrients bound up in the soil.

Animals may influence plants detrimentally by removing entire species from an area. Overgrazing, for example, has removed native steppe and grassland species from large areas in the American West. Bark beetles can have population explosions, resulting in damage to trees that can change the species composition of an area because the beetles attack only particular species of trees, leaving others untouched. Large sections of standing dead trees from beetle invasion then create fuel conditions for destructive

French Creek Valley, Alpine Lakes Wilderness. *Photo by Alan L. Bauer*

forest fires. A change in weather patterns may reduce bird populations, which in turn reduces predation on tree-eating insects, leading to an outbreak of insect damage, which in some cases can remove tree species from hundreds of acres.

Ecologists have defined a set of consistent associations of plants and animals and have extensively mapped these associations to understand their distribution. These associations are called *communities* and are typically defined and named by the dominant plants, which are those that are the most commonly found and use the most space. Communities, then, are dynamic systems exhibiting mutual dependence and accommodation among their members.

Ecologists distinguish between climax communities and seral communities. A *climax community* is one that is so well adapted to its environment that it will persist indefinitely if undisturbed. A *seral community* is one that occupies a site following natural or human disturbance, such as fire, flood, logging, or cultivation. Under natural conditions, seral vegetation will gradually revert to climax vegetation over a period of years, decades, or even longer. This process is called *succession*.

Nature is a moving tapestry of life, always changing and adapting to the existing conditions. Plant communities also change as climatic conditions change. The records from pollen found in lake bottoms tell us that since the retreat of the last glaciers, 10,000 years ago, there have been slow but steady changes in the plant life. The mountain vegetation our great-grandchildren hike through will be different from what we see today as plant species adjust to the changes in temperature and patterns of precipitation. Even over such a small scale as the last 400 years, timberline has gradually crept up in elevation as the climate has warmed.

Animals also respond to changing conditions, and inadvertent human introductions have introduced populations of animals whose native home might be half the world away. As the most successful animals occupy the best environments, those that are less successful diminish and sometimes disappear. Humans have changed vast amounts of the landscape in the past 200 years, marginalizing numerous populations of animals or leading to their outright extinction.

The transition between communities is rarely a clearly defined line but, rather, an intermingling and weaving of species, typically following elevation and aspect contours, with the dominant species that define a community commingling at the places where the communities overlap or local conditions are more attractive for one species than another. For example, a north-facing slope is cooler and holds snow longer and lower down the slope, so Pacific silver fir might be the dominant tree at 2,500 feet on the north slope, but might not dominate until 4,000 feet on the adjacent south-facing slope.

There are hundreds of documented plant communities, and describing them all is beyond the scope of this book. However, there are several common communities worth knowing, and these are described below.

FORESTS

The dominant vegetation in the mountains of the Northwest is coniferous trees, and nowhere else in the world do such superlative coniferous forests grow. The largest specimens of many species of trees are found in the temperate conditions of our mountains. In our national parks and wilderness areas there are huge trees soaring hundreds of feet tall, reminders of the vast forests of giants that once covered much of the Northwest prior to logging.

In this climate, conifers have several advantages over broadleaved deciduous trees. Resinous needles conserve moisture and also maintain photosynthesis year-round. The conical shape of conifers maximizes their ability to capture available light, as does their tall size, with mature trees soaring more than 200 feet tall. Relationships with certain fungi in the soil increase nutrient intake and provide protection against diseases.

One of the difficulties in defining plant communities is that they can operate on a time scale measured in centuries. Many forests are in a state of transition from one set of dominant species to another. In the most recent 100 years, much of the natural forest in the Cascades and Olympics, especially in the lowlands below 3,000 feet, has been severely altered by logging, herbicide applications, and monoculture replanting, so the natural patterns that emerge over time have been subverted for economic uses.

Old-growth forest. *Photo by Rob Sandelin*

TABLE I. FOREST COMMUNITIES		
COMMUNITY NAME AND DOMINANT TREES	LOCATION	ALTITUDE RANGES
Coastal Forest: western hemlock, Douglas-fir, western red cedar Sitka spruce	w slope of Cas, from BC s through Ore, and of OMtns	sea level to 2,000' in OMtns and NCas; to 5,000' in s Cas
Pacific Silver Fir: Pacific silver fir, western hemlock	w slope of Cas and OMtns	2,000–4,300' in n Cas and OMtns; 3,300–4,900' in s Cas
Ponderosa Pine: ponderosa pine, Douglas-fir	e of Cas crest	2,000–4,000' in NCas; 2,900–5,000' in s Cas
Subalpine: subalpine fir, mountain hemlock	higher elevations of Cas and OMtns	4,200–5,800' in OMtns; 4,300–7,000' in NCas; 5,600–7,800' in s Cas
Interior Fir: Douglas-fir, western hemlock, ponderosa pine, grand fir; white fir, in s Ore	e slope of Cas from s BC to s Ore	1,000–4,000' in n Cas to 6,500' in s Ore
Alpine: no trees	higher elevations of Cas and OMtns	above 5,900' in OMtns; above 7,000' in NCas; above 7,800' in s Cas

Fire is a regular natural interruption in the forests of the West and can dramatically change the plant communities over large areas. Areas deforested by fire typically go through a series of plant communities, depending on the size and heat of the fire. A low-temperature ground fire may remove only certain species, leaving other species standing. For example, much of the old-growth forest in the Coastal Forest community (see the next section) is dominated by large Douglas-fir trees. These trees have thick, corky bark that insulates the delicate inner living tissue from the heat of ground fires. This adaptation helps Douglas-firs to survive a fire that will kill the surrounding western hemlock and western red cedar trees because their much thinner bark makes them vulnerable to the heat.

Thus, the forest communities of the Cascades and Olympics are a patchwork mosaic created by a large and varied set of environmental circumstances that play out over time. Table 1 shows the most common forest communities of our mountains.

Coastal Forest

The largest trees on earth grow in the rich soils, moderate climate, and copious moisture of the Coastal Forest community. The climax species are western hemlock and, in some areas, western red cedar, but abundant historical fires have made fire-resistant, thick-barked Douglas-fir the dominant tree in many forest stands. In the Olympics, Sitka spruce is often a co-dominant, especially in the areas reached by coastal fogs that provide extra summer moisture. Along river bottoms and terraces,

Coastal forest trail. *Photo by Alan L. Bauer*

cottonwoods and moss-festooned bigleaf maples create a canopy that allows light to reach the forest floor, and often these associate with thick shrub tangles of salmonberry, elderberry, and other shrubs. This forest zone is plentiful along the river valleys of the Olympic Mountains and Cascade Range.

Access: Ohanapecosh in Mount Rainier National Park; Hoh River in Olympic National Park.
Amphibians: Rough-skinned newt, northwestern salmander, red-legged frog, Pacific chorus frog.
Reptiles: Northern alligator lizard, garter snake species, rubber boa.
Birds: Ruffed grouse, Steller's jay, chestnut-backed chickadee, winter wren, spotted towhee, song sparrow.
Mammals: Douglas squirrel, Townsend's chipmunk, deer mouse, mountain beaver, black-tailed deer.

Pacific Silver Fir

The Pacific Silver Fir community is often referred to as the montane forest. At increasing elevation on the western slopes of the Olympics and Cascades, the soils cool and patches of snow linger some years until mid-July. In these conditions, the Douglas-firs and western red cedars of the Coastal Forest zone begin to be replaced

by Pacific silver firs, which are much more tolerant of the cold conditions and are able to withstand heavy snow loads. Western hemlock is a co-dominant at lower elevations; mountain hemlock is co-dominant at the upper elevations of this zone. The soils in these snowy forests are acidic and thus poor in usable nitrates and often high in iron. These conditions favor plants of the heath family, and understory plants include thinleaf blueberry in wetter sites and salal in drier sites.

Access: Paradise Road in Mount Rainier National Park; Timberline Drive at Mount Hood.
Amphibians: Cascades frog, western toad, long-toed salamander.
Reptiles: Northern alligator lizard, garter snake species.
Birds: Varied thrush, blue grouse, northern goshawk, mountain chickadee, hermit thrush, red-breasted nuthatch, dark-eyed junco, Steller's jay.
Mammals: Douglas squirrel, deer mouse, pine marten, black bear, elk, mule deer, porcupine.

Ponderosa Pine

Ponderosa pines favor the hot, dry, lower mountain elevations on the east slope of the Cascades. This forest is very open, with trees widely spaced and often with a well-developed understory of shrubs such as serviceberry, antelope brush, and snowberry. At the lower boundaries, where annual precipitation drops below 12 to 14 inches per year, ponderosa pines are gradually replaced by the grassland and sagebrush steppes. The upper mountain limit of the Ponderosa Pine zone is determined by higher moisture, which favors Douglas-fir. One of the key environmental conditions of this zone is the long, hot, dry summer period, often with little moisture falling between June and October. Several years of seedling trees may fail because of inadequate summer moisture. Perhaps only one summer a decade is wet enough for the year's seedlings to survive. Because ponderosa pine needs less nitrogen and phosphorus to grow its needles, the tree can grow well in soils that are not fertile enough for other species, although moisture is usually the determining factor for its distribution.

Access: Interstate 90, 20 miles east of Snoqualmie Pass; east of Santiam Pass to Sisters, Oregon.
Amphibians: Western toad, spotted frog.
Reptiles: Sagebrush lizard, western fence lizard, southern alligator lizard, racer, striped whipsnake, gopher snake, northern Pacific rattlesnake.
Birds: Dusky flycatcher, chipping sparrow, flammulated owl, common nighthawk, western bluebird, calliope hummingbird, white-breasted nuthatch, Bullock's oriole.
Mammals: Least chipmunk, yellow-pine chipmunk, porcupine, deer mouse, coyote, striped skunk.

Opposite: Pacific silver fir and vanilla leaf, Mount Rainier National Park. *Photo by Alan L. Bauer*

Ponderosa pines on a dry eastern Cascades slope. *Photo by Alan L. Bauer*

Subalpine

The Subalpine forest community is defined by cold temperatures and late-lingering snowfields that create a growing season so short that trees struggle to put on new growth and harden it before the freezing temperatures destroy the tender new cells. The plants and animals here have adapted to a growing season of only eight to ten weeks. The Subalpine has two primary divisions, defined by elevation and microclimate.

In lower elevations and in protected areas, a continuous forest of trees can grow, while higher areas and those exposed to wind form extensive flowery meadows dotted with islands of trees. The continuous subalpine forest west of the Cascade crest consists typically of mountain hemlock and subalpine fir, while east of the Cascade crest, mountain hemlock is replaced with western larch and whitebark pine or lodgepole pine in the southern Cascades of Oregon.

Subalpine parklands are the highest elevations that trees can grow. Tiny, stunted trees, sometimes only a foot tall, survive killing dry winter winds under snowbanks and form sprawling mounds known as krummholz. Trees grow in groups, creating a sheltered microclimate on the downwind side of the cluster. In the drier sites of the northeastern Cascades, the deciduous alpine larch finds a foothold in rocky, thin soils, where it may be the only tree species.

The well-drained meadow areas tend to be dominated with mats of red and white mountain heathers and the delicious Cascade blueberry. In the wet, snowmelt-

Subalpine meadow with clustered subalpine firs. *Photo by Alan L. Bauer*

fed depressions are glorious gardens of dozens of herbaceous flowers. Particularly wet and cold locations are dominated by alpine sedges.

Access: Sunrise and Paradise in Mount Rainier National Park; Hurricane Ridge in Olympic National Park; Timberline at Mount Hood.
Amphibians: Western toad, Cascades frog.
Birds: Northern flicker, gray jay, Clark's nutcracker, mountain chickadee, dark-eyed junco, western tanager.
Mammals: Marmot species, golden-mantled ground squirrel, deer mouse, heather vole, coyote, black-tailed deer, Roosevelt elk, mountain goat.

Interior Fir

East of the Cascade crest, precipitation and temperature create a community of forest that is higher in elevation than the Ponderosa Pine forests and lower than the Subalpine. The soil moisture in this zone supports a community dominated by Douglas-fir and true firs. In the northern Cascades, this community is composed of Douglas-fir mixed with grand fir. Particularly moist sites support forests of western hemlock. However, south of Mount Hood, Douglas-firs begin to diminish and are replaced by grand and white firs in the southern Cascades. In places these communities are thick with low understory shrubs including blueberries and serviceberry in the north and manzanita and rhododendron in the south.

Interior fir forest. *Photo by Alan L. Bauer*

Access: Any east-west highway that crosses the mountains 5–10 miles east of and below the crest.
Amphibians: Spotted frog, western toad.
Reptiles: Garter snake species, western fence lizard, rubber boa, gopher snake.
Birds: Blue grouse, three-toed woodpecker, Hammond's flycatcher, Cassin's finch, pine siskin, dark-eyed junco, chipping sparrow.
Mammals: Snowshoe hare, yellow-pine chipmunk, Douglas squirrel, porcupine, deer mouse, mule deer.

Alpine

With a growing season of less than sixty days, the Alpine community has no trees where the average high temperature is below 50 degrees Fahrenheit. This is a narrow band, between perennial snow and glacial ice above and the Subalpine zone below. The key environmental elements that shape life here are poor soils, snowpack, low temperatures, and constant wind. Plants are small, most only a few inches tall, forming cushions of life surrounded by bare soil and rock. The soils are poor in nutrients

Plant life diminishes up the slope of Mount Aix. *Photo by Alan L. Bauer*

and often freeze, thaw, and freeze again, causing frost heave instability, which makes it impossible for any seedling to establish. There are significant patches of bare ground and rock where no plants except lichens grow. Tiny woody plants only 2 inches tall may be decades old and may be able to add new growth or produce seeds in only one of every five years. Microclimates, such as a basin on the lee side of a small rocky outcrop, create just enough shelter for a few of the hardiest plants. The wind constantly blows, distributing the snow into drifts that determine where plants can grow. Melting snow creates tiny miniature bogs, where an errant bootprint will destroy a dozen plants and remain visible for a decade. Sheltered spots may host a dozen species of flowering perennial plants such as yarrow, mountain heathers, spreading phlox, and lupines.

Access: Sunrise and Paradise in Mount Rainier National Park; Timberline at Mount Hood; Hurricane Ridge in Olympic National Park.
Birds: Gray-crowned rosy finch, white-tailed ptarmigan, horned lark, common raven.
Mammals: Mountain goat, marmot species, golden-mantled ground squirrel, heather vole.

STREAMS/RIVERS

Throughout our mountains, water is constantly moving from higher elevations downward, ultimately to the Pacific Ocean. This movement creates thousands of rivers and streams, which cut away at the mountains, moving rocks large and small, scouring blasts of sand and rocks, and bouncing large boulders downstream during river floods. Trees and shrubs along rivers and streams have to cope with moving streambeds and an often annual overabundance of water, as rainstorms combine with melting snow. Willows and alders are the trees that can withstand this environment well; their flexible stems and wide-spreading root systems help them hang on when water is raging. More important, the root systems of these plants stitch the stream banks together, holding them in place against the constant tug of water. Other shrubs commonly found along streams are ninebark, red-osier dogwood, salmonberry, and thimbleberry.

Access: Hoh River in Olympic National Park; Highway 20 east of Albany, Oregon.
Amphibians: Tailed frog, Cascades frog, torrent salamander, Pacific giant salamander.
Reptiles: Garter snake species.
Birds: Dipper, spotted sandpiper, belted kingfisher, harlequin duck, common merganser, bald eagle, American crow.
Mammals: River otter, mink, water vole, beaver, raccoon.

Opposite: Beckler River, North Cascades. *Photo by Alan L. Bauer*

AVALANCHE SLOPES

Along many trails, the mountain traveler finds a dramatic shift in vegetation, from a cool, dark forest overstory to a bright green shrub area, often with a fragrant collection of flowering plants. The transition is abrupt and startling to the senses. From a distance—for example, along the east–west mountain passes—these obvious swaths form linear chutes of a different color from the surrounding forest. These vegetation bands are caused by winter avalanches, huge movements of snow that pick up soil and rocks and form a natural bulldozer that mows down anything in its path, splintering and shredding any upright vegetation. Plants in these swaths are small enough to be protected under a layer of snow, are limber and bend with the flow, or are easily regenerated from roots. Typical Avalanche Slope species include slide alder, willows, vine maple, thimbleberry, and bracken fern. At higher elevations, Alaska yellow-cedar is the only coniferous tree flexible enough to flourish in avalanche chutes. Many herbaceous plants colonize these openings in the forest, and the variety of plants feeds many types of insects, which attracts a greater abundance of birds than in the adjacent forests.

Access: Visible on all major mountain highways; look on north- and east-facing slopes of higher ridges.
Amphibians: Northwest salamander, western red-backed salamander, western toad, Cascades frog.

Avalanche chutes run down from mountain ridges. *Photo by Alan L. Bauer*

Reptiles: Garter snake species, western fence lizard, rubber boa, gopher snake.
Birds: Olive-sided flycatcher, Townsend's warbler, rufous hummingbird, western tanager, Nashville warbler, Wilson's warbler, yellow-rumped warbler, red-naped sapsucker, Cassin's vireo, Townsend's solitaire, pine siskin, song sparrow, spotted towhee.
Mammals: Black-tailed deer, black bear, Townsend's chipmunk.

LAKESHORES/WETLANDS

As the alpine glaciers retreated from the mountains, they left behind large blocks of ice and rocky debris that dammed up creeks, or they simply gouged and scraped depressions in the valleys. As these areas filled with water, they formed the thousands of lakes that dot the Olympic Mountains and Cascade Range. As meltwater streams into these lakes, it carries with it bits of rock and sand, which over time fill the lake, creating wetlands. Often these areas are too wet for coniferous trees but form wet meadows or dense thickets of shrubs.

Lakeshore/Wetlands soils often remain cool because they are saturated with water and also because it takes about five times as much energy to raise the temperature of wet soil as it does to raise the equivalent amount of dry soil. Wetland soils typically have a great deal of decomposed plant material, forming a rich black humus that is usually fairly acidic. The combination of cold, wet, and acidic soils is a difficult environment for many plants. The most common dominant plants are sedges, which

Sheep Lake, with marshy shore. *Photo by Alan L. Bauer*

look like grasses but have sharp, triangular cross-section stems. Larger plant species include willow and slide alder, mountain spiraea, bog birch, and blueberries.

Access: Lake Wenatchee State Park on Highway 207, Washington; Crescent Lake on Highway 58, east of Eugene, Oregon.
Amphibians: Rough-skinned newt, Pacific chorus frog, red-legged frog, Cascades frog, western toad.
Reptiles: Garter snake species, rubber boa.
Birds: Spotted sandpiper, Barrow's goldeneye.
Mammals: Bat species, shrew species, raccoon, beaver, mink.

2
the geologic story

Dramatic, jagged mountain scenery is a result of geologic processes over millions of years. The rocks in mountains come in three basic varieties, based on how they were formed. Igneous rocks are formed when the rock is heated into a liquid, such as the lava associated with volcanoes. Sedimentary rocks are formed by layers upon layers of tiny particles, such as grains of sand, that settle in water and accumulate and press together over time to form rocks such as sandstone and mudstone. Metamorphic rocks form when igneous, sedimentary, or even other metamorphic rocks are subjected to enormous pressure and heat, which alters and realigns their minerals, often squeezing them into layers or streaks.

Glaciers and rock formations in the Boulder Creek Wilderness. *Photo by Alan L. Bauer*

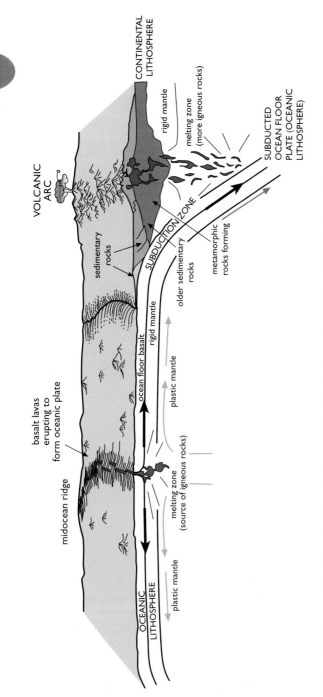

VOLCANIC ARC

CONTINENTAL LITHOSPHERE

rigid mantle

melting zone (more igneous rocks)

SUBDUCTED OCEAN FLOOR PLATE (OCEANIC LITHOSPHERE)

SUBDUCTION ZONE

older sedimentary rocks

metamorphic rocks forming

sedimentary rocks

ocean floor basalt

rigid mantle

plastic mantle

basalt lavas erupting to form oceanic plate

midocean ridge

melting zone (source of igneous rocks)

plastic mantle

OCEANIC LITHOSPHERE

Figure 2. *Plate tectonics. Illustration from* Geology of the North Cascades: A Mountain Mosaic, *used by permission.*

Since the 1960s, geologists using advanced technologies have formed a unified theory of geology called *plate tectonics* (see figure 2). The creation of metamorphic and volcanic rocks, and ultimately the mountains themselves, happens along the boundaries of huge, slowly moving plates that divide up the earth's crust. These plates, sometimes thousands of miles across, float on the denser, plastic material of the upper mantle. Upwelling basalt along midocean ridges pushes the plates away in opposite directions. As they slowly move away from the ridges, plates are pushed into other plates and these large masses are then slowly and relentlessly forced together. Measurements show that these giant plates move at about the same speed as your fingernails grow, about 2 inches a year.

The Cascades and Olympics were formed by the collision of the Juan de Fuca Plate with the North American Plate. Where these two plates collide, the lighter and thinner oceanic Juan de Fuca Plate is pushed under the heavier and thicker North American Plate in a process called *plate subduction*. During this very slow process, rocks are formed by heat and pressure, and existing rocks can be compressed and folded as they are squeezed between the plates.

As some of the oceanic plate is thrust deeper into the earth it melts, forming magma, the molten rock of volcanoes. This molten rock moves upward toward the earth's surface in cracks and fissures. When it fails to reach the surface, the molten rock slowly congeals in large underground masses. These rocks slowly cool and various types of large mineral crystals—primarily quartz, feldspars, and mica—precipitate out of solution and bond together to form granite and related rocks. When the molten rock reaches the earth's surface, it oozes over the landscape in broad basalt flows or forms discrete volcanic cones. Once on the surface, the magma cools quickly, and thus these rocks have microscopic crystals. The same molten material forms both andesite and granite, depending on whether the magma erupts on the surface or not.

When rocks are folded, sheared, buried at great depths, or intruded or heated by molten rock, minerals may rearrange or transform into new ones. The chemical and physical process of metamorphosis changes granite into gneiss, shale to slate and schist, and limestone to marble. Other types of metamorphic rocks in our mountains include phyllite and quartzite.

THE NORTH CASCADES: BATHOLITHS

The North Cascades are a confused jumble of rocks; geologists divide such a jumble into groups called *terranes*. Some of these groupings of rocks have ridden on plates and faults and moved thousands of miles from their places of origin. In some cases, as a result of the enormous pressures of colliding plates, layers of rocks have been thrust over one another or compressed into stacks, then flipped up, like turning a stack of pancakes on end. In this topsy-turvy geological wonderland, sometimes entire mountains are made from rocks flipped sideways, with the youngest rocks at the bottom and the oldest at the top!

When diving plates reach sufficient depth tens of miles beneath the earth's surface, heat and pressure become so intense that the solid rocks begin to change, which realigns their crystals. In the process, some rocks may melt and form magma while others partially melt and incorporate a portion of the overlying rocks. Along the periphery of melting rocks, the heat and pressure metamorphoses adjacent rock formations. As the molten rock slowly cools, insulated by the thick roof of older rocks, it forms large granitic formations called *batholiths*.

From Snoqualmie Pass, east of Seattle, north to the Fraser River in British Columbia, the Cascade Range consists primarily of large granitic batholiths and outcroppings of metamorphic rocks—mostly schist, phyllite, and gneiss. North Cascades granitic rocks vary a great deal in their mineral composition, ranging from almost white with a few flecks of dark minerals (granite) to almost black with a few flecks of white minerals (gabbro).

THE OLYMPICS: ANCIENT SEAFLOOR

The Olympic Mountains form an island of 6,000- to 7,000-foot peaks surrounded by lowlands. This mountain range is almost as long as it is broad, about 60 miles across, and rivers drain in all cardinal directions. The Olympics are composed mostly of sandstones, basalts, and shales that are only slightly metamorphosed. Although many Olympic peaks are composed of basalt, none of the peaks are themselves volcanoes. Instead, they are eroded remnants of a huge pile of basalt that accumulated millions of years ago on the seafloor as part of a chain of islands, perhaps like the current Hawaiian islands. The underwater origin of much of the Olympic basalts is indicated by their globular, "pillow" structure, which is evident in many outcrops and readily seen along the road to Hurricane Ridge. Some of the basalt, however, has a columnar formation, which indicates it erupted on land. The other common rocks of the Olympics are sandstones and shales, which are severely angled, flipped more than 90 degrees from the position in which they were deposited on the ocean floor. Clearly some kind of dramatic geologic process was involved in order to realign thousands of feet of rock at such odd angles.

Geologists speculate that at some point millions of years ago, as the Juan de Fuca Plate plunged beneath the North American Plate, a basalt island chain clogged the subduction trench, preventing the plate from being subducted under the continental plate. The relentless eastward push of the Juan de Fuca Plate caused huge pressures as the trench was plugged, and so part of the plate containing the islands was scraped off and squished into the continental plate. Over the course of millions of years, the pressure folded and perhaps even broke apart large chunks of the jammed plate. As the basalts and sedimentary rocks were pushed into each other, they tipped and were folded into a large, domelike mass, with additional younger sedimentary rocks from the western side of the plate getting shoved into the jumble. The result is a large mass of folded, tipped, and broken sedimentary rocks to the west and in the center of the range, as well as a ring of basalt rocks around the north, east, and south edges. As uplift continued, streams and glaciers scoured the resulting dome, eroding away the softer sedimentary rocks and incising the radial pattern of ridges and valleys that exists today. The continental glaciers that scooped out Puget Sound also helped shape the Olympics by carving away at the north and east sides of the range.

THE SOUTHERN CASCADES: VOLCANOES

As plates rub together, significant amounts of molten rock typically rise to the earth's surface by way of faults and fissures in the overlying rocks. Upon reaching the surface, the molten rock erupts from volcanic vents in the form of lava. As lava pours out, the flows can—depending on the composition of minerals—stack up in large cones of mixed lava and debris, creating *stratovolcanoes,* the symmetrical cone shapes we associate with classic volcanoes such as Mounts Rainier, Baker, and Hood. Smaller cones are numerous throughout the southern Cascades, including Broken Top, Mount Bachelor, and Mount McLoughlin.

Lava can also pile up in more or less horizontal layers. From Mount Rainier to Lassen Peak, the Cascade Range is a broad highland of volcanic layers surmounted at intervals by volcanoes. This portion of the range is made up almost entirely of volcanic rocks, primarily basalt and andesite, as old as 40 million years and as young as the 1980 eruption of Mount St. Helens.

Some kinds of magma, such as rhyolite, can absorb considerable water. When water is present during volcanic eruptions, it can cause the rocks to melt at lower temperatures, and the resulting gas pressure can spew out materials with great violence and speed. Some past eruptions have spread volcanic material thousands of miles. Crater Lake, for example, is a former volcano (Mount Mazama) that completely destroyed itself in a massive, explosive eruption. The recent destructive explosion of Mount St. Helens is only a small example of the kind of volcanic violence that created the Cascades. When magma is under pressure, gases in the molten rock remain in solution, like carbon dioxide in a can of pop. When a volcano erupts, it can release pressure very quickly, so that gases trapped in the magma create holes in the rock as it cools. These porous rocks are called lava cinders. When eruptions happen very quickly, the molten rock can create a sort of foam, which hardens into pumice, a rock with so much air space in it that it floats.

Volcanic eruptions are not always violent; often they are slow and steady, with molten rock the consistency of peanut butter pouring out. In many places in the Cascades, large volcanic flows oozed out in layer after layer to cover hundreds of miles of land thousands of feet deep in lava. Much of the area around Mount Rainier is an example of andesite flows that are perhaps 10,000 feet deep. Andesite contains more silica than basalt and so it is lighter in color and also holds a bit more water. Andesite is the primary building block of our stratovolcanoes such as Mounts Rainier and Hood, because when water is present, it tends to create blocky sorts of rocks that pile up nicely into mounds. Basalt, on the other hand, tends to erupt in big oozing flows that spread widely.

KNIVES OF WATER AND ICE

The rugged and spectacular alpine topography of the North Cascades and Olympic Mountains is the product of glacial erosion in terrain already deeply cut by streams.

Alpine glaciers form when the snows that fall in successive winters exceed the amounts that melt during the intervening summers. The accumulated snow becomes compacted and gradually turns to ice. When a body of ice becomes large enough, it begins to flow plastically downslope in response to gravity. In the process, it quarries huge amounts of rock from the confining walls and floors of its valley and transports these materials downslope, eventually depositing the rubble in ridges called *moraines.*

Many of the river valleys of the Olympics and Cascades show evidence that alpine glaciers have been much larger than they are today. As a glacier moves into a river valley, it scours the sides of the valley, creating steep sidewalls and a broad, flat basin. This classic **U** shape is widely evident through river valleys in our mountains. As glaciers melt back, they litter their beds with stranded boulders—called *erratics*—which they earlier had plucked from upstream and transported downslope. As a result, erratics may be entirely different types of rocks from those upon which they finally come to rest. For example, in the Olympic Mountains it is possible to find rounded and polished boulders and rocks of granite, even as high as 3,500 feet. Since there is no granite in the bedrock of the Olympics, these rocks are erratics from the large Cordilleran Ice Sheet that flowed south from British Columbia some 14,000 years ago and carved out Puget Sound.

Glaciers strip the land of vegetation and soil and polish the underlying rock to a high sheen. Remnants of glacial polish persisting from the last ice age exist throughout our mountains. Rock materials embedded in the bottom of a glacier also cut shallow, parallel grooves, or *striations,* into the rock, and by examining the grooves, geologists can determine which direction a glacier was flowing.

As water is deposited on the landscape, it seeks the lowest point. Water seeps into cracks and crevasses in the rock and, should it freeze, the expanding force physically breaks apart the rock. Small flows of water carry particles that rasp and abrade the rocks further and, eventually over millions of years, wear away even the most resistant rock. Rivers and streams carve away deep channels and valleys, depositing smaller particles in slack water downstream. The Cascade Range and Olympic Mountains were once much higher than they are today. The force of moving water, both liquid and frozen, has ground them to their present heights and will eventually, over tens of millions of years, return all the rock of our mountains to the ocean, where it will become sandstone, continuing the ever ongoing cycle of rock making.

ROCKS OF OUR MOUNTAINS

Identifying rocks can be both satisfying and confusing. Some of the most common rocks have similarities that confuse casual identification and confound even experts. The basic properties of a rock that to help identify it in the field include:

- **Hardness:** Can you scratch it with a knife blade or a coin?
- **Breakability:** Can you break it by hitting it with another rock?
- **Minerals:** Can you see grains or specks of minerals in the rock?
- **Cleavage:** Does it break in sheets or with many right angles?

- **Color:** Is it all one color, or does it have multiple colors?
- **Streaking:** Do the minerals all line up in one direction, or are they random?

    Note: Often weathering can change the color of rocks, and so rock hounds often break a rock to get a fresh, nonweathered surface. Be careful when breaking rocks, as flying rock chips are sharp.

PLATE 1

IGNEOUS ROCKS

Basalt. Blk, brown to reddish, occas dk green. No apparent grains, oft angular in form, sometimes forming distinctive 5- to 6-sided columns, smooth, dull. Hard, not scratchable. Mt. Rainier National Park, Wn. Basalt cinders are highly porous, rough, oft reddish from iron oxide content. Mackenzie Pass, Highway 242, Ore. Pillow basalts are smooth bowls or domes, 1–5' in diam, closely fitted together. Hurricane Ridge Road, Olympic National Park, Wn.

Andesite. Gray to brown, no apparent grains, oft angular in form, smooth, dull. Hard, not scratchable. Andesite cinders highly porous, rough. Occas pores filled with lighter minerals, resulting in a spotted appearance. Typically extensive flows as part of stratovolcanoes. Mt. Rainier, Mt. Baker, Mt. Hood.

Rhyolite. Light gray to light yellow, occas pink, no apparent grains, oft angular in form, smooth, dull. Com mixed in with other volcanic rocks in debris flows. Three Sisters, OR; Mt. Hood.

Ash. Light gray powder in a layer in the soil, ¼"–½" in depth, occas several inches deep. Typically found along trail cuts in Cas. Mt. Baker, Mt. Mazama, and Mt. St. Helens all have contributed ash layers.

Pumice. Light gray, highly porous, spongelike, very light, smaller pieces float on water. Soft, easily breakable. Abundant around Mt. St. Helens and Crater Lake National Park, Ore.

Granite. White or pinkish, sprinkled with blk flecks (less than 30% of total). Crystals visible with naked eye. Mostly feldspars (milky white or pink) with quartz (clear), and dk minerals (mostly biotite mica with occas hornblende). Hard, not scratchable. Exposures in NCas include peaks and rocks at Washington Pass Overlook; widespread in NCas and Stuart Range; absent from OMtns.

Basalt Cinder

Andesite

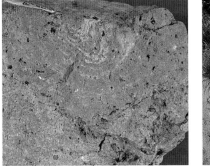

Rhyolite

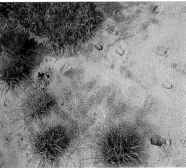

Ash

Pumice

Granite

PLATE 2

IGNEOUS ROCKS

Granodiorite. Similar in appearance to granite but with blk flecks 30–50% of total and with more white than pink feldspars. Coarse-grained, with crystals visible to naked eye. Widespread in NCas; absent from OMtns.

Diorite (not pictured). Intermediate in color and mineral composition between granodiorite and gabbro and is rare in Cas; absent from OMtns.

Gabbro. Dk gray, green, or blk, with more than 70% dk minerals, mostly amphibole and pyroxene, and less than 30% white feldspar. Coarse-grained, with crystals visible to naked eye. Hard, not scratchable. Throughout North Cascades National Park, Wn; absent from OMtns.

SEDIMENTARY ROCKS

Sandstone. Fine grains, usually light gray color, layered rock. Grains feel gritty when rubbed between fingers. Breaks when hit with another rock, scratchable. Outcroppings common in lowl Cas road cuts, OMtns.

Mudstone. Fine grains, dk blk. Crumbles easily in hand; grains feel slippery, like clay when rubbed between fingers. Com in lowl Cas r valleys, OMtns.

Limestone. Fine-grained; white, pinkish, or reddish; grains feel slippery when rubbed between fingers. Bubbles in solution of weak acid such as vinegar. Hurricane Ridge Road, Olympic National Park, Wn.

Conglomerate. Rounded pebbles and rock pieces in a matrix of sandstone or mudstone. Various colors depending on pebbles. Low coastal areas and valleys. Hoh R, Skagit R, Hood R.

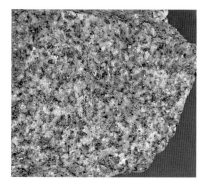

Granodiorite

Gabbro

Sandstone

Mudstone

Limestone

Conglomerate

PLATE 3

SEDIMENTARY ROCKS

Breccia. Angular pebbles and rock pieces in a matrix of sandstone or mudstone. Can also be of volcanic origin with angular pieces in a matrix of basalt or andesite. Mt. Hood, Mt. Rainier.

METAMORPHIC ROCKS

Slate. Fine-grained blk rock that forms thin plates. Oft found in large sheetlike exposures, with small knifelike pieces accumulating at the bottom of the exposures. Breakable, scratchable. Hurricane Hill Road, Olympic National Park, Wn.

Gneiss. Light-colored; rough texture similar to granite, except crystals aligned in one direction. Visible crystals, hard, not scratchable. Oft found in alternating bands with dk gray schist contrasting with white or light gray gneiss. Highway 20, North Cascades National Park, Wn.

Schist. Dk gray, occas reddish, fine layers, visible grains. Hard, not scratchable. Mica schist is shiny gray; green schist is dull green. Oft breaks along planes although not platelike as in shale. Schist often hosts garnets, small red gems. Throughout North Cascades National Park, Snoqualimie and Stevens Pass areas, Wn.

Phyllite. Dk brown to gray, obvious layers, oft curved or wrinkled. Scratchable. Slight sheen, mostly dull. Oft breaks in angular chunks that come apart at the layers. Intermediate between shale and schist. Throughout North Cascades National Park, Wn, lowl.

Quartzite. White or crystalline, sometimes red or pink. Typically angular. Hard, not scratchable. Oft in seams or filling holes and chambers in other types of rock. Throughout North Cascades National Park, Wn.

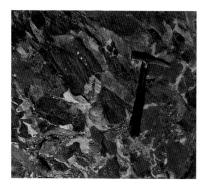

Breccia

Slate

Gneiss

Schist

Phyllite

Quartzite

PART II
Mushrooms and Plants

3

mushrooms

The moist and relatively warm west side of the Cascade Range and Olympic Mountains forms an excellent habitat for hundreds of species of mushrooms. A mushroom is the above-ground fruiting body of a fungus, an organism that typically lives in the upper soil layer as a large mass of microscopic cobwebby material. This material, called *mycelium,* may extend for a considerable distance; in some cases the mycelia from an individual fungus can cover hundreds of acres. Fungi lack chlorophyll and live on organic matter, either by decomposing dead material, interconnecting with roots, or parasitizing living organisms. Enzymes secreted by fungi are exceptionally effective at decomposing and releasing nutrients, converting once-living matter into organic

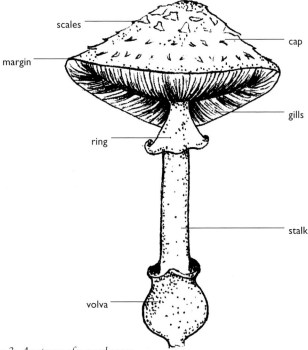

Figure 3. *Anatomy of a mushroom*

compounds that can then be utilized by other organisms. Coupled with insects and bacteria, they recycle the dead material in any biome.

Some fungi are parasites, attacking living plants or animals and feeding off them, occasionally killing the host. The organism that causes athlete's foot and ringworm is a form of parasitic fungus.

Many species form mutually beneficial *(symbiotic)* relationships with plants, invading the plants' root hairs and exchanging nutrients dissolved from the soil for carbohydrates from the photosynthetic process. This association between mushroom and plant is called *mycorrhiza,* and it plays a crucial role in the health of all our Northwest forests. As a young tree seedling becomes established in the soil, its tiny root system is often inadequate to fully support the fast-growing seedling. The association with the mycorrhizal fungi extends the root system of the tree or shrub far beyond the reach of its unaided roots. Many species of mycorrhyzal fungi are especially good at releasing nitrogen and phosphorus bound in soil material, key elements for plant growth. Trees and shrubs with this mycorrhizal connection grow faster and stronger and are more disease-resistant than those without mycorrhyzae. Sometimes specific fungi partner with specific species of trees or shrubs. For example, the early morel *(Verpa bohemica)* seems to partner closely with cottonwood trees.

Fungi reproduce by spores released from the fruits (mushrooms), which come in a wide a variety of shapes. The classic mushroom shape, which resembles a thick-handled miniature umbrella, is typical of the *gilled fungi.* However, mushrooms also come shaped like heads of lettuce, cones, gelatin cups, coral, fingers, and oozy blobs.

IDENTIFYING MUSHROOMS

The mushrooms selected for this book are both common and have distinctive macroscopic features (see figure 3). Key features for identifying mushrooms in this book are: the overall shape, the color, where it grows, and features of the stalk. Gilled mushrooms have a round, oval, or domed *cap,* which often has a distinctive marking or color. The underside of the cap is where the spores are produced in either *gills, pores,* or *teeth.* Gills are *free* from or *attached* to the stalk. *Scales* are small shinglelike patches, often dry, on the cap. The edge of the cap is called the *margin,* and sometimes this has a color, is rolled inward, or has other attributes. Sometimes in younger specimens the gills are covered with a cobwebby material called a *veil.* As the mushroom matures, often this veil breaks apart and forms a *ring* on the stalk. The nongilled mushrooms are identified by their overall shape and color.

Mushrooms grow either on the ground or on wood—logs, stumps, or snags. Mushrooms tend to fruit in the spring or fall in relation to moisture and temperature. Mushroom hunters eagerly await the first solid rains in September or October and concentrate their forays during those months. Often by mid- to late November, the hard frosts coupled with heavy rains will reduce the fruiting bodies to piles of mush. Seasonal conditions vary, so there can be a few mushrooms out even in the coldest months in the lowlands, and some are present year-round. A period of mild weather in December or January can bring forth another fruiting of some lowland species.

ABOUT EATING MUSHROOMS

In this guide, information about edibility has been deliberately left out. It cannot be overstated that before consuming any mushroom, an absolute positive identification should be made, including spore color and other technical attributes beyond the scope of this book. While the majority of mushrooms are benign, a few are highly poisonous, and many edible mushrooms have close look-alikes that may make you quite ill if you eat them. Even commercially raised mushrooms disagree with some people, leading to flulike symptoms. One person's edible mushroom is another's allergen. Do not assume that if a mushroom is eaten by a squirrel or other animal, that makes it safe for human consumption. For references to mushroom edibility and absolute identification, consult the books in the Selected References at the back of this book. If you are inclined to harvest mushrooms, keep in mind that you are not the only consumer in the woods and, in addition, little is known about how human harvests are affecting the organisms and their other relationships. Be judicious in collecting to minimize your impacts. Check for harvesting regulations for the area you are visiting.

PLATE 4

AGARICUS FAMILY (AGARICACEAE)

The prince, *Agaricus augustus.* Cap 4"–10" diam, yellowish brown, heavily scaled, bruising yellow, fragrant almond-anise. Gills free, whitish to pinkish young, brown with age. Stalk L 3"–5", stout with perst veil ring, scaled below ring. Forests, mdws, oft in disturbed sites, along trails, roads, on grnd. Lowl-mont in all our mtns. June-Oct.

Meadow mushroom, *Agaricus campestris.* Cap 1"–4" diam, whitish to gray-brown, smooth or lightly scaled. Gills free, pinkish, turning deep brown with age. Stalk L 1"–2", thick, partial veil leaving thin ring. Grassy areas, fields, on grnd. Lowl-mont in all our mtns. All year.

Shaggy parasol, *Macrolepiota rachodes.* Cap 3"–8" diam, pink to reddish brown, egg-shaped when young, scaled, center brown and smooth, margin fringed. Gills free, white. Stalk L 4"–8", turns orange when cut; ring. In woods, grassy areas, on grnd. Lowl in all our mtns. Sept.-Nov. Shaggy-stalked lepiota, *Lepiota clypeolaria,* cap 1"–3" diam, with scales, smooth brown center. Gills free, white. Stalk L 2"–4", densely scaly, does not stain when cut. Conif woods on grnd. Lowl, W Cas, occas E Cas, OPen. Sept.-Nov.

AMANITA FAMILY (AMANITACEAE)

Fly amanita, *Amanita muscaria.* Cap 2"–10" diam, brilliant red to orange with angular white patches. Gills whitish, free or slightly att. Stalk L 2"–7", oft with large, skirtlike ring, with series of rings near bulbous base with volva. Conif forests, on grnd, oft at forest edges. Lowl-subalp in all our mtns. July-Nov.

Panther amanita, *Amanita pantherina.* Cap 1"–6" diam, yellowish brown to dk brown, with angular white patches, margin lined. Gills whitish, free or slightly att. Stalk L 2"–7", with large skirtlike ring, base bulbous with volva. Conif forests, on grnd. Lowl-mont in all our mtns. Apr.-Sept.

CHANTERELLE FAMILY (CANTHARELLACEAE)

Golden chanterelle, *Cantharellus formosus.* Cap ½"–6" diam, yellow to orange, oft with wavy margin. Gills yellow, blunt ridges, extend down stalk, well separated. Stalk L 1"–3". On grnd, Douglas-fir forests, lowl, in all our mtns. July-Dec. White chanterelle, *C. subalbidus,* similar to golden chanterelle only white, thicker, mostly E Cas, OPen. False chanterelle, *Hygrophorpsis aurantiaca,* similar to golden chanterelle. Cap 1"–2½" diam, orange, oft concave, with inrolled margin, dry. Gills orange, thin, close together, not blunt or ridgelike. Stalk narrow, occas off center. Conif forests, on grnd. Lowl-mont in all our mtns. Aug.-Nov.

Woolly chanterelle, *Gomphus floccosus.* Cap 2"–6"diam, yellowish orange or reddish with distinctive vase shape and coarse, curled scales on top. Gills as veined ridges or wrinkles. Stalk short and hollow, oft not apparent below vaselike cap. Conif forests, on grnd. Lowl-mont, in all our mtns. July-Dec.

Pig's ears, *Gomphus clavatus.* Cap 1"–4" diam, light purple-tan, thin, broad, oft bowl shaped, lacks scales, clustered, occas fused. Underside purplish, with blunt veined gills to near base. Stalk short, 2", occas fused with other stalks. Conif forests, on grnd. Lowl-mont, W Cas, OMtns. July-Dec.

The Prince

Meadow Mushroom

Shaggy Parasol

Fly Amanita

Panther Amanita

Golden Chanterelle

Woolly Chanterelle

Pig's Ears

PLATE 5

RUSSULA FAMILY (RUSSULACEAE)

Short-stemmed russula, *Russula brevipes*. Cap 4"–10" diam, dull white with sunken center, stains yellow to brown. Gills att to stem and descend down upper stem. Stalk L 1"–3", stout, firm, breaks cleanly in two like a piece of chalk. On grnd in woods, oft makes larges lumps in forest duff. Lowl-mont in all our mtns. July-Dec.

Shrimp mushroom, *Russula xerampelina*. Cap 1"–6" diam, purplish red, sometimes greenish at margin, sticky. Distinctive odor of shellfish. Gills att to stem, creamish white, yellowing with age. Stalk L 2"–3", slightly pink-purple, enlarges toward base, stains yellow. Conif forests, on grnd. Lowl-mont in all our mtns. July-Nov.

Delicious milky cap, *Lactarius deliciosus*. Cap 2"–5½" diam, orange, staining green with age, sticky. Gills orange, att to stem, bleed orange "milk" when cut. Stalk L 1"–3¼", orange. Conif forests, on grnd. Lowl-mont in all our mtns. Aug-Nov. Many *Lactarius* spp ooze sap from cut gills.

INKY CAP FAMILY (COPRINACEAE)

Shaggy mane, *Coprinus comatus*. Cap 2"–14" tall, cone shaped, white with large brown scales, rapidly decays into blk ink. Gills free, turning blk. Stalk L 2¼"–8". On grnd in roadsides, parking areas, disturbed sites. Lowl in all our mtns. May-Dec. Inky cap, *C. atramentarius,* similar, smaller, cap 2"–6" tall, lacks scales.

TRICHOLOMA FAMILY (TRICHOLOMATACEAE)

White matsutake, *Tricholoma magnilevere*. Cap 2"–8" diam, white with reddish brown scales, inrolled cottony margin, spicy-sweet odor. Gills att, white, stain brown. Stalk L 2"–6", cottony skirtlike ring on upper stalk. Conif forests, pines, coastal forests, on grnd. Lowl-mont, E Cas, occas W Cas. Aug-Nov.

Oyster mushroom, *Pleurotus ostreatus*. Cap 2"–8" diam, broad, white, gray or brown. Gills white, aging yellow. Stalk L ¼" to absent. In clusters on wood, stumps, logs of decid trees, alder, oak, maple. Lowl-mont in all our mtns. Year-round. Angel wings, *P. porrigens,* similar but thinner and growing on conif logs. Montane in W Cas, OMtns, stream valleys in E Cas. Sept-Nov.

Honey mushroom, *Armillaria ostoyae*. Cap 1"–5" diam, light brown, yellowish. Gills att, white, staining yellow or reddish. Stalk L 2"–6", stout ring, stringy pith inside stalk. In large clusters on wood, roots, stumps. In all our mtns. Aug-Dec.

Short-stemmed Russula

Shrimp Mushroom

Delicious Milky Cap

Shaggy Mane

White Matsutake

Oyster Mushroom

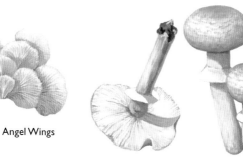

Angel Wings

Honey Mushroom

PLATE 6

CORTINARIUS FAMILY (CORTINARIACEAE)

Purple cortinarius, *Cortinarius violaceus.* Cap 2"–4½" diam, dry, rough with scales or hairs, deep purple. Gills att, purple. Stalk L 2"–7", slightly woolly. Old-growth forests, on grnd. Lowl-mont, mostly W Cas, occas in creek drainages and bogs E Cas, OPen. Sept-Nov.

STROPHARIA FAMILY (STROPHARIACEAE)

Questionable stropharia, *Stropharia ambigua.* Cap 2"–6" diam, yellow-gold, slimy with cottony scales along margin. Gills att, gray, aging purple-brown. Stalk L 3"–6", with cottony scales. Lowl, mixed woods oft in decid forests, on grnd, in all our mtns. Aug-Nov.

Scaly pholiota, *Pholiota squarrosa.* Cap 1"–4" diam, yellowish, distinctive pointed yellow-brown scales. Gills att, aging brown. Stalk L 2"–4", yellowish, heavily scaled. In clusters on trees or logs. Lowl-mont. in all our mtns. July-Nov. Golden pholiota, *P. aurea*, and lemon pholiota, *P. limonella,* similar; caps more yellowish, lighter scaled, slimy. In clusters on tree wounds, trunks, or logs. In all our mtns.

Sulfur tuft, *Hypholoma fasciculare.* Cap 1"–3" diam, yellowish to orange, greenish. Gills att, yellow-green, aging to gray. Stalk L 2"–4¾", slender. Conif forests, in clusters on logs and stumps. Lowl-mont in all our mtns. Aug-Nov.

GOMPHIDIUS FAMILY (GOMPHIDIACEAE)

Woolly spike, *Chroogomphus tomentosus.* Cap 1"–3" diam, dry, rough-scaly-hairy, dull orange. Gills orange, widely spaced, run down stem. Stalk L 2"–7", thick, narrowing toward base. Hemlock-fir forests, in clusters on grnd. Lowl, in all our mtns. Aug-Dec.

TOOTH FUNGI FAMILY (HYDNACEAE)

Scaly hydnum, *Sarcodon imbricatum.* Cap 2"–8" diam, dry, covered with large brown-blk scales, oft raised, oft forming rosette in center of cap. Spines brown, brittle. Stalk L 1½"–4", thick, light brown, hollow when aged. In many forest types, on grnd. Lowl-mont in all our mtns. May-Oct.

Spreading hedgehog, *Hydnum (Dentinum) repandum.* Cap ½"–6" diam, orange to off-white, white cap bruising orange, oft irreg, oft scaly. Spines white to orange. Stalk L 1"–4". Conif forests, on grnd. Lowl-mont in all our mtns. July-Nov.

Goat's beard, *Hericium abietis.* Mass 6"–14" diam, white, many clusters of spines, oft like mass of icicles hanging in clusters. Spine tips color reddish with age. Conif forests, stumps, logs, lowl-mont in all our mtns. Sept-Dec.

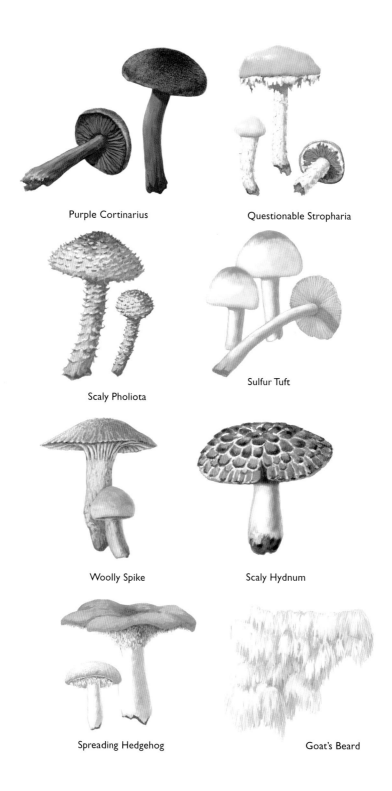

Purple Cortinarius

Questionable Stropharia

Scaly Pholiota

Sulfur Tuft

Woolly Spike

Scaly Hydnum

Spreading Hedgehog

Goat's Beard

PLATE 7

BOLETE FAMILY (BOLETACEAE)

King bolete, *Boletus edulis.* Cap 3"–10" diam, reddish brown to yellowish red, moist, sticky when wet, cracking when dry. Pores spongelike, white, not staining when bruised. Stalk L 4"–10", white-brown, thick, widening at base. Many forest types, mostly conif, on grnd. Lowl-mont in all our mtns. Aug-Nov. Admirable bolete, *B. mirabilis,* cap 2½"–6" diam, dk brown, reddish brown with small scales or hairs. Pores yellow. Does not stain when bruised. Stalk L 2"–4", same color as cap, conif forests, on rotting wood. Lowl-mont, W Cas, OPen. June-Nov. Zeller's bolete, *B. zelleri,* cap 2"–4" diam, dk gray, blk with occas red tinge, not cracked or fissured. Pores yellow, oft bruise blue. Stalk oft red or tinged red. Conif forests, on grnd. Lowl-mont in all our mtns. July-Jan.

Common slippery jack, *Suillus brevipes.* Cap 2"–4" diam, brownish, occas yellowish, slimy. Pores yellow. Stalk L 1"–2", white, occas dotted. Pines, on grnd, lowl-mont. Mostly E Cas, occas W Cas. May-June, Sept-Nov. Lake's bolete, *S. lakei,* cap 2½"–5½" diam, covered with dry, brown scales. Pores yellowish. Stalk L 1"–2½", yellowish, bruising blue. Conif, on grnd in groups. Lowl W Cas, OMtns. Aug-Oct.

LACQUERED BRACKET FAMILY (GANODERMATACEAE)

Artist's conk, *Ganoderma applanatum.* Cap 3"–20" diam, shelflike, top hard, woody, brown, gray, blk, concentric rings, colors lighter toward margin. Underside white, pores soft, bruise dk, marks perst. Dead trees, most oft decid. Lowl-mont in all our mtns. Year-round.

Varnished conk, *Ganoderma tsugae.* Cap 2"–12" diam, fan- to kidney-shaped, top soft, aging corky, reddish to orangish, oft white to orange margin, shiny, with obvious zones. Underside white. Occas stalk, L 1"–6". On logs, stumps, dead conifs. Lowl-mont in all our mtns. Year-round.

SHELF FUNGUS FAMILY (POLYPORACEAE)

Turkey tail, *Trametes versicolor.* Cap 1"–4" diam, multicolored bands, thin, fan- to kidney-shaped, oft many overlapping, leathery. Underside white-yellowish. Dense clusters on sticks, logs, stumps. Lowl-mont in all our mtns. Year-round.

Sulfur shelf, *Laetiporus sulphureus.* Cap 2"–12" diam, orange to yellow-orange, fan- to kidney-shaped, overlapping. Underside yellow. On stumps, logs, snags, occas on living trees. Lowl-mont in all our mtns. Aug-Nov.

CORAL FUNGUS FAMILY (CLAVARIACEAE)

Cauliflower mushroom, *Sparassis crispa.* Mass 6"–30" diam, white to yellowish, densely clustered, folded, curled, noodlelike growth, fragrant. Base of conifs, oft true firs. Lowl-mont in all our mtns. Aug-Oct.

Coral mushroom, *Ramaria botrytis.* Mass 2"–5" wide, 2"–4" tall, coral-like with many branches from a stout stem. Branches oft red, pink tipped. Mixed forests, on grnd. Lowl-subalp in all our mtns. Many spp of coral mushrooms, widespread and com. Aug-Dec, Apr-June.

King Bolete

Common Slippery Jack

Artist's Conk

Varnished Conk

Turkey Tail

Sulfur Shelf

Cauliflower Mushroom

Coral Mushroom

PLATE 8

PUFFBALL FAMILY (LYCOPERDACEAE)
Gem-studded puffball, *Lycoperdon perlatum.* Turban shaped, ht 1"–2½", dull white with brownish center, small spines easily detached, stalklike base. Mixed forests, clusters on grnd. Lowl-mont in all our mtns. Several spp of puffball, all release spores in a puff (like smoke) from center of top hole. July-Oct.

CUP FUNGI FAMILY (SARCOSCYPHACEAE, PYRONEMATACEAE)
Scarlet cup, *Sarcoscypha coccinea.* Bright red cup, ¾"–2½" diam, outer surface white with tiny hairs. Mixed forest, on grnd, on branches or buried wood. Lowl-mont in all our mtns. Oct-Mar.

Orange peel fungus, *Aleuria aurantia.* Lobed or cup shaped, ¾"–4" diam, bright orange, outer surface whitish or light orange. Disturbed areas, paths, road edges, on grnd, oft in groups. Lowl-mont in all our mtns. May-Nov.

Wood ear, *Auricularia auricula.* Lobed or cup shaped, 2¾"–4½" diam, brown, many folded, rubbery when fresh. Fallen logs, usu logs with bark on them. Lowl-mont in all our mtns. June-Feb.

HELVELLA FAMILY (HELVELLACEAE)
Elfin saddle, *Helvella lacunosa.* Cap ½"–2¼" wide, blk, occas gray, saddle shaped, wrinkled. Stalk L 1½"–4", white to gray, occas blk, deeply fluted with grooves, complexly folded in cross section. Mixed forests on grnd. Lowl-mont in all our mtns. Oct-May. Several similar spp.

MOREL FAMILY (MORCHELLACEAE)
Early morel, *Verpa bohemica.* Cap L ½"–1", yellowish, thimble shaped, deeply wrinkled, attached to stalk only at top of cap, sides hang free. Stalk L 2½"–3¼", white, hollow. Cottonwoods, on grnd. Lowl-mont in all our mtns. Apr-July.

Black morel, *Morchella elata.* Cap L ¾"–4", blk, conical, honeycombed with pits and ridges, insides of pits lighter, occas yellowish, entire length of cap attached to stalk. Stalk L 2"–4", white. Conif woods, oft in burns, logged areas, pines, on grnd. E Cas, occas W Cas. Apr-May. Yellow morel, *M. esculenta,* similar, with yellow cap.

JELLY FUNGI FAMILY (TREMELLACEAE)
Witch's butter, *Tremella mesenterica.* Cap 1"–4" diam, bright orange–yellow orange, gelatinous blobs, lobed, wrinkled. On dead trees. Lowl-mont in all our mtns. Wet months fall or spring.

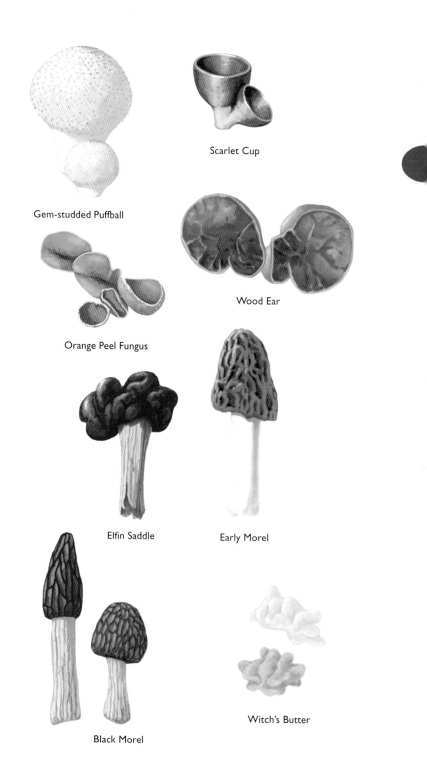

Gem-studded Puffball

Scarlet Cup

Orange Peel Fungus

Wood Ear

Elfin Saddle

Early Morel

Black Morel

Witch's Butter

4

ferns

Ferns, like flowering plants, have vascular tissue for support and for circulating water and nutrients. Unlike flowering plants, ferns reproduce from spores rather than seeds. Seed-bearing plants, no matter how fernlike their leaves, are not ferns. Ferns are among the oldest vascular plants in the fossil record, first appearing about 500 million years ago. During the Carboniferous period, about 300 million years ago, they were the dominant land plants. Today there are about 10,000 species, of which just over 30 occur in our region. Of the 30 species depicted in this guide, 10 occur throughout the northern hemisphere, 9 are endemic to western North America, 5 occur throughout North America, and 4 range throughout Eurasia and western North America but not east of the Rocky Mountains. The 2 remaining species have curious ranges that are mentioned in the species descriptions.

Ferns are an important, highly distinctive element in the humid forests of the Pacific Northwest and British Columbia. They are closely associated with those forests in the popular imagination and, along with mosses and lichens, are largely responsible for their lush, verdant appearance. Sword fern is the most common understory plant in many forest environments, providing a delicate, lacy contrast to the massive solemnity of the dominant trees. Several other species, though less common, are present in large numbers. Bracken is one of the first plants to relieve the devastation of clear-cuts and fires. It also grows abundantly along roads and in sunny fields throughout the region, commonly preferring open, disturbed habitats. Other ferns add a touch of green to rocky alpine slopes or combine with mosses and other moisture-loving plants to produce exquisite emerald gardens near seeps and streamlets.

The ferns of our region fall into two broad groups by habitat. One group prefers damp, shaded sites, often in the forest. The other prefers rocky habitats—cliffs, talus, ledges, crevices—which may be sunny or shaded, damp or dry. Ferns of one kind or another may be found nearly anywhere from sea level to above timberline. Some species are extremely local in their distribution but most are fairly widespread in suitable habitats.

The life cycle of a fern consists of two distinct stages or generations, each represented by a separate plant. The plant we normally call a fern actually represents only the asexual, spore-bearing generation. Spores are produced in minute cases called *sporangia*. Clusters of sporangia form *sori*, which are borne on the underside of fertile leaves. Sori usually appear in summer and in some species are covered by a thin membrane called the *indusium*. In other species, portions of the leaf margin curl

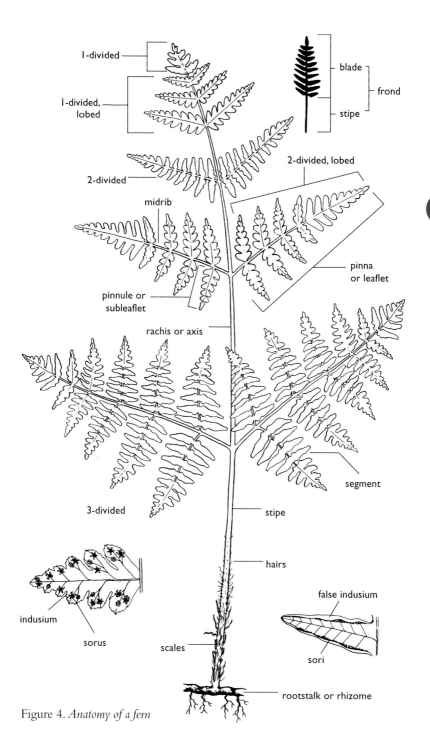

Figure 4. *Anatomy of a fern*

under to cover the sori and thereby serve as indusia. Sori may be missing if a plant is immature or if the season or growing conditions are inappropriate.

Upon maturity, sporangia slowly open and then snap shut, in the process slinging out thousands of spores, which are broadcast by the wind. Those landing in suitable habitats germinate to form tiny, simple, heart-shaped plants, each called a *prothallus*. Smaller than a thumbnail, a prothallus is a self-supporting green plant bearing the male and female reproductive cells that, upon uniting, grow into the plant we know as a fern.

When identifying ferns, one must pay special attention to the structure of the leaves and both the location of the sori and the nature of their indusium (see figure 4). If sori are not present, some species may be difficult or impossible to distinguish, though careful attention to other features, as well as habitat and range, will yield results in many cases.

Scientific names conform to those in *USDA Plant Database* (U.S. Department of Agriculture, Natural Resources Conservation Service; 2002; version 3.5; *http:// plants.usda.gov;* National Plant Data Center). The common names, with some exceptions, are from the same source.

PLATE 9

COMMON FERN FAMILY (POLYPODIACEAE)

Aleutian maidenhair fern (northern maidenhair), *Adiantum aleuticum.* Fronds decid, L to 28", stipes shiny blk or dk brown, forked to form 2 curved rachises, ea bearing 2 to several pinnae with 15–35 pinnules on ea side of midrib. Sori covered by folded marginal lobes. Moist woods, low-mid el, in all our mtns, Alas e across Can, s to Cal, e Utah, Wyo.

Maidenhair spleenwort, *Asplenium trichomanes.* Fronds evergreen, narrow, 1-divided, L to 7" with purplish brown stipes and rachises. Pinnae margins slightly toothed. Lvs decid but rachises perst. Sori along veinlets with thin, flaplike indusia. Moist rock ledges and crevices, oft limestones, in all our mtns, se Alas to e Can, s to Ore, Ariz, se US. Green spleenwort, *A. t. ramosum,* similar but rachises green.

Indian dream, *Aspidotis densa.* Fronds evergreen, densely clumped, L 4"–8"; sterile ones few or absent, 3-divided, with broad, flat, sharply toothed segm; fertile ones numerous, 3-divided with narrow segm having stiff, sharp tips and tightly curled margins covering sori. Moist crevices, talus, esp limestone or serpentine in all our mtns, s BC to Cal, e to RM and e Can.

Lady fern, *Athyrium filix-femina.* Fronds decid, gen 2-divided, L 12"–60", broadest in middle, tapering at ea end, tightly clumped amid more numerous dead stipe bases; stipes short, furrowed, straw colored, scaly at base. Sori along veinlets with flaplike but soon decid indusia. Com, damp, shaded places, forest in all our mtns; Alas to e Can and US, s to Cal. Alpine lady fern, *A. americanum,* similar but fronds gen 3-divided and indusia lacking; moist, rocky places, streamsides, mont-alp, oft near timberline in all our mtns; Alas s to Cal, Nev, Colo; e Can.

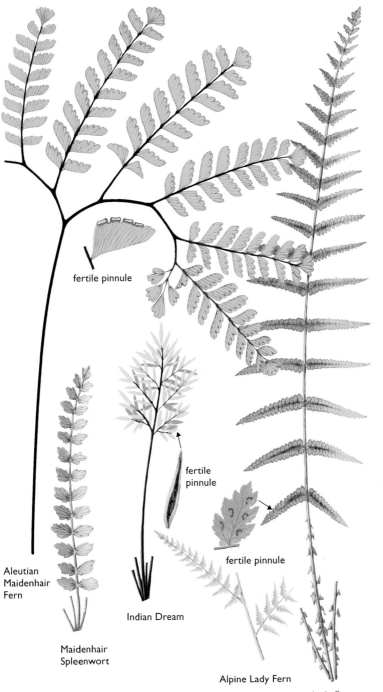

fertile pinnule

fertile pinnule

fertile pinnule

Aleutian
Maidenhair
Fern

Indian Dream

Maidenhair
Spleenwort

Alpine Lady Fern

Lady Fern

PLATE 10

COMMON FERN FAMILY (POLYPODIACEAE)

Deer fern, *Blechnum spicant.* Fronds evergreen, leathery, tapering toward base, with short brownish stipes; sterile fronds peripheral, erect or spreading, L 8"–32", with broad, crowded pinnae; fertile fronds taller, erect from center of plant, with narrow, widely spaced pinnae and sori parallel to midribs, with flaplike indusia attached to margins. Com, damp or wet woods, low-mid el, in all our mtns, mostly W CMtns–Cas, Alas to Cal.

Lace fern, *Cheilanthes gracillima.* Fronds evergreen, L 2¾"–8", 2-divided, with usu smooth stipes and scaly rachises and pinna midribs. Pinnae with round or oval pinnules, rolled margins, and dense, woolly, matted brown hairs below. Sori partly covered by curled margins. Rock ledges and crevices, low el–subalp in all our mtns, s to Cal, e to Mont. Hairy lip-fern, C. *lanosa,* similar but has long, soft hairs on underside of pinnae; in our region found only at one place in OMtns.

Rock brake, *Cryptogramma acrostichoides.* Fronds evergreen, L 3"–6", numerous, densely clustered, hairless, 2- to 3-divided, with slender green or straw-colored stipes; fertile fronds stiff, erect, with narrow pinnules, margins entirely curled to form continuous indusia; sterile fronds more numerous, shorter, with ovate to oblong pinnules, margins scalloped or sharply lobed. Talus, rocky places, in all our mtns; Alas to e Can, ne US, s to Cal, NMex.

Brittle bladder fern, *Cystopteris fragilis.* Frond decid, L to 12", delicate, erect or spreading, gen 2-divided; rachis green; stipe straw colored or brown; pinnules very thin, sharply lobed. Sori on veinlets, with hoodlike indusia. Com, damp woods, rocky places low el–alp in all our mtns; Alas to e Can, s to Cal, se US.

Wood fern, *Dryopteris carthusiana.* Fronds decid, L to 18"–40", gen 3-divided, ultimate segm with serrated margins and sharp tips, stipes brown-scaly, lowest pinnae asymmetrical. Sori on veins with kidney-shaped indusia. Moist woods, stream banks, in all our mtns; Alas to e Can, ne US, se US.

Male fern, *Dryopteris filix-mas.* Fronds decid, ± 2-divided, L 24"–48", with stipe, rachises, and midribs covered with pale brown, hairlike scales. Sori and indusia similar to those of above sp but confined to upper half of frond. Woods, shaded talus, CMtns, Wn Cas; BC to e Can, s to Cal, e US.

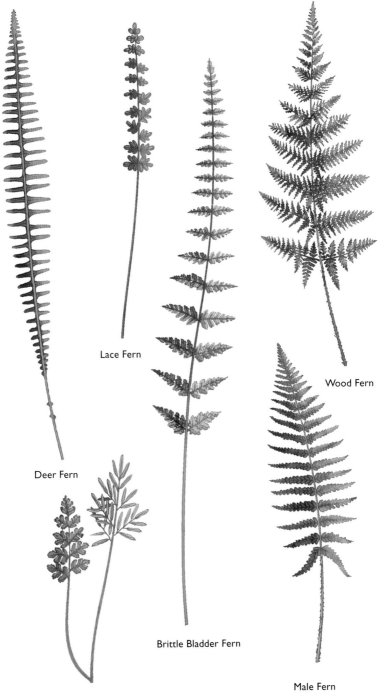

Lace Fern

Deer Fern

Wood Fern

Brittle Bladder Fern

Male Fern

Rock Brake

PLATE 11

COMMON FERN FAMILY (POLYPODIACEAE)

Smooth cliff brake, *Pellaea glabella.* Similar to *P. breweri* but upper pinnae entire or barely lobed and basal ones oft divided again, with 3–5 pinnules; stipes reddish brown, hairless or nearly so, with or without cross-grooves, some perst but fewer than lvs. Dry rocky places, E Cas, CR Gorge, n to s BC; ne Ore and Idaho s to SNev.

Pacific oak fern, *Gymnocarpium disjunctum.* Fronds decid, L to 16", few in number, 2- to 3-divided, with basal pinnae asymmetrical, ea ± as large as rest of blade; stipe smooth, shiny, pale yellow, up to 2x as long as blade. Sori on veinlets, no indusia. Damp woods, shaded rocky places, in all our mtns s to n Ore; Alas to e Can, s to Ore, e Wyo.

Brewer's cliff brake, *Pellaea breweri.* Fronds decid, L 2"–8", pinnate, with deeply 2-lobed pinnae; stipes brown, cross-grooved, slightly hairy, old ones perst and oft more numerous than lvs. Sori partly covered by curled margins. Rocky places, low el–subalp, E Cas, Wn; e to Utah, Wyo, s to Nev, Cal.

Goldback fern, *Pentagramma triangularis.* Fronds evergreen, L to 14", pinnate near top, 2- to 3-divided near base, with yellowish waxy powder beneath; stipe stiff, wiry, dk brown, ca ⅔ length of blade; blade triangular, with asymmetrical basal pinnae much larger than the rest. Sori along veins, no indusia. Rocky places in all our mtns; sw BC to Baja, e to Idaho, Utah, NMex.

Licorice fern, *Polypodium glycyrrhiza.* Plant evergreen. Fronds pinnate, with narrow, pointed, finely toothed pinnae; stipe L 2½"–12", stout; blade L 6"–20". Sori near veins, no indusia. Com, epiphytic, growing on trees and rocks in shady, damp woods, low el, W CMtns–Cas, Alas to Cal. Western polypody, *P. hesperum,* similar but pinnae rounded or blunt at tip; crevices, rocky slopes, Cas, BC to Ore; Alas, Ariz, NMex.

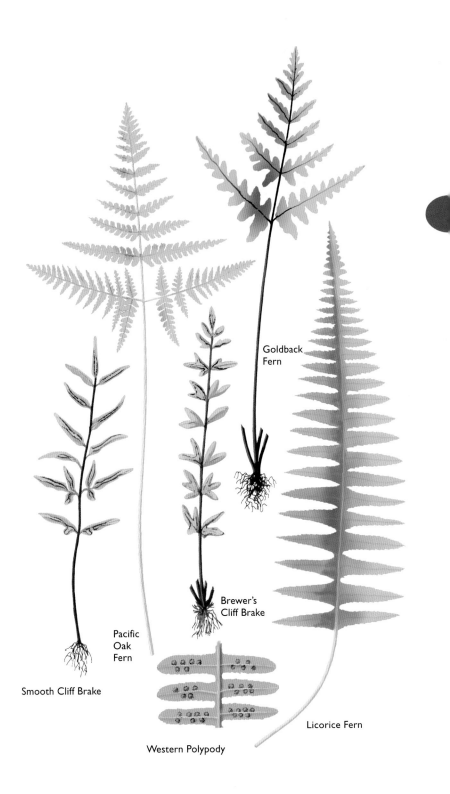

Goldback
Fern

Pacific
Oak
Fern

Brewer's
Cliff Brake

Smooth Cliff Brake

Western Polypody

Licorice Fern

PLATE 12

COMMON FERN FAMILY (POLYPODIACEAE)

Common sword fern, *Polystichum munitum.* Fronds evergreen, pinnate, L 8"–60", swordlike; stipes and rachises densely brown-scaly; pinnae asymmetrical, undivided, with scaly midrib and spinelets along margins and at tip. Sori large, in 1+ rows, with shieldlike indusia. Moist forest, low-mid el in all our mtns, Alas to Cal, e to n RM. Imbricate sword fern, *P. imbricans,* similar but smaller (fronds to 20"), sparsely or not scaled, and prefers drier woods and rocky places; OMtns and Cas s to SNev.

Northern holly fern, *Polystichum lonchitis.* Fronds evergreen, pinnate, L 4"–24", with short stipe and slender blade that narrows toward both ends; pinnae leathery, asymmetrical, undivided, with spinelets along margins and at tip. Sori in 2 rows with shieldlike indusia. Rocky places, occas forest, mont-alp, in all our mtns; Alas s to e Can, n Cal, RM.

Anderson's sword fern, *Polystichum andersonii.* Fronds evergreen, usu pinnate, relatively soft, L 12"–40", with short, very scaly stipes and one or more scaly buds beneath near tip of rachis; pinnae deeply cleft or occas pinnate, smoother or nearly so above, scaly beneath, with serrated margins. Sori in 1+ rows, with shieldlike indusia. Moist woods, Alas s in all our mtns to n Ore, e to Idaho and Mont. Braun's sword fern, *P. braunii,* very similar but without frond buds; BC only in our range.

Shasta fern, *Polystichum lemmonii.* Fronds evergreen, 2-divided, relatively soft, L 4"–20"; pinnae overlapping, with pinnules lobed or toothed but never prickly or spiny; stipe straw colored, somewhat sticky or with fine hairs, scaly only toward base. Sori gen only on mid and upper pinnae, indusia shieldlike. Rocky slopes, oft on serpentine, mont-subalp, Wenatchee mtns, Cal Cas.

Rock sword fern, *Polystichum scopulinum.* Fronds evergreen, pinnate, L 4"–16", with scaly stipe and pale green blade, stipe brown toward base, straw colored above; pinnae with stiff marginal prickles (*not* spines) and only one free pinnule. Sori in 2 rows near midrib, with shieldlike indusia. Rocky slopes, mid-high el, lower in CRGorge, mostly E Cas, BC to Cal; e to RM and e Can. Kruckeberg's sword fern, *P. kruckebergii,* similar but pinnules only 1–2x as long as wide and marginal spaces more prominent; rocky places, subalp-alp, s BC to Cal and Utah.

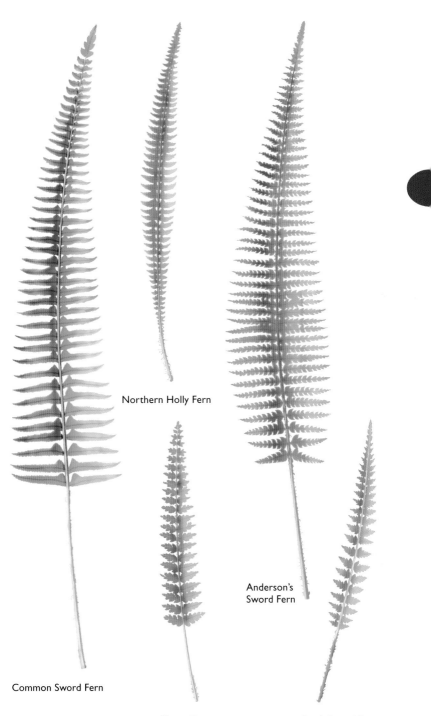

Northern Holly Fern

Anderson's
Sword Fern

Common Sword Fern

Shasta Fern

Rock Sword Fern

PLATE 13

COMMON FERN FAMILY (POLYPODIACEAE)

Bracken, *Pteridium aquilinum.* Fronds large, decid, L gen 20"–80", 3-divided, coarse, stiff, densely hairy beneath, ± smooth above; stipe stout, straw colored. Sori covered by curled margins. Com, open places, low-mid el in all our mtns; widespread throughout the world.

Oregon woodsia, *Woodsia oregana.* Fronds 1- to 2-divided, L gen 4"–8", bright green, hairless; pinnae lobed; stipe stiff, slender, brown and scaly at base, smooth and straw colored above. Indusia minute, divided into threadlike segm. Dry, rocky places, CMtns, Cas s to Ore; e to RM, mid US, e Can. Rocky Mountain woodsia, *W. scopulina,* similar but lvs sticky and white haired.

Beechfern, *Phegopteris connectilis.* Fronds decid, L 8"–18", pinnate, nearly triangular, ± hairy above and beneath, with lobed pinnae and straw-colored stipe much longer than blade. Sori on veins, not marginal, no indusia. Moist, open woods, rocky places in all our mtns, Alas to e Can, e US, s to Ore.

Mountain fern, *Thelypteris quelpaertensis.* Fronds decid, pinnate, L to 40", pinnae lobed; stipe short, scaly, straw colored with dker base. Sori marginal, on veins, indusia horseshoe shaped. Open woods, subalp mdws, Vanc I, CMtns, Wn Cas; Alas to n Wn. Sierra wood fern, *T. nevadensis,* similar but smaller, more delicate, with narrower blades; uncom, Cas s of Rainier, s to Cal.

Chain fern, *Woodwardia fimbriata.* Fronds decid, L gen 20"–80", firm, pinnate; pinnae with long, sharp-tipped, serrated lobes; stipe stout. Sori in 2 chainlike rows near midrib, indusia flaplike. Moist woods, stream banks, mostly near coast, but to mid el in mtns, s BC to Cal and Ariz.

Bracken

Oregon
Woodsia

Beechfern

Mountain Fern

Chain Fern

5
flowering plants

The mountains of our region, with their varied topography and climate, support a few thousand species of flowering plants. Species that are at once common, conspicuous, distinctive, and showy, however, make up only a fraction of the total. This guide depicts more than 320 species and provides information for identifying several dozen more.

The term *wildflower* has no precise botanical meaning and may refer to any flowering plant growing outside of cultivation. In common parlance, however, it usually refers to herbaceous plants, which have nonwoody stems that grow anew each year and die back after seed production. Annuals sprout each year from seed and complete their life cycles in a single growing season. Biennials require two years. Perennial herbs live for several seasons, but during months of dormancy, they persist in the form of mostly underground parts such as bulbs, corms, tubers, rhizomes, or root crowns. Some perennial herbs die back to woody bases, but each year's new growth is herbaceous. Such plants are called subshrubs. In addition to reproducing from seed, some perennials may form new plants through such means as the division of bulbs and corms, the sprouting of tubers, and the formation of new plantlets along rhizomes and runners.

As used here, the term *flowering plant* includes cone-bearing plants *(gymnosperms)* and true flowering plants *(angiosperms)*. Gymnosperms bear naked seeds on the undersides of cone scales. Angiosperms bear seeds in protective capsules called ovaries.

Scientific names conform to those in *USDA Plant Database* (U.S. Department of Agriculture, Natural Resources Conservation Service; 2002; version 3.5; *http://plants.usda.gov;* National Plant Data Center). The common names, with some exceptions, are from the same source.

The following glossary defines the technical terms used in the species descriptions. Most terms, in addition, are illustrated in figures 5 through 8, which depict types of flowers and leaves as well as plant parts. Wherever possible, common words have been used to replace technical terms.

GLOSSARY

Alternate: *Having one leaf per node (see figure 7).*
Anther: *The pollen-bearing part of the stamen (see figure 5).*
Axil: *The point of the upper angle formed where a leaf or petiole joins a stem (see figure 7).*

Basal:	*Referring to leaves that emerge from the base of a flowering stem, either from the stem itself, a woody base, runners, or underground parts (see figure 7).*
Blade:	*The expanded part of a leaf or petal (see figure 7).*
Bract:	*Any more or less modified or reduced leaf associated with an inflorescence (see figures 5 and 6).*
Calyx:	*All the sepals of a flower considered together; the outer set of modified floral leaves (see figure 5).*
Catkin:	*An erect or drooping spikelike inflorescence consisting of numerous tiny flowers and their associated bracts (see figure 6).*
Clasping:	*Referring to leaves that partially wrap around a stem at the point of attachment (see figure 7).*
Composite head:	*An inflorescence typical of the sunflower family (Asteraceae) that consists of numerous tubular disk flowers surrounded by a few to many straplike ray flowers, the whole resembling a single regular flower; examples include asters, daisies, and sunflowers (see figures 5 and 6).*
Compound:	*Referring to leaves with two or more distinct leaflets (see figure 7).*
Compound-pinnate:	*Referring to compound leaves having two or more pinnate leaflets (see figure 7).*
Corolla:	*All the petals of a flower considered together; the innermost set of modified floral leaves (see figure 5).*
Corymb:	*A round- or flat-topped inflorescence in which the lower (outer) pedicels are progressively longer (see figure 6).*
Deciduous:	*Falling off, as leaves in autumn or petals after flowering.*
Disk flower:	*The generally small, tubular flowers making up the central disk of a composite head (see figures 5 and 6).*
Dissected:	*Cut or divided into lobes or segments; said of leaves.*
Double-toothed:	*Referring to leaf margins divided into large teeth that are themselves divided into smaller teeth (see figure 8).*
Elliptic:	*Referring to a leaf shape resembling an ellipse (see figure 8).*
Entire:	*Referring to undivided leaf margins (see figure 8).*
Evergreen:	*Referring to plants that retain leaves throughout the year.*
Fascicled:	*Referring to leaves that are attached to a stem in tight bundles, or fascicles (see figure 7).*
Filament:	*The stalk of a stamen (see figure 5).*
Glandular:	*Plant parts having glands that secrete a sticky or greasy substance.*
Inflorescence:	*A flower cluster sharing a single main stem (see figure 6).*
Involucre:	*A set of bracts beneath an inflorescence (see figure 5).*
Irregular flower:	*A flower displaying bilateral, rather than radial, symmetry (see figure 6).*
Leaflet:	*The ultimate division of a compound leaf that resembles a single, simple leaf (see figure 7).*
Linear:	*Referring to leaves that are long, narrow, of more or less uniform width (see figure 8).*

Lobe: *A segment of a leaf blade, usually blunt or rounded and not cut all the way from margin to midrib (see figure 8); a projecting segment of a corolla or calyx.*

Node: *Place on a stem where a leaf is or was attached (see figure 7).*

Oblanceolate: *Referring to leaves that are inversely lancelike (see figure 8).*

Oblong: *Referring to leaves that are much longer than broad, with nearly parallel sides (see figure 8).*

Obovate: *Referring to leaves that are inversely egg shaped (see figure 8).*

Opposite: *Having a pair of leaves per node (see figure 7).*

Oval: *Referring to leaves that are broadly elliptic (see figure 8).*

Ovary: *The swollen, seed-bearing portion of the pistil (see figure 5).*

Ovate: *Referring to leaves that are egg shaped (see figure 8).*

Ovule: *Unfertilized or undeveloped seed; borne in the ovary (see figure 5).*

Palmate: *Referring to leaves resembling the palm of a hand; having leaves or veins radiating from a central point (see figure 8).*

Panicle: *An inflorescence with branched pedicels (see figure 6).*

Pedicel: *The stalk of a single flower in an inflorescence (see figures 5 and 6).*

Peduncle: *The stalk of an inflorescence.*

Perfoliate: *With a leaf completely surrounding the stem (see figure 7).*

Petal: *One of the modified leaves making up the corolla of a flower; usually brightly colored to attract insects (see figure 5).*

Petiole: *Leaf stalk (see figure 7).*

Petioled: *Having a petiole.*

Pinnate: *A compound leaf with the leaflets arranged on each side of a common axis (see figure 7).*

Pistil: *The female reproductive organ of a flower, consisting of a stigma, style, and ovary (see figure 5).*

Raceme: *An inflorescence bearing flowers on pedicels (see figure 6).*

Ray *or* ray flower: *The strap-shaped, petal-like peripheral flowers of a composite head (see figures 5 and 6).*

Receptacle: *The swollen part of a floral stalk to which the flower parts are attached (see figure 5).*

Regular flower: *A flower displaying radial symmetry (see figure 6).*

Rhizome: *A trailing underground stem producing leafy shoots on the upper side and roots on the underside.*

Rosette: *A leaf cluster, usually basal, in which the leaves are arranged in a concentric configuration like that of the petals of a rose.*

Samara: *Dry, generally one-seeded, winged fruit, as in maples (see plates 49, 61).*

Scalloped: *Referring to leaves having shallow, rounded divisions (see figure 8).*

Sepal: *One of the modified leaves making up the calyx of a flower (see figure 5).*

Sessile: *Referring to leaves attached directly to the stem; said of leaves without petioles (see figure 7).*

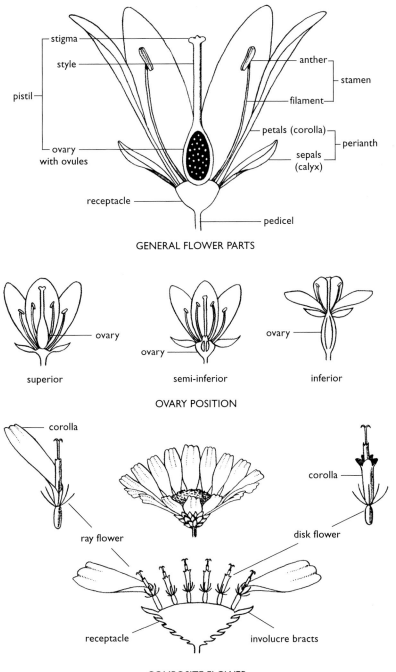

stigma

style

pistil

anther
stamen
filament

ovary
with ovules

petals (corolla)
perianth
sepals
(calyx)

receptacle

pedicel

GENERAL FLOWER PARTS

ovary

superior

ovary

ovary

semi-inferior

ovary

inferior

OVARY POSITION

corolla

corolla

ray flower

disk flower

receptacle

involucre bracts

COMPOSITE FLOWER

Figure 5. *Anatomy of a flower*

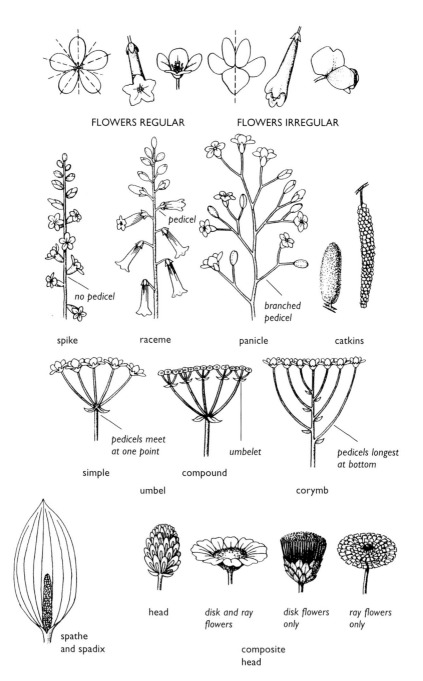

FLOWERS REGULAR   FLOWERS IRREGULAR

pedicel

no pedicel

branched
pedicel

spike   raceme   panicle   catkins

pedicels meet
at one point

umbelet

pedicels longest
at bottom

simple   compound   corymb

umbel

spathe
and spadix

head   disk and ray
flowers   disk flowers
only   ray flowers
only

composite
head

Figure 6. *Types of inflorescence*

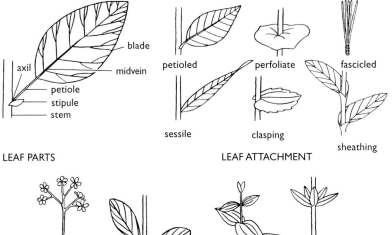

blade

axil

midvein

petiole

stipule

stem

LEAF PARTS

petioled

perfoliate

fascicled

sessile

clasping

sheathing

LEAF ATTACHMENT

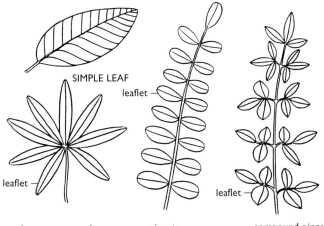

basal

alternate

opposite

whorled

LEAF ARRANGEMENT

SIMPLE LEAF

leaflet

leaflet

leaflet

palmate compound

pinnate

compound-pinnate

COMPOUND LEAVES

Figure 7. *Anatomy of leaves*

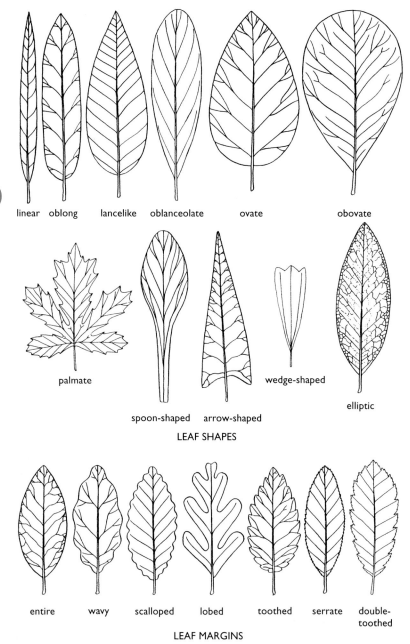

linear oblong lancelike oblanceolate ovate obovate

palmate spoon-shaped arrow-shaped wedge-shaped elliptic

LEAF SHAPES

entire wavy scalloped lobed toothed serrate double-toothed

LEAF MARGINS

Figure 8. *Leaf shapes and margins*

Sheathing:	*Referring to leaves wrapping around the stem like a sheath (see figure 7).*
Simple leaf:	*A leaf with a blade undivided into leaflets; opposite of a compound leaf (see figure 7).*
Spadix:	*A floral spike with tiny flowers crowded on a fleshy stem (see figure 6).*
Spathe:	*A large, usually solitary bract partly surrounding a spadix or other inflorescence (see figure 6).*
Spike:	*An inflorescence in which flowers are attached directly to a central stem (see figure 6).*
Spur:	*A slender, hollow projection from a petal or sepal.*
Stamen:	*The male reproductive organ of a flower, consisting of the anther and filament (see figure 5).*
Stigma:	*The pollen receptacle on the tip of a pistil (see figure 5).*
Stipule:	*One of a pair of leaflike structures found at the base of leaves on many types of plants (see figure 7).*
Style:	*The stalk of a pistil (see figure 5).*
Tepal:	*A modified floral leaf performing the function of both sepal and petal when those are lacking.*
Toothed:	*Referring to leaves having margins divided into pointed segments (see figure 8).*
Tufted:	*Referring to leaves growing in basal tufts or fascicles.*
Umbel:	*Inflorescence in which all the pedicels arise from a central hub (see figure 6).*
Whorled:	*Having three or more leaves or flowers radiating from a single node on a stem (see figure 7).*

WILDFLOWERS

More than 200 of the more common or showy species of wildflowers found in our mountains are described and illustrated in the rest of this chapter. They include representatives from each vegetation zone and from most of the important families and genera. The great majority are native to our region, but a few are exotics that have become naturalized.

For easy reference, the flowers are grouped by color. A word of caution is in order, however, for color by itself is not always a reliable field mark. First, many species are variable in color. Second, flowers may change color with age. Third, closely related species may have flowers of identical colors. Fourth, some flowers are more than one color and are therefore difficult to assign to a single color group. Fifth, people differ markedly in their perception of color: what appears creamy white to me may seem pale yellow to you; what I call rosy pink you may consider reddish purple. Therefore, when searching for a wildflower in this guide, turn first to the appropriate color group, but if you do not find your specimen, consult the list of color variations found at the beginning of each color section. This list will direct you to species in other sections that sometimes have flowers the color of your specimen. In addition, don't rely on color alone. Pay equal attention to flower structure, leaves, stems, general growth habit, habitat, and range. Figures 5 through 8 will help you recognize flowers and leaves.

Under each color heading, species are grouped by family. To assist your search, immediately following each family name is a brief statement characterizing the flowers of family members appearing on each plate. If you find a species that does not exactly match your specimen but is very similar, refer to the brief descriptions of similar species that may be included in the species description. Your specimen may be included there, or you may have to settle for identifying it by genus alone. It is also possible, of course, that you have found a species not covered in this book, in which case you should consult Hitchcock and Cronquist's *Flora of the Pacific Northwest* or one of the other exhaustive floras covering our region.

For information on the organization and use of the species descriptions and illustrations, as well as for a list of the abbreviations used in the accounts, see the Introduction. The general flowering period for each species is indicated at the end of each account.

I. White Flowers

This section includes not only flowers that are truly white but also those that appear white even though lightly tinged with other colors. The following species from other color sections sometimes have white or whitish flowers.

Sulfur-flowered buckwheat, *plate 26*

Oval-leaved buckwheat, *plate 26*

Martindale's lomatium, *plate 28*

Coiled-beak lousewort, *plate 29*

Rosy twisted stalk, *plate 31*

Western spring beauty, *plate 31*

Steer's head, *plate 32*

Alpine willowherb, *plate 33*

Candystick, *plate 33*

Skyrocket, *plate 34*

Spreading phlox, *plate 34*

Foxglove, *plate 35*

Common camas, *plate 37*

Monkshood, *plate 37*

Cut-leaf anemone, *plate 37*

Oregon anemone, *plate 37*

Nuttall's pea, *plate 38*

Marsh violet, *plate 38*

Mountain pennyroyal, *plate 40*

Western meadowrue, *plate 43*

Fringecup, *plate 43*

Pinedrops, *plate 43*

PLATE 14

LILY FAMILY (LILIACEAE): USUALLY 3 PETALS AND 3 SEPALS, OR 6 TEPALS, BUT SEE *MAIANTHEMUM* BELOW

Subalpine mariposa lily, *Calochortus subalpinus.* Flr creamy white, occas lavender tinged; petals broadly ovate, yellow haired, oft with purple crescent at base. Single grasslike basal lf as long or longer than stem. Ht 2"–12". Volcanic soils in open woods, mid-high el, Cas, s Wn to cen Ore. Sum.

Lyall's mariposa lily, *Calochortus lyallii.* Similar to *C. subalpinus* but petals lancelike, fringed, without yellow hairs. Dry woods and brush, low el, E Cas, BC to cen Wn. Late spr–midsum.

Hooker's fairy bell, *Disporum hookeri.* Flr L to ¾", creamy white, with undivided stigma, usu in pairs, nodding. Lvs sessile, nearly clasping, hairy, wavy margined. Ht 12"–24". Dense woods in all our mtns, BC to Cal, E Cas to coast; n RM. Spr-midsum. Fairy lantern, *D. smithii,* similar but flr L ca 1", with divided stigma and lvs broader, not clasping, hairless above; BC to n Cal, coast to W Cas.

Queen's cup (bead lily), *Clintonia uniflora.* Flrs bell shaped with spreading tepals, 1 (occas 2) per stem. Lvs 2–3, basal, oblong, L 3"–10". Fruit a turquoise berry. Ht ca 4". Com, forest, open places, low-high el, in all our mtns, Alas to Cal, e to RM, e Ore. Sum.

False lily-of-the-valley, *Maianthemum dilatatum.* Flrs tiny, in raceme; only lily with 2 petals, 2 sepals. Lvs heart shaped, glossy green, usu 2 (1–3) per stem, lower one(s) L 2"–4½", upper one smaller. Fruit a red berry ¼" diam. Ht 4"–8". Moist woods, low-mid el, in all our mtns, Alas to Cal, e to n RM. Late spr–early sum.

Avalanche lily, *Erythronium montanum.* Flrs white with yellow throat, nod-ding, ca 2½" diam, usu 1–3 on lfless stem. Lvs basal, broadly ovate or lance shaped, L 4"–8". Ht to 10". Abun, wet mdws, mid-high el, Vanc I, OMtns, s Wn Cas s to Mt. Hood. Early sum to midsum, just after snow melts.

Washington lily, *Lilium washingtonianum.* Flrs white or pale pink, oft with purplish spots, aging purple, fragrant, in loose raceme, 3"–4" diam, nearly as long. Lvs 1 lancelike, L 2"–4", alt on lower stem, whorled on upper stem. Ht 24"–80". Open forest, brush, Cas of Ore and Cal, s in SNev. Sum.

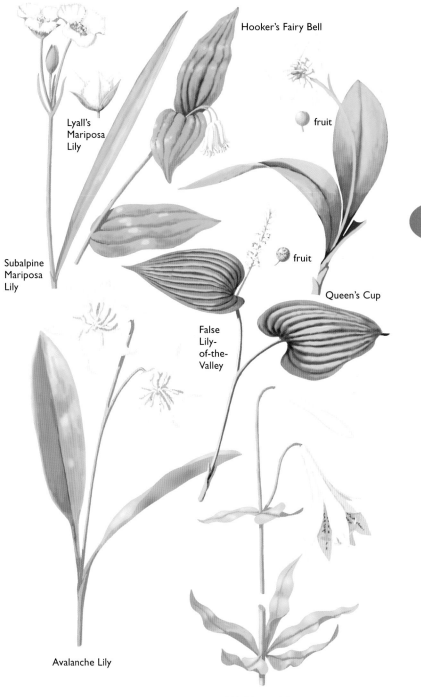

Hooker's Fairy Bell

fruit

Lyall's
Mariposa
Lily

Subalpine
Mariposa
Lily

fruit

Queen's Cup

False
Lily-
of-the-
Valley

Avalanche Lily

Washington Lily

PLATE 15

LILY FAMILY (LILIACEAE): 3 PETALS AND 3 SEPALS, OR 6 TEPALS

Starry solomon's plume (false solomon's seal), *Maianthemum stellatum.* Flrs starlike, ca ¼" diam, 5–10+ in zigzag raceme. Lvs lancelike to elliptic, clasping stem, gen glossy green above, sometimes downy beneath. Fruit a greenish berry, aging black. Ht 8"–28". Com, usu moist woods to open rocky slopes in all our mtns, Alas to Cal; RM s to Ariz, e to Atl. Late spr–midsum. False solomon's seal (false spikenard), *M. racemosum,* similar but flrs tiny, numerous in panicle, lvs broader, berries red; moist woods, stream banks, low-mid el in all our mtns, Alas to Cal, e to Atl; early spr–midsum.

Clasping-leaved twisted stalk, *Streptopus amplexifolius.* Flrs white, green tinged, usu 1 borne below ea lf. Stems oft kinked or zigzag, freely branching, ht 12"–36". Lvs ± ovate, clasping. Fruit a translucent red berry. Moist forest, stream banks in all our mtns, Alas to Cal, e in much of US and Can. Late spr. Cf other twisted stalks, plates 31 and 42.

Sticky tofieldia, *Tofieldia glutinosa.* Flrs greenish white, to ¼" diam, in cluster atop sticky, lfless stem. Lvs grasslike, clasping, basal. Ht 4"–20". Wet mdws, bogs, low-high el in all our mtns, Alas to Cal, e to Atl. Sum.

Western trillium (wake-robin), *Trillium ovatum.* Flrs 1½"–3" diam, gen white, aging pink to dark red, 1 above whorl of 3 (occas 4–5) ovate lvs. Ht 4"–16". Com, moist, oft shaded sites lowl–mid el, in all our mtns, Alas to Cal, e to RM. Late win–early sum.

Corn-lily (white false-hellebore), *Veratrum californicum.* Flrs white or occas greenish, numerous in dense, upright terminal panicle. Lvs gen ovate to oval, L 8"–12", numerous. Ht 3'–7'+. Wet places, lowl–subalp, W Cas (occas E Cas), Wn s to SNev. Sum. Cf green false-hellebore, plate 42.

Beargrass, *Xerophyllum tenax.* Flrs tiny, creamy, starlike, in dense terminal inflor. Lvs grasslike, stiff, basal ones gen 6"–24" long, clumped, stem lvs shorter, numerous. Ht 2'–5'. Open woods, clearings, gen mid-high el, in all our mtns, BC to cen Cal, e to RM. Sum.

Elegant death-camas, *Zigadenus elegans.* Flrs creamy or green tinged, with green glands at base, in terminal inflor. Lvs mostly basal, grasslike, L 6"–12", with powdery bloom. Ht 6"–28". Mdws, rocky places, gen mid-high el, Alas and BC s to Wn Cas and OMtns; e to RM, s to Ariz and n Mex. Sum.

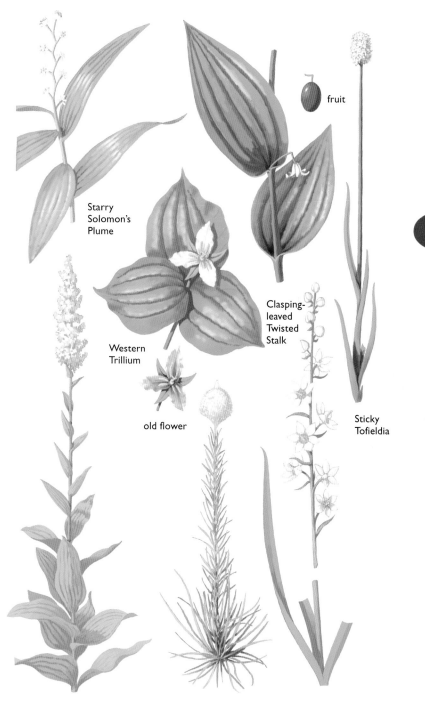

Starry
Solomon's
Plume

fruit

Western
Trillium

Clasping-
leaved
Twisted
Stalk

old flower

Sticky
Tofieldia

Corn-lily

Beargrass

Elegant Death-camas

PLATE 16

ORCHID FAMILY (ORCHIDACEAE): FLOWERS IRREGULAR, 3 PETALS, 3 SEPALS

Mountain ladyslipper (moccasin flower), *Cypripedium montanum.* Flrs usu 2, orchidlike; sepals brownish purple, 2 lower ones fused; 2 upper petals like sepals but twisted, lower one white, pouchlike, occas purple veined. Lvs oval to ovate, L 2"–6", sheathing stem. Ht 4"–24"; stem leafy, sticky haired. Mostly E Cas, Alas to Cal, e to RM. Late spr–sum. Cf clustered ladyslipper, plate 42.

Phantom (snow) orchid, *Eburophyton austiniae.* Entire plant white, aging brown, with 5–20 fragrant flrs on single stem. Lvs bractlke on lower stem. Ht 8"–20". Moist, shady forest, OMtns, Cas, Wn to s Cal, e to Idaho. Sum.

Rattlesnake-plantain (orchid), *Goodyera oblongifolia.* Flrs small, gen in 1-sided raceme on sticky-haired stem. Lvs basal, dk green, mottled or striped with white. Ht gen 10"–16". Shady woods in all our mtns, Alas e to Atl, s in most of w Can and US. Sum–early fall.

Roundleaf bog orchid (rein orchis), *Platanthera orbiculata.* Flrs creamy white to greenish, 5–25 per stem, with spur L to 1". Lvs round, rather fleshy, L ca 2½"–6", 2 (3) at base, lying flat on ground. Ht 8"–24". Moist, mossy forest in our mtns s to Ore, Alas e to Atl and RM. Sum.

White bog orchid, *Platanthera dilatata.* Flrs white, fragrant, spurred. Lvs clasping, lower ones ± lancelike, L to 4", upper ones linear, L 2"–12". Ht 6"–40". Wet places in all our mtns, Alas s in w Can and US, e to e Can, ne US. Sum–early fall. Short-spurred bog orchid (elegant bog orchid), *Piperia elegans,* has nearly basal lvs and green flrs with white spur; prefers dry woods. Slender bog orchid, *Platanthera stricta,* has green flrs with sack-shaped spur.

Lady's tresses, *Spiranthes romanzoffiana.* Flrs white or creamy to greenish white, up to 60 in dense, spiraling spike. Lvs linear, L 2"–10", ± basal, bractlike above. Ht 4"–24". Moist or wet places in all our mtns, Alas s to Cal, Ariz, NMex, e to e Can, ne US. Late sum–early fall.

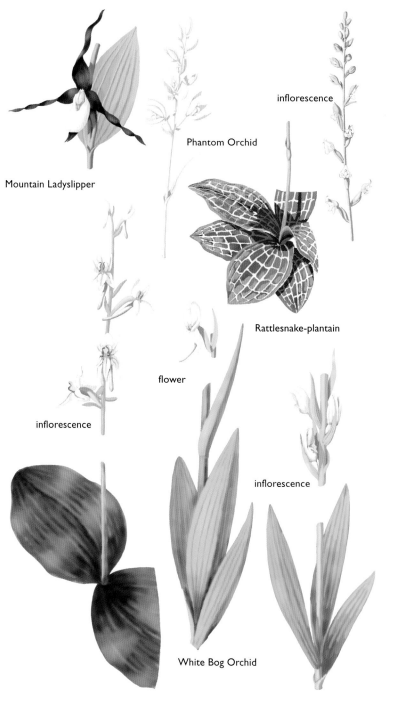

Mountain Ladyslipper

Phantom Orchid

inflorescence

Rattlesnake-plantain

flower

inflorescence

inflorescence

Roundleaf Bog Orchid

White Bog Orchid

Lady's Tresses

PLATE 17

BUCKWHEAT FAMILY (POLYGONACEAE): NO PETALS, 4–9 PETAL-LIKE SEPALS

Alpine (pyrola-leaved) buckwheat, *Eriogonum pyrolifolium.* Flrs creamy or greenish white, aging pink, in umbels with 2 linear bracts at base. Lvs numerous, ± oval, basal, petioled. Ht 2"–4". Subalp-alp, Wn Cas to Cal, e to RM. Sum.

Common (American, mountain, western) bistort, *Polygonum bistortoides.* Flrs tiny, in dense clublike inflor. Lvs mostly basal, elliptic to oblong, L to 8"; stem lvs smaller, bractlike. Ht 12"–24". Abun, subalp-alp mdws, stream banks, in all our mtns, BC to Cal, e to RM. Showiest and commonest of more than a dozen knotweeds in our range. Sum.

PURSLANE FAMILY (PORTULACACEAE): GENERALLY 5 PETALS, 2 SEPALS

Miner's lettuce, *Claytonia perfoliata.* Flrs small, in raceme above round, perfoliate lf (2 lvs fused). Basal lvs usu spoon shaped. Ht 1"–14". Plant edible. Moist places, low-mid el, Cas, BC s to Baja; e to RM and mid US. Spr-sum.

Siberian miner's lettuce (western spring beauty, candyflower), *Claytonia sibirica.* Flrs white or pale pink, lined with darker pink, in loose racemes. Basal lvs numerous, broadly spoon shaped, long petioled; stem lvs opp, 1 pair per stem, oval, sessile. Ht 2"–16". Moist, shaded places, low-mid el, in all our mtns, Alas to Cal, e to RM. Sum. Heartleaf montia, *C. cordifolia,* has broad, heart-shaped lvs. Littleleaf montia, *C. parvifolia,* has alt stem lvs and spoon-shaped basal lvs. Cf western spring beauty, plate 31.

Pygmy (dwarf, alpine) lewisia, *Lewisia pygmaea.* Flrs white to pink or rose, 1 per stem, with 2 sepals, 5–9 petals. Lvs fleshy, basal, linear, L 1½"–6". Ht to 4". Open, rocky places, Cas and OMtns, Wn to Cal, e to RM. Sum.

PINK FAMILY (CARYOPHYLLACEAE): 5 PETALS, 5 SEPALS

Mountain (beautiful, fescue) sandwort, *Arenaria capillaris.* Flrs to ½" diam, in open, branched inflor. Lvs grasslike, mostly basal, but with 2–5 opp pairs on stems. Ht 4"–8", mat forming. Dry, rocky places, in all our mtns, Alas to n Ore, e to Mont, s to Nev. Sum. Other sandworts in our range ± similar.

Parry's (white, fescue) silene (campion, catchfly), *Silene parryi.* Plant hairy, ± sticky. Flrs white, aging pink, with 4-lobed petals L ca ¼"; calyx tubular, 5-lobed, with green or purplish veins. Lvs linear-oblanceolate, basal and in 2–3 opp pairs on stem. Ht 4"–24". Mdws, mont-alp, in all our mtns, BC and Wn e to RM. Sum.

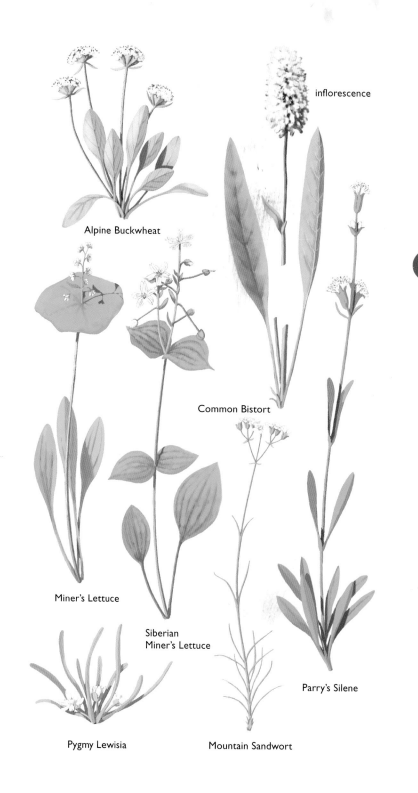

inflorescence

Alpine Buckwheat

Common Bistort

Miner's Lettuce

Siberian
Miner's Lettuce

Parry's Silene

Pygmy Lewisia

Mountain Sandwort

PLATE 18

BUTTERCUP FAMILY (RANUNCULACEAE): 5–12 PETAL-LIKE SEPALS

Western red baneberry, *Actaea rubra.* Flrs tiny, tinged purple, in dense racemes. Lvs compound pinnate, long petioled, ultimate segm toothed and lobed. Fruit is clusters of poisonous red berries. Ht 16"–40". Moist places, in all our mtns, Alas to Cal, e to RM, e Can, ne US. Late spr–midsum.

Columbia windflower (anemone), *Anemone deltoidea.* Flrs solitary, tinged blue, 1½" diam, with 5 petal-like sepals. Basal lf usu solitary with 3 ovate, toothed lflets; 3 simple, toothed stem lvs in whorl. Ht 4"–12". Forest, W Cas, Wn to n Cal. Spr. Lyall's anemone, *A. lyalli,* similar but stem lvs ea have 3 lflets. Northern anemone, *A. parvaflora,* has numerous basal lvs and simple, 3-lobed stem lvs and is usu less than 6" tall. Cf Oregon anemone, plate 37.

Globeflower, *Trollius laxus.* Flr solitary, creamy or greenish white, ca 1½" diam. Lvs palmately 5-lobed or divided, basal and alt on stem. Ht 4"–20". Wet places, mid-high el, mtns of BC, OMtns, Wn Cas, e to RM and in US to Atl. Late spr–early sum.

Drummond's anemone, *Anemone drummondii.* Flrs gen 1 per stem, ca 1" diam, 5 petal-like sepals white tinged with blue. Lvs finely divided, silky haired, several on long petioles from base; smaller but similar lvs in whorl on upper stem. Ht 4"–12". Alp-subalp in all our mtns, Alas to Cal, e to RM. Sum. Cliff anemone, *A. multifida,* similar but flrs oft 2–3 per stem, usu yellowish, tinged with red, blue, or purple.

False bugbane, *Trautvetteria caroliniensis.* Flrs with 3–7 tiny greenish sepals and numerous white stamens, in loose corymbs. Lvs mostly basal, 4"–12" broad, palmately lobed and toothed. Ht 6"–40". Moist places in all our mtns; N Amer, Japan. Late spr–sum.

Western pasqueflower, *Pulsatilla occidentalis.* Entire plant hairy. Flrs 1"–2" diam, occas blue tinged, with 5–7 petal-like sepals. Lvs basal, downy, finely divided, ultimate segm linear. Stems ca 4" tall at flowering, to 24" at maturity. Fruit a mop of feathery seeds. Wet mdws, mont-alp, in all our mtns, BC to Cal, e to RM. Early sum.

Twin marsh-marigold, *Caltha leptosepala.* Flrs white with yellow center, ca 1½" diam, 5–12 petal-like sepals, usu 2 flrs per stem. Lvs basal, nearly round to ovate, L to 4", nearly as wide or wider. Wet places, subalp-alp, in all our mtns, Alas to Cal, e to RM. Sum.

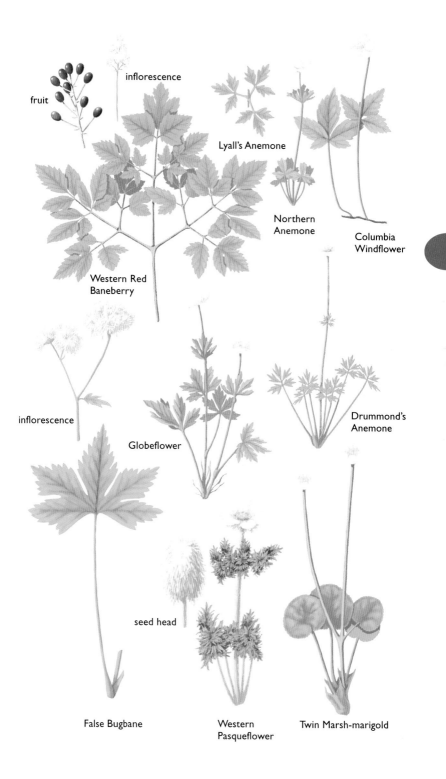

fruit

inflorescence

Lyall's Anemone

Northern
Anemone

Columbia
Windflower

Western Red
Baneberry

inflorescence

Globeflower

Drummond's
Anemone

seed head

False Bugbane

Western
Pasqueflower

Twin Marsh-marigold

PLATE 19

BARBERRY FAMILY (BERBERIDACEAE): FLOWERS 3-PARTED
Vanilla leaf, *Achlys triphylla*. Flrs inconspicuous, numerous in dense spike l"–2" long. Lvs basal, long petioled, compound, 3 lflets fan shaped with wavy, toothed margins. Ht 8"–16". Moist forest, stream banks, low-mid el, in all our mtns, BC to Cal. Spr–sum.

MUSTARD FAMILY (BRASSICACEAE): 4 PETALS IN A CROSS
Alpine smelowskia, *Smelowskia calycina*. Flrs white, creamy, or purple tinged, in racemes. Lvs mostly basal, pinnately lobed, gray haired, with long, stiff hairs on petioles. Cushion plant, ht 2"–8". Subalp-alp, BC s to Wn Cas, OMtns; widespread in N Amer e to RM; Asia. Sum. Shortleaf smelowskia, *S. ovalis,* very similar but without long, stiff hairs on petioles; Cas, Wn to Cal.

SUNDEW FAMILY (DROSERACEAE): USUALLY 5 PETALS, 5 SEPALS
Round-leaf sundew, *Drosera rotundifolia*. Flrs white or pinkish, small, on slender, bent stalk. Lvs basal, spreading, long petioled, covered with sticky red hairs. Ht to 10". Insectivorous. Bogs, in all our mtns, Alas s to Cal and Nev, e in Can and n US to Atl. Sum–early fall. Great sundew, *D. anglica,* very similar but lvs ± oblong and gen upright, not spreading.

SAXIFRAGE FAMILY (SAXIFRAGACEAE): 5 PETALS, 5 SEPALS
Elmera (alumroot), *Elmera racemosa* var *puberulenta*. Flrs 10–35 in raceme, with tiny, white and greenish yellow calyx. Lvs basal and on flr stem, kidney shaped, sticky haired, margins lobed. Ht 4"–10". Rock crevices, mont-subalp, OMtns, Wn Cas, se Ore. Sum–early fall. *E. r.* var *racemosa* has longer hairs.

Small-flowered alumroot, *Heuchera micrantha* var *micrantha*. Similar to elmera but flrs in panicle and lvs gen basal, with white or red hairs on petioles and base of flr stem. Ht to 36". Stream banks, moist rock crevices, lowl–subalp, in all our mtns, BC to Cal, e to ne Ore, Idaho. Late spr–sum. *H. m.* var *diversifolia,* leaves are more acutely lobed. Smooth alumroot, *H. glabra,* very similar but petioles hairless. Other spp similar, but flrs yellow or greenish.

Fringed grass-of-Parnassus, *Parnassia fimbriata*. Flrs solitary on stem, ca 1" diam, with 5 fringed petals and feathery structure at base of stamens. Lvs basal, long petioled, heart- to kidney-shaped. Ht 6"–20". Wet places, mont-alp, in all our mtns, Alas to Cal, e to RM. Midsum–early fall.

Foamflower (false miterwort, coolwort), *Tiarella trifoliata*. Flrs tiny, nodding, in branched inflor. Lvs gen basal, hairy, toothed, either compound with 3 lflets or simple and palmately lobed. Plants with simple lvs oft considered a separate sp, *T. unifoliata.* Ht to 16". Damp forest in all our mtns, Alas to Cal, e to RM. Late spr–fall.

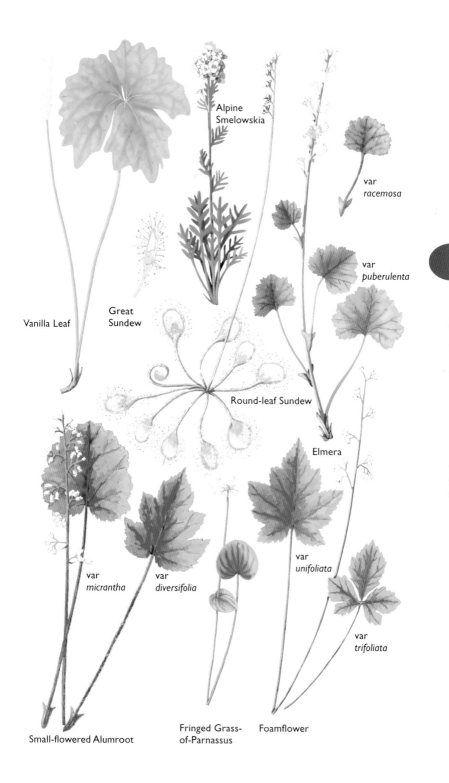

Alpine
Smelowskia

var
racemosa

var
puberulenta

Vanilla Leaf

Great
Sundew

Round-leaf Sundew

Elmera

var
micrantha

var
diversifolia

var
unifoliata

var
trifoliata

Small-flowered Alumroot

Fringed Grass-
of-Parnassus

Foamflower

PLATE 20

SAXIFRAGE FAMILY (SAXIFRAGACEAE): 5 PETALS, 5 SEPALS

Brook saxifrage, *Saxifraga odontoloma.* Flrs in sticky, red-haired panicles, petals round and oval. Lvs kidney shaped, toothed, basal, on long petioles. Ht 8"–24". Wet places, mont-alp, in all our mtns, Alas to Cal, e to RM. Sum. Dotted saxifrage, S. *nelsoniana,* similar but petals oblong and inflor white haired, not sticky.

Tufted saxifrage, *Saxifraga caespitosa.* Flrs plain white. Lvs tiny, wedge shaped, sticky, 3-lobed at tip, in basal tufts. Stems sticky, 2"–6" tall; mat-forming plant. Rocky places, in all our mtns; widespread in n hemis. Sum.

Spotted (matted, common) saxifrage, *Saxifraga bronchialis.* Flrs with many yellow, orange, red, and/or maroon spots. Lvs tiny, leathery, fringed, in basal tufts. Ht 2"–6", mat forming. Rocky places, lowl-alp, in all our mtns, Alas to n Ore, Ida, e Colo; Greenland, Eurasia. Sum.

Lyall's saxifrage, *Saxifraga lyallii.* Flrs white, aging pink, with 2 yellow spots on ea petal. Lvs basal, fan shaped, nearly as broad as long, petioled, toothed. Plant matlike, sparsely downy. Ht to 12". Moist places, mont-alp, in all our mtns, Alas to NCas, e to RM. Sum.

Rusty saxifrage, *Saxifraga ferruginea.* Flrs irreg, 2 lower petals spoon shaped, white; 3 upper petals lancelike, slender stalked, white with 2 yellow spots. Lvs basal, spoon shaped, toothed. Plant hairy. Ht 4"–24". Flrs oft replaced by leafy bulblets. Moist cliffs, stream banks, in all our mtns, Alas to Cal, e to RM. Sum.

Merten's saxifrage, *Saxifraga mertensiana.* Flrs tiny, white with pink anthers, oft replaced by pinkish bulblets. Lvs round, sparsely hairy, succulent, doubly toothed, 1"–4" diam, on long-haired petioles with membranous sheathing stipules. Flr stem branched, hairy, 4"–16" tall. Stream banks, low-mid el, in all our mtns, Alas to Cal, e to RM. Spr-sum.

Western saxifrage, *Saxifraga occidentalis.* Flrs white (purple in OMtns), with or without yellow spots; inflor variable. Lvs ovate, petioled, strongly toothed, gen with red hairs beneath. Highly variable sp. Ht 2"–12". Mdws, cliffs, stream banks, in all our mtns, BC to n Ore, e to RM. Spr-sum.

Tolmie's (alpine) saxifrage, *Saxifraga tolmiei.* Flrs white with smooth, bowl-shaped calyx. Lvs fleshy, thick, L to ½", basal. Ht ca 1"–3", mat forming. Mdws, stream banks, wet rocks, gen alp, Alas to Cal, e to RM. Sum.

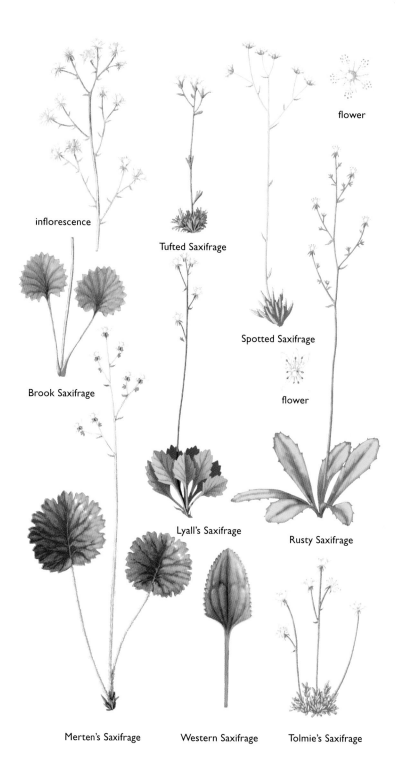

flower

inflorescence

Tufted Saxifrage

Spotted Saxifrage

flower

Brook Saxifrage

Lyall's Saxifrage

Rusty Saxifrage

Merten's Saxifrage

Western Saxifrage

Tolmie's Saxifrage

PLATE 21

ROSE FAMILY (ROSACEAE): 5 PETALS, 5 SEPALS

Goatsbeard, *Aruncus dioicus.* Flrs tiny, in plumelike panicles. Lvs compound, large, long petioled, with ovate, toothed, slender-tipped lflets to 6" long. Ht 3'–7'. Moist places, in all our mtns, Alas to n Cal, e in BC to RM; Eurasia. Spr-sum.

Woods strawberry, *Fragaria vesca.* Flrs, lvs, fruit like domestic strawberries. Mdws, stream banks, open woods, in all our mtns; widespread in N Amer, Eurasia. Sum.

Strawberry bramble, *Rubus pedatus.* Flrs similar to above. Lvs compound, with 5- (or 3-) toothed lflets. Stems trailing, to 7' long. Forest, lowl-subalp, in all our mtns, Alas to s Ore, e to Mont, Idaho. Late spr. Dwarf bramble, *R. lasiococcus,* very similar but lvs gen 3- to 5-lobed, not compound.

Partridgefoot, *Luetkea pectinata.* Flrs tiny, creamy white, in headlike racemes. Lvs finely divided, tiny, numerous at base, fewer on stems. Ht 2"–6", mat forming. Moist or shaded places, subalp-alp, Vanc I, OMtns, W CMtns–Cas, Alas to n Cal, e to RM. Sum.

OXALIS FAMILY (OXALIDACEAE): 5 SEPALS, 5 PETALS

Oregon oxalis (wood sorrel, redwood sorrel), *Oxalis oregana.* Flrs single on long stalks, white to pink with yellow in center, ½"–¾" diam. Lvs 3-divided, cloverlike, lflets heart shaped. Ht 2"–6". Moist, dense forest, OPen s to Cal, e to Cas, CR Gorge. Spr-fall.

VIOLET FAMILY (VIOLACEAE): FLOWERS IRREGULAR, 5 SEPALS, 5 PETALS

Small white violet, *Viola macloskeyi.* Flrs to ½" wide, lower 3 petals purple veined. Lvs heart shaped, not tapering to slender tip. Ht ca 1½"–2½". Mtn bogs, in all our mtns; widespread in N Amer. Late spr–sum. Canada violet, *V. canadensis,* ht 4"–15", flrs with yellow centers and without purple veins.

PARSLEY FAMILY (APIACEAE): FLOWERS IN UMBELS, 5 PETALS

Cow parsnip, *Heracleum maximum.* Flrs in compound, flat-topped umbel to 12" diam. Lvs 3-divided, lflet L 6"–16", nearly as wide, deeply 3-lobed, coarsely toothed. Stem single, smooth to woolly. Ht 3'–10'. Widespread in N Amer; Siberia. Sum.

Gray's lovage, *Ligusticum grayi.* Flrs tiny, in compound umbel. Lvs compound-pinnate, finely divided, ultimate segm lancelike, L 4"–12", all but 1–2 gen basal. Stem smooth, solitary, ht 8"–24". Open woods, dry mdws, gen mid el, Cas, BC to SNev, also n RM. Sum-fall.

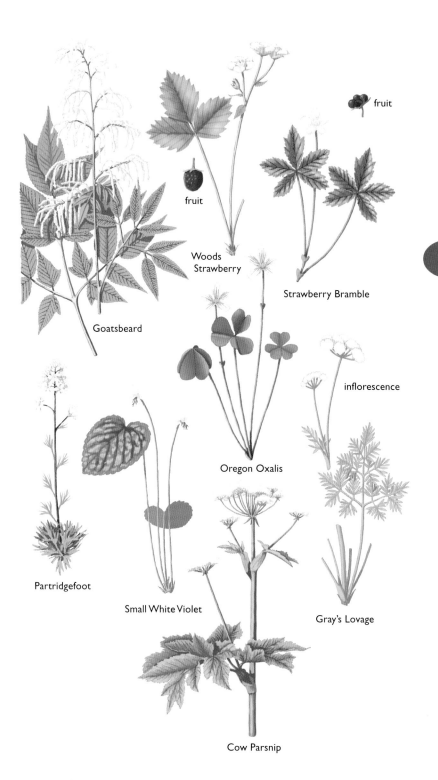

fruit

Woods
Strawberry

fruit

Strawberry Bramble

Goatsbeard

inflorescence

Oregon Oxalis

Partridgefoot

Small White Violet

Gray's Lovage

Cow Parsnip

PLATE 22

HEATH FAMILY (ERICACEAE): 5 PETALS, 5 SEPALS

Indian pipe, *Monotropa uniflora.* Entire plant white. Flrs nodding. Lvs scalelike. Stems clustered, thick, succulent. Ht 2"–6". Shady forest in all our mtns, Alas to Cal, e to Atl. Sum.

Pinesap, *Hypopitys monotropa.* Flrs white, yellowish, or pinkish, with hairy petals, in nodding racemes. Lvs scalelike. Stem pinkish or pale yellow, drying black, fleshy, stout, unbranched. Ht 2"–10". OMtns, W Cas, s Wn to n Cal, e to Atl; Europe. Sum. Fringed pinesap, *Pleuricospora fimbriolata,* very similar but flrs in erect spikelike raceme, petals not hairy.

White-veined wintergreen, *Pyrola picta.* Flrs greenish white, creamy, or pink. Lvs sometimes absent; if present, oval or ovate, leathery, dk green mottled with white along veins, mostly basal, long petioled. Stems reddish brown. Ht 4"–10". Forest, in all our mtns, BC to S Cal, e to RM. Sum.

One-sided wintergreen, *Orthilia secunda.* Flrs greenish white, 6–20 in 1-sided raceme. Lvs ovate, clear green, toothed or scalloped. Ht 2"–6". Moist forest in all our mtns, Alas s to s Cal, e to RM and Atl. Sum.

Wood nymph (one-flowered wintergreen), *Moneses uniflora.* Flr white or pink, solitary. Lvs oval or ovate, on lower part of stem, long petioled, fine toothed. Ht 1½"–6". Moist forest, rotting wood, in all our mtns, Alas to Cal, e to RM, e Can, e US. Sum.

PRIMROSE FAMILY (PRIMULACEAE): FLOWERS GENERALLY 5-LOBED

Fairy candelabra, *Androsace septentrionalis.* Flrs tiny, tubular, with spreading lobes, in open umbels. Lvs straplike, toothed toward tip, in basal rosette. Ht 1"–10". Dry, rocky places in all our mtns; widespread in mtns of N Amer and Eurasia. Spr-sum.

White shooting star, *Dodecatheon dentatum.* Flrs with short tubes and longer, reflexed lobes; white with yellow center and purplish stamens in umbel. Lvs basal, ovate, toothed or scalloped, petioled. Ht 6"–16". Wet places, E Cas, BC to n Ore, e to Idaho. Spr-sum.

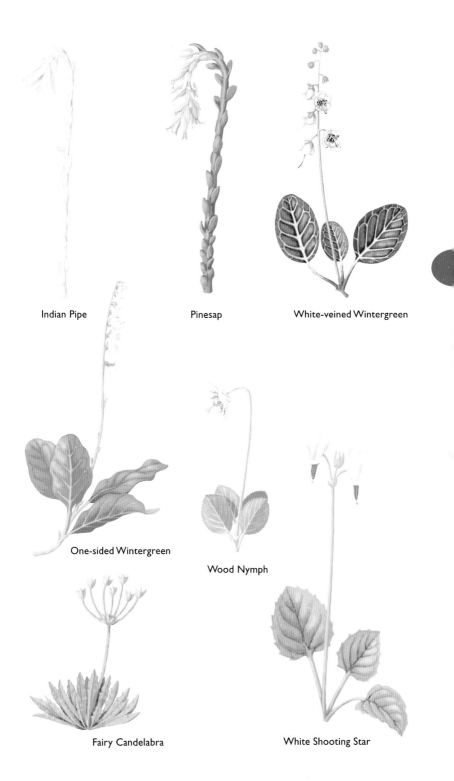

Indian Pipe

Pinesap

White-veined Wintergreen

One-sided Wintergreen

Wood Nymph

Fairy Candelabra

White Shooting Star

PLATE 23

PHLOX FAMILY (POLEMONIACEAE): 5-LOBED FLOWERS
Alpine collomia, *Collomia debilis* var *larsenii*. Flrs white to pale blue or pink, tubular, L ½"–1½", to ¾" diam. Lf L ½"–1¼", variable (lancelike to finely divided). Ht ca 2", mat forming. Talus, subalp-alp, OMtns, Cas, Wn to Cal. Sum. *C. d.* var *debilis,* leaves entire or only slightly divided near tip.

WATERLEAF FAMILY (HYDROPHYLLACEAE): 5-LOBED FLOWERS
Fendler's waterleaf, *Hydrophyllum fendleri*. Flr L to ¾", bell shaped, white to lavender, in terminal inflor. Lvs pinnate, L to 10", 6" wide, hairy, with 7–15 sharp-toothed lflets. Stems hairy. Ht 8"–32". Moist, open places, thickets, lowl–subalp, OMtns, Cas s to Cal; e to Idaho, Utah, NMex. Spr-sum.

Varileaf phacelia, *Phacelia heterophylla*. Flrs white, in bristly-hairy inflor. Lvs gray-green, entire on upper stem, pinnate or pinnately lobed on lower stem, with 1 terminal lflet or lobe and 1–2 pairs of basal lflets or lobes. Plant hairy, sticky, oft bristly. Ht usu to 20". Dry, open places, low-mid el, E Cas. Spr-sum.

FIGWORT FAMILY (SCROPHULARIACEAE): FLOWERS IRREGULAR
Ramshorn (sickletop) lousewort, *Pedicularis racemosa*. Flr L ca ½", white or pink, 2-lipped, upper one beaklike, twisted on one side, lower one 3-lobed. Lvs lancelike, L 2"–4", toothed. Ht 6"–20". Open forest in all our mtns, BC to Cal, e to RM. Sum.

Small-flowered paintbrush, *Castilleja parviflora* var *albida*. Corolla white or pink, tiny, tubular, 2-lipped; flrs in terminal spike, with numerous white, 3- to 5-lobed bracts. Lvs 3- to 5-lobed, numerous on stem. Ht to 12". Subalp-alp mdws, NCas s to Cascade Pass. Sum. Cf magenta paintbrush, plate 35.

MINT FAMILY (LAMIACEAE): FLOWERS IRREGULAR, 2-LIPPED
Yerba buena, *Clinopodium douglasii*. Flrs small, white or pale purple, 1 in ea upper lf axil. Lvs opp, ± round, L ½"–1". Creeping plant with erect flr stems to 12" tall, trailing stems to 36" long. Shaded woods, low el, W Cas to coast, BC to Baja, n Idaho. Spr-fall.

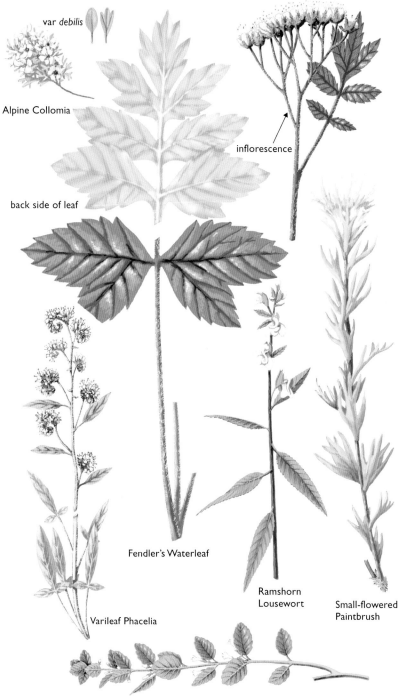

var *debilis*

Alpine Collomia

back side of leaf

inflorescence

Fendler's Waterleaf

Varileaf Phacelia

Ramshorn
Lousewort

Small-flowered
Paintbrush

Yerba Buena

PLATE 24

MADDER FAMILY (RUBIACEAE): 3- TO 4-LOBED FLOWERS
Sweet-scented bedstraw, *Galium triflorum.* Flrs tiny, greenish white, in 3s from upper lf axils and stem tip, fragrant. Lvs vanilla scented, narrow to oval or oblanceolate, pointed, usu 5–6 in whorls. Stems gen trailing, L to 32". Moist woods, oft near seeps or streams, low-mid el, in all our mtns; widespread in N Amer. Sum.

VALERIAN FAMILY (VALERIANACEAE): 5-LOBED FLOWERS
Sitka valerian, *Valeriana sitchensis.* Flrs small, slightly irreg, fragrant, in round heads. Lvs mostly in 2–5 pairs on stem, pinnate, long petioled, lflets toothed, terminal one longest. Ht 12"–48". Moist open or wooded places, esp in wet subalp mdws, mid-high el, CMtns, Cas, BC to n Cal. Sum. Scouler's valerian, *V. scouleri,* similar but smaller, ht 6"–7", with lflts smooth edged; moist areas, low-mid el, Cas to n Cal; sum.

ASTER OR SUNFLOWER FAMILY (ASTERACEAE): FLOWERS IN COMPOSITE HEADS
Woolly pussytoes (everlasting), *Antennaria lanata.* Flrs very like those of above sp, but plant ht only 4"–8", densely woolly throughout. Lvs mostly basal, oblanceolate, L to 4", stem lvs narrower. Not mat forming. Subalp-alp, s BC to Ore, e to n RM. Sum.

Trail plant, *Adenocaulon bicolor.* Flr heads tiny, with disk flrs only, at ends of short, thin stems. Lvs mostly near base, broadly arrow shaped, with wavy margins, smooth above, white-woolly beneath, long petioled. Ht to ca 36". Moist forest, low-mid el, in all our mtns, BC to Cal, e to mid US. Sum.

Pearly everlasting, *Anaphalis margaritacea.* Flr heads small, with numerous minute yellow disk flrs and white, papery bracts. Lf L ca 2"–4", linear or lancelike, numerous, white-woolly. Stems 8"–36" tall, white-woolly. Dry, open places, lowl-suhalp, in all our mtns, Alas s to s Cal, e to ne US; Eurasia. Sum.

Alpine pussytoes (everlasting), *Antennaria alpina.* Flrs white to yellowish, similar to those of above 2 spp. Stem lvs linear; basal lvs ± spoon shaped, L to 1", mostly on runners. Entire plant woolly, mat forming. Ht to 4". Moist, gravelly sites, subalp-alp, in all our mtns, BC to Cal, e to RM. Sum.

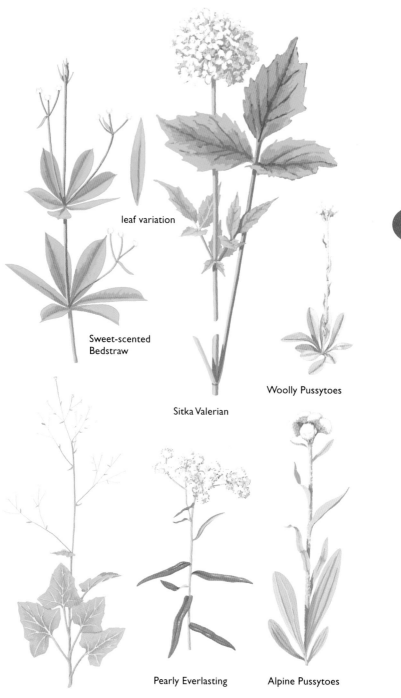

leaf variation

Sweet-scented
Bedstraw

Sitka Valerian

Woolly Pussytoes

Trail Plant

Pearly Everlasting

Alpine Pussytoes

PLATE 25

ASTER OR SUNFLOWER FAMILY (ASTERACEAE): FLOWERS IN COMPOSITE HEADS

Yarrow, *Achillea millefolium.* Disk flrs yellow, ray flrs white or pink; heads small, in terminal inflor. Lvs finely divided, fernlike, aromatic. Stems mostly unbranched and solitary, covered with cottony hairs. Ht 4"–30"+. Lowl-alp in all our mtns; widespread in n hemis. Spr-fall.

Olympic aster, *Eucephalus paucicapitatus.* Flr heads ca 1" diam, with tiny yellow disk flrs and gen 13 white, straplike ray flrs, 1 or few heads per stem. Lvs elliptic, sessile, L 1"–2", alt on stem. Plant downy or sticky. Ht 8"–20". Open subalp slopes, OMtns, Vanc I. Sum.

Oxeye daisy, *Leucanthemum vulgare.* Flr heads 1"–3" diam, with yellow disk flrs, gen 15–30 ray flrs. Lvs cleft and scalloped, lower ones wedge- or spoon-shaped, L 1½"–6", long petioled; upper ones smaller, narrower, sessile. Ht 8"–32". Com disturbed places, esp roadsides, in all our mtns; widespread in N Amer; introduced from Europe. Spr-fall.

Dwarf mountain (cutleaf) daisy (fleabane), *Erigeron compositus.* Flr heads ca 1" diam, with yellow disk and white (pink or blue), slender ray flrs, solitary. Mostly basal lvs, finely cleft, fernlike. Plant sticky-hairy to nearly smooth. Flr stems 1½"–10" tall. Gen rocky places, low-high el, in all our mtns; widespread in N Amer. Sum. Several other spp very similar.

White-flowered hawkweed, *Hieracium albiflorum.* Flr heads with rays only. Lvs oblong, basal ones hairy, L 2"–6", ± entire, petioled; stem lvs smaller, without petioles, less hairy. Stems long haired below, ± hairless above. Ht 12"–48". Moist slopes, open woods in all our mtns but E CMtns–Cas, Alas to Cal and Colo. Sum.

Coltsfoot, *Petasites frigidus.* Flr heads white or pinkish, usu with disk flrs only, in dense terminal inflor. Lvs basal, palmate, ± hairy, deeply lobed and toothed, up to 12" diam. Stems coarse, thick, succulent, with large, sheathing, parallel-veined bracts. Ht 6"–24". Moist places, lowl-subalp. Circumboreal. Late win–midsum.

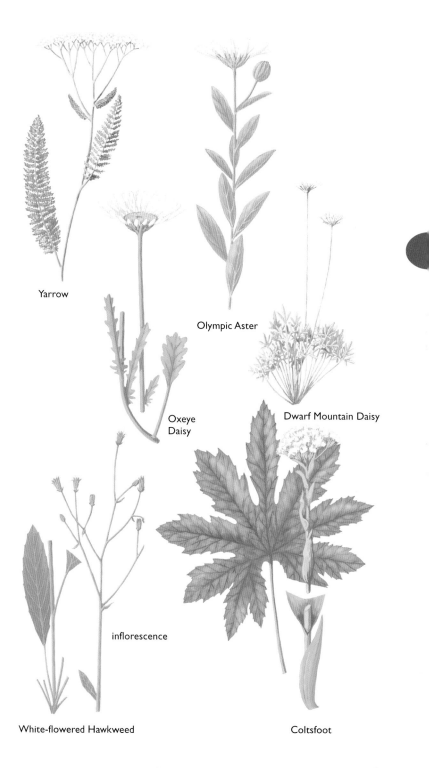

Yarrow

Olympic Aster

Oxeye
Daisy

Dwarf Mountain Daisy

inflorescence

White-flowered Hawkweed

Coltsfoot

II. Yellow and Orange Flowers

This section includes only flowers that are distinctly yellow or truly orange. Cream-colored flowers are covered in section I, White Flowers; red-orange flowers in section III, Pink to Red Flowers. Asteraceae (members of the sunflower family) with yellow disks but ray flowers of other colors are grouped according to the color of the rays. The following species from other color sections sometimes have yellowish or orangish flowers.

Cliff anemone, cf Drummond's anemone, *plate 18*
Indian pipe, *plate 22*
Alpine pussytoes, *plate 24*
Yarrow, *plate 25*
Coltsfoot, *plate 25*
Rosy twisted stalk, *plate 31*
Western spring beauty, *plate 31*
Tweedy's pussypaws, cf pussypaws, *plate 31*
Applegate paintbrush, *plate 35*
Common paintbrush, *plate 35*
Explorer's gentian, *plate 39*
Brewer's mitrewort, *plate 43*
Pinedrops, *plate 43*

PLATE 26

ARUM FAMILY (ARACEAE): FLOWERS IN SPIKE (SPADIX) PARTLY ENCLOSED BY SHOWY BRACT (SPATHE)

Skunk cabbage, *Lysichiton americanus.* Flrs tiny, on fleshy spadix L 1½"–4", ½"–1" diam, spathe L up to 8". Lvs oval, basal, L 12"–36", half as wide. Wet places, in all our mtns, Alas to Cal, e to Mont, Idaho. Spr–early sum.

LILY FAMILY (LILIACEAE): 3 PETALS AND 3 SEPALS, OR 6 TEPALS

Glacier lily (yellow fawn-lily), *Erythronium grandiflorum.* Flrs 1–2 per stem, with 6 reflexed tepals L ca ½". Lvs basal, elliptic, L 4"–8". Ht 6"–12". Damp, recently snow-free sites, mont-subalp, in all our mtns, s BC to n Ore, e to RM. Sum.

Tiger (columbia) lily, *Lilium columbianum.* Flrs 2"–3" diam, with strongly reflexed tepals. Lvs lancelike, usu in whorls, but may be scattered on stem. Ht 12"–48". Open areas, dry woods, BC to n Cal, e to Idaho, Nev. Sum.

BUCKWHEAT FAMILY (POLYGONACEAE): NO PETALS, 4–9 PETAL-LIKE SEPALS

Sulfur-flowered buckwheat, *Eriogonum umbellatum.* Flrs tiny, occas cream colored, hairy, in compound umbels. Lvs spoon shaped, mostly in basal tufts, L ½"–1½", smooth or hairy on 1 or both sides; whorl of smaller lvs at base of umbel, but not at midstem. Dwarf plants, ht under 4"; others to 12". Dry, rocky places, lowl-alp, mostly E Cas, s BC to Cal, e to RM. Sum.

Oval-leaved buckwheat, *Eriogonum ovalifolium.* Similar to above sp, but inflor not branched, lvs rounder, no whorl of lvs at base of umbel. Flrs occas pinkish; lvs silvery to pale green. Various habitats, lowl-alp, BC s in OMtns, Cas and RM to Cal and NMex. Late spr–sum. This and above sp are 2 of many, very similar yellow-flowered buckwheats in our region.

WATER-LILY FAMILY (NYMPHAECEAE): TINY PETALS, 9 SEPALS

Yellow pond-lily (water-lily), *Nuphar polysepalum.* Flrs with tiny, inconspicuous petals, small outer green sepals, large yellow inner sepals, to 2" diam. Lvs heart shaped, L 6"–8", nearly as wide, floating on pond surfaces. Aquatic plant in ponds, other standing water, low-mid el, in all our mtns, Alas to s Cal, e to Colo. Sum-fall.

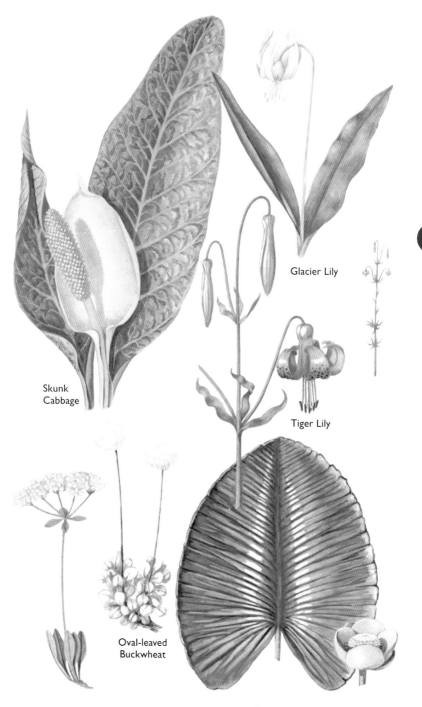

Glacier Lily

Skunk
Cabbage

Tiger Lily

Sulfur-flowered Buckwheat

Oval-leaved
Buckwheat

Yellow Pond-lily

PLATE 27

BUTTERCUP FAMILY (RANUNCULACEAE): 5 PETALS, 5 SEPALS

Yellow columbine, *Aquilegia flavescens.* Flrs nodding, with spurred petals and spreading petal-like sepals. Lvs mainly basal, compound, long petioled, ea lflet 3-lobed and toothed, waxy blue-green. Ht 18"–24". Moist mdws, subalp-alp, Cas, BC to s Wn, e to RM. Sum.

Subalpine (mountain) buttercup, *Ranunculus eschscholtzii.* Flrs glossy yellow, ca ½" diam. Basal lvs long petioled, blade 3-lobed, L to 1⅛", lobes toothed or mid one sometimes entire. Ht to 8". Moist, oft rocky places, subalp-alp, in all our mtns, Alas to Cal, e to RM. Sum. Several other similar spp found at all elevations.

MUSTARD FAMILY (BRASSICACEAE): 4 PETALS IN A CROSS

Payson's whitlow-grass, *Draba paysonii.* Flrs in small racemes. Lvs slender, L to ½", basal, fringed with forked and unforked hairs, old lvs persisting. Cushion plant, ht to 2". Rocky places, subalp-alp, BC to Cal, e to RM. Sum. One of several very similar spp in our range.

Mountain wallflower, *Erysimum arenicola.* Flrs in short racemes. Lvs toothed, ± linear to narrowly oblanceolate, numerous at or near base, several to many on stem. Ht gen 4"–10". Dry, rocky places, mont-alp, OMtns, Cas, Wn to s Ore. Sum. Rough wallflower, *E. asperum,* of E Cas s to CR Gorge, is very similar.

STONECROP FAMILY (CRASSULACEAE)

Spreading stonecrop, *Sedum divergens.* Flrs starlike, with petals distinct. Lvs opp, ± oval, thick, fleshy, sessile. Flr stems branching from prostrate, rooting stems. Ht to 6". Rocky places at high el, OMtns, CMtns–Cas, s BC to n Ore. Sum. Oregon stonecrop, *S. oreganum,* has petals united near base, alt lvs, flr stems sprouting from rhizomes. Creamy stonecrop, *S. oregonense,* has white to creamy flrs, spoon-shaped lvs. Lanceleaf stonecrop, *S. lanceolatum,* has alt linear to lancelike lvs with many basal rosettes. Rough stonecrop, *S. stenopetalum,* has slender, pointed lvs and bulblets in upper lf axils oft replacing flrs.

ROSE FAMILY (ROSACEAE)

Fanleaf cinquefoil, *Potentilla flabellifolia.* Flrs ca 1" diam, not waxy, petals notched. Lvs compound, with 3 toothed lflets. Ht 4"–14". Moist mdws, talus, high el in all our mtns, s to Cal, e to RM. Sum. Varileaf cinquefoil, *P. diversifolia,* has 5–7 lflets, white haired beneath. Hairy cinquefoil. *P. villosa,* is a cushion plant with small hairy lvs. Drummond's cinquefoil, *P. drummondii,* has 5–7 lflets, 3 upper fused at base. Cf shrubby cinquefoil, plate 47.

Sibbaldia, *Sibbaldia procumbens.* Flrs ca ⅓" diam, with greenish sepals far exceeding petals. Lvs compound, with 3 toothed, wedge-shaped lflets and membranous stipules. Stems prostrate, mat forming. Ht to 3". Alp, N Amer; Eurasia. Sum.

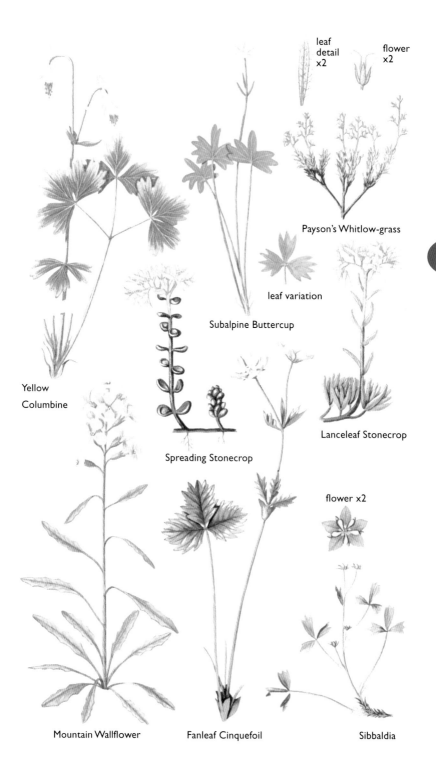

leaf
detail
x2

flower
x2

Payson's Whitlow-grass

leaf variation

Subalpine Buttercup

Yellow
Columbine

Spreading Stonecrop

Lanceleaf Stonecrop

flower x2

Mountain Wallflower

Fanleaf Cinquefoil

Sibbaldia

PLATE 28

PEA FAMILY (FABACEAE): FLOWERS IRREGULAR
Golden pea, *Thermopsis montana.* Flrs sweetpealike, L ¾"–1", in racemes. Lvs compound, with 3 broadly lancelike lflets ea 2"–4" long and large lflike stipules. Fruit erect, hairy pods L 1½"–3". Ht 12"–48". Mdws, forest openings, BC to n Cal, e to RM. Spr–sum.

VIOLET FAMILY (VIOLACEAE): FLOWERS IRREGULAR, 5 PETALS, 5 SEPALS
Wood (pioneer) violet, *Viola glabella.* Flrs pansylike, with maroon lines on lower petals, ¾"–1" wide. Lf L to 2", heart shaped, toothed, with slender tip. Ht to 12". Moist places, in all our mtns, Alas to Cal, e to Mont. Spr–sum. Our most com yellow violet. Evergreen violet, *V. sempervirens,* has thick, glossy green, round-tipped, heart-shaped lvs, creeping stems. Round-leaved violet, *V. orbiculata,* has thin, round or heart-shaped lvs, erect stems.

EVENING-PRIMROSE FAMILY (ONAGRACEAE): 4 PETALS, 4 SEPALS
Yellow willowherb, *Epilobium luteum.* Flrs 1"–1½" diam, petals notched. Lvs lancelike, toothed, L ¾"–3", opp. Ht 8"–28". Moist sites, mont-alp, in all our mtns, Alas to Ore. Midsum–early fall.

PARSLEY FAMILY (APIACEAE): FLOWERS IN UMBELS, 5 PETALS
Martindale's lomatium, *Lomatium martindalei.* Flrs yellow or white, small, in flat-topped umbels. Lvs finely dissected, parsleylike. Ht 2"–8". Late spr–sum. Barestem lomatium, *L. nudicaule,* has oval lflets. Other spp similar to Martindale's lomatium.

FIGWORT FAMILY (SCROPHULARIACEAE): FLOWERS TUBULAR, 2-LIPPED
Alpine yellow (mountain) monkeyflower, *Mimulus tilingii.* Flrs ca 1" diam, 2-lipped, lower red spotted with calyx teeth of uneven length. Lvs opp, smooth, toothed, on prostrate stems. Mat forming, ht 2"–4". Wet mdws, bogs, subalp-alp, BC to s Cal, e to RM. Sum. Common monkeyflower, *M. guttatus,* very similar but not mat forming, ht 2"–24", commoner at lower el. Coast monkeyflower, *M. dentatus,* ht 4"–12", but not mat forming, calyx teeth of equal length; OMtns only. Primrose monkeyflower, *M. primuloides,* has solitary flr on erect stem rising above basal rosette. Musk-flowered monkeyflower, *M. moschatus,* has musky scent, slimy, sticky-haired lvs. Chickweed monkeyflower, *M. alsinoides,* is a tiny lowland sp with long-petioled lvs, single reddish spot on base of lower corolla lip.

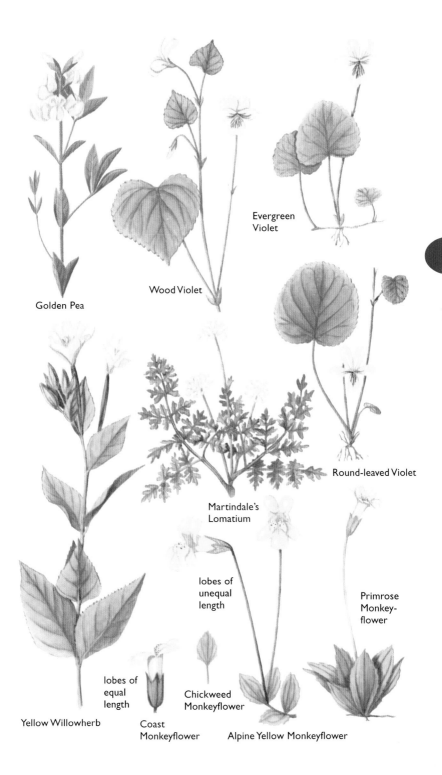

Golden Pea

Wood Violet

Evergreen Violet

Round-leaved Violet

Martindale's Lomatium

Yellow Willowherb

lobes of equal length

Coast Monkeyflower

Chickweed Monkeyflower

lobes of unequal length

Alpine Yellow Monkeyflower

Primrose Monkey-flower

PLATE 29

FIGWORT FAMILY (SCROPHULARIACEAE): FLOWERS 2-LIPPED OR 5-LOBED

Bracted lousewort (wood betony), *Pedicularis bracteosa.* Flrs yellow, red, or purple, 2-lipped, upper lip hoodlike, ± beakless. Lvs pinnate, L 3"–10", lflets ± double toothed; stem lvs as large as those, if any, at base. Ht 12"–36". Moist mdws, forest openings, mont-alp, BC to n Cal, e to RM. Sum. Mount Rainier lousewort, *P. rainierensis,* very similar but ht only 6"–16", with many basal lvs and fewer, smaller stem lvs; Mt. Rainier only.

Coiled-beak lousewort, *Pedicularis contorta.* Flrs yellow or creamy, 2-lipped, upper lip beaklike, slender, strongly curved or coiled downward. Lvs pinnate, long petioled, lflets toothed. Ht 8"–20". Mdws, open places, mont-alp, mostly Cas, Wn to n Cal. Sum.

Woolly mullein, *Verbascum thapsus.* Flrs nearly reg, 5-lobed, in dense bracteose spike. Lvs of 1st year basal, oblong to oblanceolate, L 4"–16"; lvs of 2nd year on flr stem, elliptic to lancelike, sheathing, oft droopy, L 2"–12". Plant woolly throughout. Ht 12"–78". Disturbed places, esp roadsides; widespread in N Amer; introduced from Europe. Sum.

ASTER OR SUNFLOWER FAMILY (ASTERACEAE): FLOWERS IN COMPOSITE HEADS

Orange mountain-dandelion, *Agoseris aurantiaca.* Flr heads dandelion-like, ca 1" diam, distinctly burnt-orange, unique. Lvs basal, variable, broadest above mid, oft slightly toothed. Ht 4"–24". Grassy places, mdws, in all our mtns; widespread in mtns of w N Amer. Sum.

Pale mountain-dandelion, *Agoseris glauca.* Flr heads like those of common dandelion, ½"–1¼" diam. Lvs basal, variable, L 2"–14", lancelike to oblanceolate, nearly smooth or finely haired, entire or slightly toothed. Ht 4"–30". Mdws, rocky places, lowl–alp, in all our mtns, w Can s to Cal and NMex, e to Minn. Late spr–sum. Other yellow mountain-dandelions very similar, but this sp the most com in our range.

Mountain (broadleaf) arnica, *Arnica latifolia.* Flr heads 1 to few per stem, with both disk and ray flrs. Lvs opp, ovate, sessile above, petioled below, sharply toothed, in 24 pairs on stem. Ht 8"–18". Gen moist, open places, in all our mtns, Alas to Cal and Colo. Sum. Most com of several similar spp in our range.

Arrowleaf balsamroot, *Balsamorhiza sagittata.* Flr heads very large (4"–5" diam), with 8–25 rays, ea 1"–1½" long. Lvs basal, arrow shaped, long petioled, blade L to 12". Open places, pine-fir forests, E Cas, BC to SNev, e to RM. Sum. Com and conspicuous.

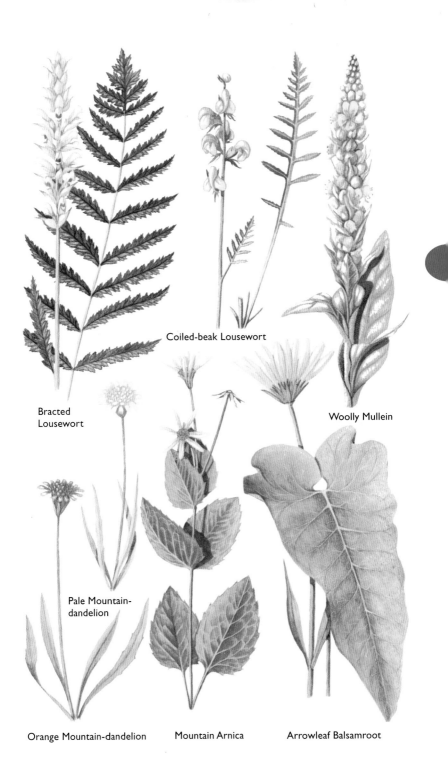

Coiled-beak Lousewort

Bracted
Lousewort

Woolly Mullein

Pale Mountain-
dandelion

Orange Mountain-dandelion   Mountain Arnica   Arrowleaf Balsamroot

PLATE 30

ASTER OR SUNFLOWER FAMILY (ASTERACEAE): FLOWERS IN COMPOSITE HEADS

Golden fleabane (daisy), *Erigeron aureus.* Flr heads solitary, ½"–1" diam. Lvs mostly basal, petioled, spoon shaped. Plant woolly. Ht 2"–6". Rocky places, subalp-alp, Wn Cas, n to s BC and Albta. Sum.

Woolly sunflower, *Eriophyllum lanatum.* Flr heads 1"–1½" diam, with 9–11 ray flrs. Lvs entire to deeply pinnately cut, very woolly. Ht 4"–12". Dry, open places, lowl-mont (subalp in OMtns), BC to Cal, e to RM. Late spr–sum.

Lyall's goldenweed, *Tonestus lyallii.* Flr heads solitary, ca 1" diam. Lvs + oblanceolate, sessile, sticky haired, L ½"–3". Stems sticky haired, 2"–6" tall. Rocky places, gen alp, BC and Wn e to Albta, ne Ore, ne Nev, Colo. Midsum–early fall.

Silverback luina, *Luina hypoleuca.* Flr heads rayless, in branched, terminal inflor on ea stem. Lvs sessile, oval or ovate, densely white-haired below. Stems numerous, clustered. Ht 6"–16". Rocky places w of Cas, BC to Cal. Sum.

Arrowhead groundsel, *Senecio triangularis.* Flr heads 1"–1½" diam, with 5–10 rays, in branched inflor. Lvs like arrowheads, L 2"–6", sharply toothed. Ht 12"–36". Moist places, lowl–high el, in all our mtns, Alas to Cal, Ariz, NMex. Late sum.

Tall western groundsel, *Senecio integerrimus.* Flr heads usu yellow, occas white or rayless in Wn Cas, with black-tipped involucre bracts. Basal lvs, L 2½"–10", gen oblanceolate or elliptic, long petioled; stem lvs alt, smaller upward, becoming sessile, lancelike. Ht 12"–36". Open places below timberline in all our mtns; widespread in N Amer. Late spr–midsum.

Creek (meadow, Canada) goldenrod, *Solidago canadensis.* Flr heads small, numerous, in dense spraylike panicles. Lvs lancelike, toothed, numerous, L 2"–5". Ht 12"–36". Moist places, lowl-mont, in all our mtns; widespread in N Amer. Late sum–fall. Other tall spp similar.

Northern (alpine) goldenrod, *Solidago multiradiata.* Flr heads small, gen with 13 rays, in panicles. Stem lvs spoon shaped or lancelike, gen pointed, sessile, ± entire. Basal lvs spoon shaped, ± toothed, with bristly hairs along petiole margins. Ht gen to 12". Subalp-alp, mtns of w N Amer, but missing from Ore Cas. Sum.

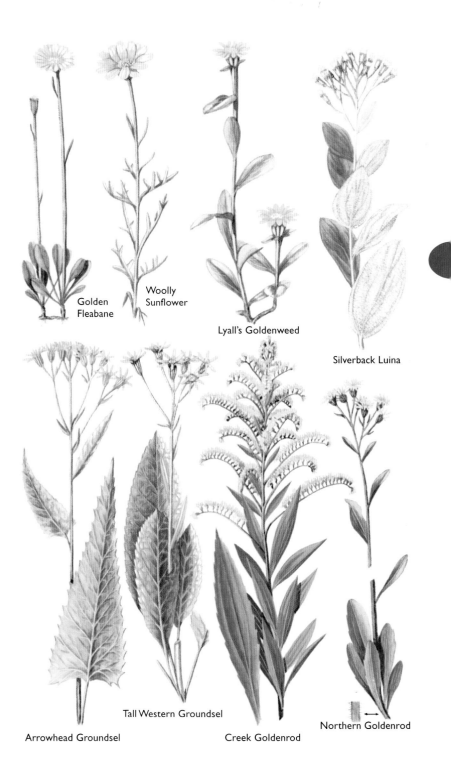

Golden
Fleabane

Woolly
Sunflower

Lyall's Goldenweed

Silverback Luina

Tall Western Groundsel

Arrowhead Groundsel

Creek Goldenrod

Northern Goldenrod

III. Pink to Red Flowers

Flowers in this section range in color from pale pink to red-orange or reddish purple. Compounded of red and blue, purple comes in shades that are difficult to assign to one color or the other. When attempting to identify plants with reddish purple flowers, also consult section IV, Blue to Purple Flowers. Truly orange flowers are covered in section II, Yellow and Orange Flowers. White flowers tinged with pink are found in section I, White Flowers. The following species sometimes have pink or reddish flowers.

Washington lily, *plate 14*
Western trillium, *plate 15*
Alpine buckwheat, *plate 17*
Miner's lettuce, *plate 17*
Siberian miner's lettuce, *plate 17*
Pygmy lewisia, *plate 17*
Round-leaf sundew, *plate 19*
Lyall's saxifrage, *plate 20*
Oregon oxalis, *plate 21*
Indian pipe, *plate 22*
Wood nymph, *plate 22*
Alpine collomia, *plate 23*
Small-flowered paintbrush, *plate 23*
Ramshorn lousewort, *plate 23*
Yarrow, *plate 25*
Dwarf mountain daisy, *plate 25*
Tiger lily, *plate 26*
Oval-leaved buckwheat, *plate 26*
Bracted lousewort, *plate 29*
Oregon anemone, *plate 37*
Nuttall's pea, *plate 38*
Flett's violet, *plate 38*
Davidson's penstemon, *plate 40*
Cascade aster, *plate 41*
Wandering daisy, *plate 41*
Giant helleborine, *plate 42*
Heartleaf twayblade, *plate 42*
Mountain-sorrel, *plate 43*
Fringecup, *plate 43*
Pinedrops, *plate 43*

PLATE 31

LILY FAMILY (LILIACEAE): 6 TEPALS

Olympic onion, *Allium crenulatum.* Flrs pink or white with pink lines on lancelike tepals, in upright umbel. Lvs 2, fleshy, narrow, basal, oft coiled at tip, present with flrs. Stem ± flattened and winged. Ht 3"–8". Dry, gravelly places, subalp–alp, Vanc I, OMtns, Cas, cen Wn s to sw Ore. Sum. Nodding onion, *A. cernuum,* has nodding head, ± oval tepals. Tapertip onion, *A. acuminatum,* is dk rose; lvs wither before flowering.

Rosy twisted stalk, *Streptopus lanceolatus.* Flrs rosy to white or greenish with magenta spots, 1–2 below ea lf. Lvs ovate, sessile, minutely toothed. Stems zigzag, gen unbranched. Ht 12"–24". Damp forest, mid-high el in all our mtns, Alas to Ore. Sum. Cf plates 15 and 42.

ORCHID FAMILY (ORCHIDACEAE): 3 PETALS, 3 SEPALS, FLOWERS IRREGULAR

Fairy (venus) slipper, *Calypso bulbosa.* Flr solitary on single unbranched stalk. One (occas 2) basal lf, oval to ovate, L 1¼"–2½"; 2–3 bracts on stem. Ht 2"–8". Moist forest, lowl-mont, in all our mtns, Alas to Cal; Ariz, Colo, e across Can to Atl. Spr–early sum.

Spotted coralroot, *Corallorrhiza maculata.* Flrs ca ¾" diam, with 3 sepals, 2 sepal-like petals, a 3rd, lower, drooping 3-lobed lip. Lvs scalelike. Ht 8"–32". Forest in all our mtns; widespread in N Amer. Late spr–sum. Striped coralroot, *C. striata,* similar but petals red striped, lip unlobed. Western coralroot, *C. mertensiana,* has ± uniformly reddish brown flrs.

PURSLANE FAMILY (PORTULACEAE): 5+ PETALS, 2+ SEPALS

Western spring beauty, *Claytonia lanceolata.* Flrs pink or white (occas yellow), red lined, with 2 sepals, 5 petals, in 1-sided racemes. Lvs 2 per stem, opp, lancelike, ¾"–3" long, just below inflor; occas 1–2 basal lvs. Ht 2¾"–6". Open places, lowl-alp, in all our mtns, BC to Cal, e to RM. Spr-sum.

Columbia lewisia, *Lewisia columbiana.* Flrs with 2 sepals, 6–11 petals, ¾"–1" diam, several per stem. Lvs basal, fleshy, straplike. Ht 4"–8". Open, rocky places, s BC to Cal, e to ne Ore, Idaho. Late spr–sum. Threeleaf lewisia, *L. triphylla,* lacks basal lvs when in flower.

Pussypaws, *Cistanthe umbellata.* Flrs in fuzzy, round headlike umbels. Lvs basal, spoon shaped, leathery. Mat forming, ht to 6", either perennial with branched woody base (var *caudicifera*) or annual without woody base (var *umbellifera*). Dry, open places, E Cas, BC to Cal, e to RM. Spr-sum. Tweedy's pussypaws, *Cistanthe tweedyi,* has pale pink to peach or apricot flrs, ½"–3" diam; endemic to Wenatchee Mtns.

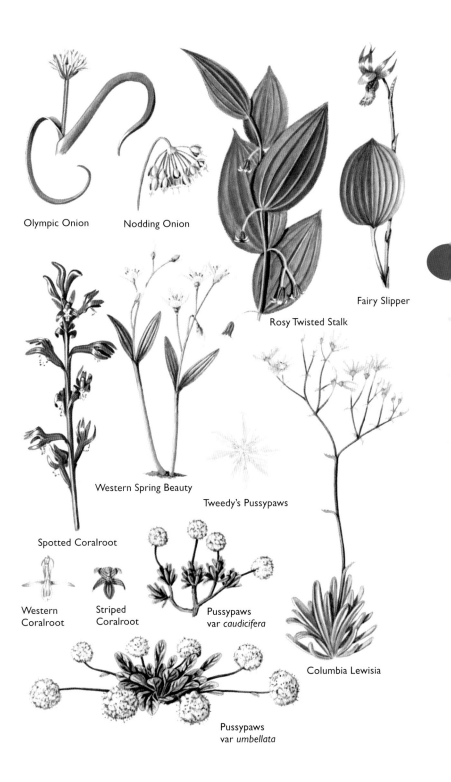

Olympic Onion

Nodding Onion

Rosy Twisted Stalk

Fairy Slipper

Western Spring Beauty

Tweedy's Pussypaws

Spotted Coralroot

Western
Coralroot

Striped
Coralroot

Pussypaws
var *caudicifera*

Columbia Lewisia

Pussypaws
var *umbellata*

PLATE 32

BUTTERCUP FAMILY (RANUNCULACEAE): 5 PETALS, 5 SEPALS

Red columbine, *Aquilegia formosa.* Flrs with flaring petal-like sepals and scooplike, spurred petals. Lvs gen basal, long petioled, compound, lflets lobed. Ht 12"–36". Woods, moist mdws, lowl-mont, in all our mtns, Alas to Cal, e to RM. Spr-sum.

PINK FAMILY (CARYOPHYLLACEAE): 5 PETALS, 5 SEPALS

Moss campion, *Silene acaulis.* Flrs pink to lavender, numerous, ca ½" diam, with tubular calyx. Lvs needlelike, ca ½" diam, mostly basal. Ht 2"–4¾", mat or cushion forming. Rocky places, subalp-alp in all our mtns, Alas s in mtns of N Amer; arctic tundra. Sum.

FUMITORY FAMILY (FUMARIACEAE): 4 PETALS, 2 SEPALS

Scouler's (western) corydalis, *Corydalis scouleri.* Flrs irreg, spurred. Lvs usu 3, gen compound-pinnate. Ht 12"–48". Moist, shaded places, Cas to coast, BC to Ore. Spr-sum.

Steer's head, *Dicentra uniflora.* Flrs pink to white, resembling cow's skull, with 2 outer petals forming horns, 2 inner petals the skull. Lvs basal, L 1"–4", 3-compound, lflets lobed. Ht 1½"–4". Open places, lowl-subalp, Wn Cas s to Cal, e to Idaho, Wyo, Utah. Spr-sum.

Western bleeding heart, *Dicentra formosa.* Flrs nodding, heart shaped. Lvs compound-pinnate, lflets lobed and toothed, long petioled. Ht gen 6"–26". Moist woods, low-mid el, BC to Cal, e to Cas. Spr-sum.

MUSTARD FAMILY (BRASSICACEAE): 4 PETALS IN A CROSS

Lyall's rockcress, *Arabis lyalli.* Flr L to ½", in racemes. Lvs both basal and on stem, rather fleshy, entire, linear to lancelike or spoon shaped, ± smooth. Ht 4"–10". Subalp-alp, BC to Cal, e to RM. Sum. One of several very similar spp in our range.

Slender toothwort (large-flowered bittercress), *Cardamine nuttallii.* Flrs pink to reddish or purplish, in racemes. Lvs basal, long petioled, either compound with lobed lflets or simple, round, lobed. Ht gen 4"–8". Moist woods, BC to Cal, W Cas to coast. Spr.

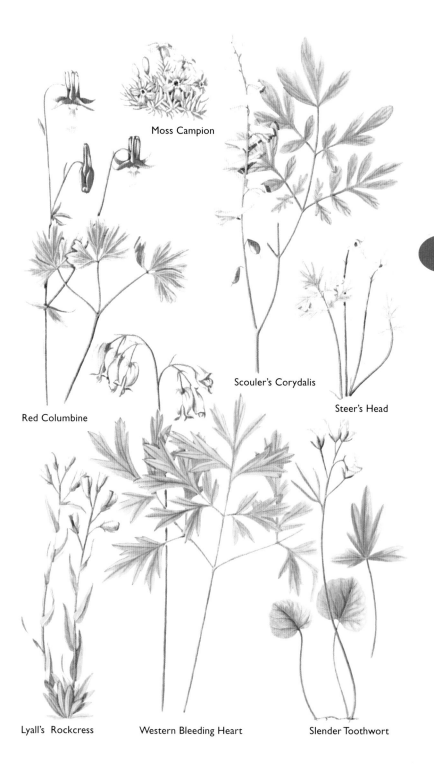

Moss Campion

Scouler's Corydalis

Steer's Head

Red Columbine

Lyall's Rockcress

Western Bleeding Heart

Slender Toothwort

PLATE 33

STONECROP FAMILY (CRASSULACEAE): 5 PETALS, 5 SEPALS

Roseroot (rosy sedum or stonecrop), *Rhodiola integrifolia.* Flrs fleshy, tiny, crowded in flat inflor. Lvs fleshy, lancelike, alt, crowded on stem. Ht to 6". Moist, rocky places, subalp–alp, BC to Cal, e to RM; Greenland, Eurasia. Sum.

SAXIFRAGE FAMILY (SAXIFRAGACEAE): 5 PETALS, 5 SEPALS

Purple saxifrage, *Saxifraga oppositifolia.* Flrs starlike, pink to reddish purple, petals much smaller than sepals and "stemmed" at base. Lvs ovate, gen opp, in 4 overlapping rows on stems. Cushion plant to 2" tall. Rocky alp slopes, tundra, N Amer s to Wn, ne Ore, Wyo, RM. Sum.

ROSE FAMILY (ROSACEAE): 5 PETALS, 5 SEPALS

Marsh cinquefoil, *Comarum palustre.* Flrs starlike, deep wine red to purple. Lvs pinnate, with 5–7 sharply toothed lflets. Stems oft trailing or floating. Wet places, lowl–subalp, Alas to Cal, e to mid US, e Can. Sum.

EVENING-PRIMROSE FAMILY (ONAGRACEAE): 4 PETALS, 4 SEPALS

Alpine willowherb, *Epilobium clavatum.* Flrs occas white, to ½" diam, petals notched. Lvs ovate to elliptic, L to 2", opp, occas alt near tip of stem. Ht 2"–12". Moist places, subalp–alp, Alas to Cal, e to RM and Atl; Eurasia. Sum.

Red willowherb, *Chamerion latifolium.* Flrs to 1½" diam; raceme not spirelike. Lvs opp, lancelike, L 1"–2". Ht to 16". Moist rocky or gravelly places, subalp–alp, Alas to Cal, e to e Ore and RM. Sum.

Fireweed, *Chamerion angustifolium.* Flrs in spirelike raceme, opening from bottom to top of inflor. Lvs alt, willowlike, L 3"–6". Ht 3'–10'. Abun on burns, clear-cuts, other disturbed places, Alas to Cal, e to Atl; Eurasia. Late spr–sum.

HEATH FAMILY (ERICACEAE): 5 PETALS, 5 SEPALS

Candystick, *Allotropa virgata.* Flrs urn shaped, in spikelike raceme. Lvs scalelike, brownish. Stem fleshy, striped like a candy cane. Ht 4"–16". Moist, shady forest, E Cas to coast, BC to Cal. Sum.

Prince's pine (pipsissewa), *Chimaphila umbellata.* Flrs gen 5–15 in oft ± nodding inflor. Lvs evergreen, leathery, oblanceolate, toothed, L 1"–3", in 1–2 whorls. Stems slightly woody. Ht 4"–12". Gen conif forest, Alas to s Cal, e to RM and e US; Eurasia. Sum. Little prince's pine, *C. menziesii,* similar but lvs elliptic, gen 1–3 flrs.

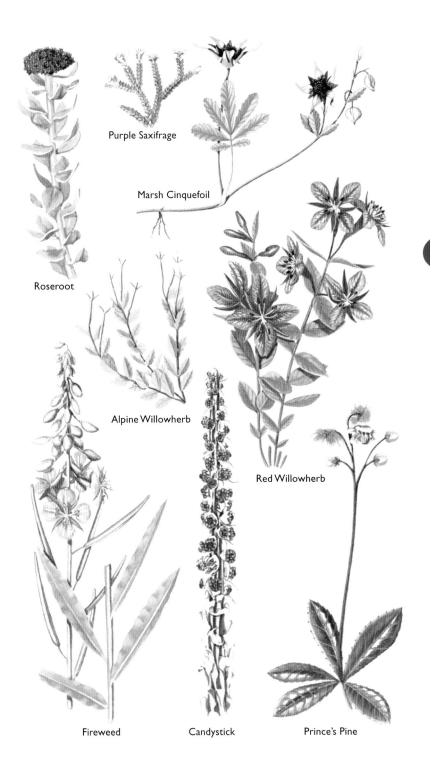

Purple Saxifrage

Marsh Cinquefoil

Roseroot

Alpine Willowherb

Red Willowherb

Fireweed

Candystick

Prince's Pine

PLATE 34

HEATH FAMILY (ERICACEAE): 5 PETALS, 5 SEPALS

Pink wintergreen, *Pyrola asarifolia.* Flrs 10–25 in raceme. Lvs basal, heart shaped to ± oval, minutely toothed to nearly entire, petiole and blade ea to ca 3" long, lvs occas absent. Ht to 16". Moist woods, Alas s in most of w N Amer, e across Can and n US. Sum–early fall.

PRIMROSE FAMILY (PRIMULACEAE): 4–9 PETALS, 4–9 SEPALS

Jeffrey's shooting star, *Dodecatheon jeffreyi.* Flrs gen with 5 (occas 4) reflexed petals and enlarged stigma tip, in sticky-haired umbel. Lvs spoon shaped, smooth or sticky haired, broad petioled, basal, L 2"–16", entire or scalloped or slightly toothed. Ht to 24". Moist places, Alas to Cal, e to n RM. Sum. One of several very similar spp in our range. Cf white shooting star, plate 22.

Smooth douglasia, *Douglasia laevigata.* Flrs ca ¾" diam, tubular with flaring lobes. Lf L to ¾", smooth or hairy margined, lancelike, in rosettes at stem ends. Stems creeping, L to 12", with flr stalk ht to 2½"; mat forming. Open, rocky places, W Cas to coast, Wn and Ore, very rare in w BC. Spr-sum.

Western starflower, *Trientalis borealis.* Flrs white to rose, ca ½" diam. Lvs elliptic, L 1¾"–4", 4–8 in whorl right below flrs. Ht 4"–6". Woods, mdws, s BC to Cal, e to n RM. Spr-sum. Northern starflower, *T. europaea,* a bog plant, has white flrs, lvs along entire stem.

DOGBANE FAMILY (APOCYNACEAE): 5-LOBED FLOWERS

Spreading dogbane, *Apocynum androsaemifolium.* Flrs tubular or bell shaped, to ½" diam, gen in terminal inflor, occas in lf axils. Lvs ovate to elliptic, opp, L 1"–2½". Ht 8"–20". Dry places, lowl-subalp, in all our mtns; widespread in N Amer. Sum–early fall.

PHLOX FAMILY (POLEMONIACEAE): 5-LOBED FLOWERS

Skyrocket, *Ipomopsis aggregata.* Flr L ¾"–1¼", occas white. Lf L 1"–2", most numerous near base of stem, divided into linear segm. Ht 8"–40". Dry, open places, E Cas, BC to Cal, e to RM and s to n Mex. Sum.

Spreading phlox, *Phlox diffusa.* Flrs usu pink, occas pale blue or white, ¾" diam, oft hiding lvs. Lvs opp, needlelike, L ¼"–¾". Stems woody at base, prostrate, mat forming. Ht 4"–12". Dry, rocky places, gen subalp-alp, in all our mtns; widespread in w N Amer. Early sum.

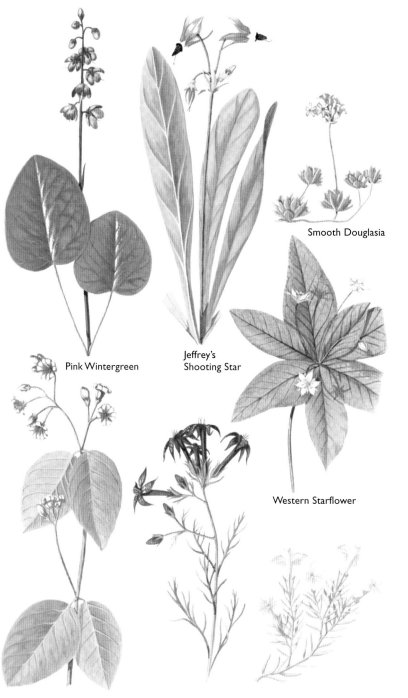

Pink Wintergreen

Jeffrey's
Shooting Star

Smooth Douglasia

Western Starflower

Spreading Dogbane

Skyrocket

Spreading Phlox

PLATE 35

FIGWORT FAMILY (SCROPHULARIACEAE): FLOWERS IRREGULAR, 5-LOBED

Applegate paintbrush, *Castilleja applegatei.* Flrs slender, tubular, spoutlike, gen inconspicuous among scarlet (occas orange or yellow) 3- to 5-lobed bracts. Lvs either 3-lobed on upper stem and entire below, or all entire; margins wavy. Stems sticky haired below inflor. Ht 4"–24". Open woods, rocky places, Cas, Ore to Cal; e to e Ore, Idaho, Nev. Sum.

Common (scarlet) paintbrush, *Castilleja miniata* var *miniata.* Flrs similar to those of *C. applegatei;* floral bracts scarlet to crimson (occas orange or yellow), 3-lobed. Lvs entire, lancelike, margins not wavy. Ht 12"–36". Moist places, lowl-mont, s Alas, w Can, s in w US to Cal, e to NMex. Late spr–early fall. Elmer's paintbrush, *C. elmeri,* also has entire lvs, but inflor gen crimson to purplish, strongly sticky haired; subalp-alp, cen Wn Cas n to s BC.

Magenta paintbrush, *Castilleja parviflora* vars *oreopola* and *olympica.* Flrs similar to those of *C. applegatei,* but corolla obscured by calyx. Floral bracts 3- to 5-lobed, gen magenta or rose. Ht to 12". Subalp mdws, OMtns, Cas, Rainier to cen Ore. Sum. Cf small-flowered paintbrush, plate 23.

Cliff paintbrush, *Castilleja rupicola.* Flrs similar to those of *C. applegatei,* but corolla beak extends far beyond calyx; floral bracts entirely red, 3- to 7-lobed. Densely hairy. Ht to 8". Rocky places, subalp-alp, Cas, BC to s Ore. Sum. Harsh paintbrush, *C. hispida,* also densely hairy but gen taller, with flr bracts green at base.

Suksdorf's paintbrush, *Castilleja suksdorfii.* Flrs similar to those of *C. applegatei,* with beak extending well beyond calyx; floral bracts gen 5-lobed, yellow at base, red toward tips. Lvs + smooth, entire or lobed. Ht to 20". Moist subalp mdws, Cas, cen Wn to s Ore. Sum–early fall.

Foxglove, *Digitalis purpurea.* Flrs pink to lavender, purple, and white, L 1"–2", in dense 1-sided raceme. Lvs ovate, toothed or scalloped, to L 12" at base, smaller upward on stem. Ht to 6'. Moist sites, roadsides and waste places, lowl-mont throughout our region; introduced from Europe. Late spr–sum.

Brewer's monkeyflower, *Mimulus breweri.* Flrs very nearly reg, ca ¼" diam. Lvs entire, lancelike. Plant sticky haired. Ht to 6". Dry places, E Cas, low-mid el, BC s to Cal. Sum.

Lewis' monkeyflower, *Mimulus lewisii.* Flr L 1¼"–2¼". Lvs opp, ovate, toothed, clasping stem. Ht 12"–24". Moist-wet subalp-alp in all our mtns, w Can s to Cal, e to n RM. Sum.

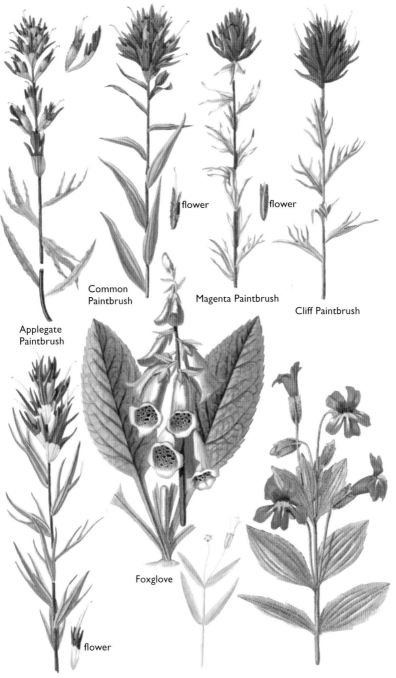

Common
Paintbrush

flower

Magenta Paintbrush

flower

Cliff Paintbrush

Applegate
Paintbrush

Foxglove

flower

Suksdorf's Paintbrush

Brewer's Monkeyflower

Lewis' Monkeyflower

PLATE 36

FIGWORT FAMILY (SCROPHULARIACEAE): FLOWERS IRREGULAR, 2-LIPPED

Elephant's head, *Pedicularis groenlandica.* Flrs rose to purple, like tiny elephant heads, upper lip forming trunk, lateral lobes forming ears. Lvs pinnate, L to 6", basal, reduced upward on stem. Plant hairless. Ht to ca 24". Wet mdws in all our mtns; widespread in w N Amer. Sum.

Little elephant's head, *Pedicularis attollens.* Similar to above sp but plant hairy and "trunk" no longer than lower lip. Ht to 16". Wet mdws, Ore Cas s to SNev. Sum.

Birdsbeak lousewort, *Pedicularis ornithorhyncha.* Flrs dark rose to purple, with short, straight "beak." Lvs pinnate, basal, up to 3 small ones on stem. Ht to 6". Subalp–alp mdws, s Alas in CMtns and Vanc I, to Wn Cas. Sum.

Woodland beardtongue, *Nothochelone nemorosa.* Flr L to 1", 2–5 in terminal panicle. Lvs ovate, opp, toothed, L 2"–3". Ht to 24". Moist places, W Cas to coast, BC to n Cal. Sum.

Cliff (rock) penstemon, *Penstemon rupicola.* Flrs rose to lavender or red, L 1"–1½". Lvs opp, ovate, thick, toothed, L to ¾". Stems creeping, woody at base. Ht 3"–6". Cliffs, rocky places, Cas, Wn to Cal. Sum. Cf Davidson's penstemon, small-flowered penstemon, plate 40.

ASTER OR SUNFLOWER FAMILY (ASTERACEAE): FLOWERS IN COMPOSITE HEADS

Rosy pussytoes, *Antennaria microphylla.* Flr heads with tiny yellow disk flrs bordered by pink or rosy bracts, in tight inflor. Basal lvs spoon shaped, pointed; stem lvs linear, all white-woolly. Ht to 18", mat forming. Open places, mtns of w N Amer. Late spring–sum. Cf woolly pussytoes, alpine pussytoes, plate 24.

Edible thistle, *Cirsium edule.* Flr heads with disk flrs only, 2"–3" diam, surrounded by spiny bracts. Lvs pinnately lobed, spiny margined, mostly basal, L to 16", fewer and smaller on stem. Ht 24"–28". Plant webby haired. Moist mdws, open woods, lowl–alp, cen BC to n Ore, e to W Cas. Sum–early fall.

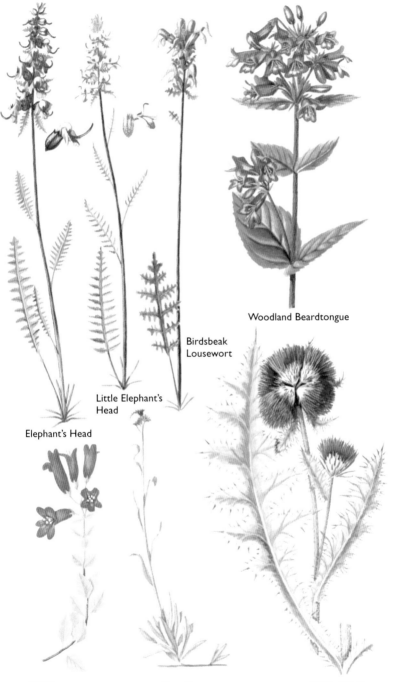

Woodland Beardtongue

Birdsbeak
Lousewort

Little Elephant's
Head

Elephant's Head

Cliff Penstemon

Rosy Pussytoes

Edible Thistle

IV. Blue to Purple Flowers

This section includes flowers that are distinctly blue, violet, or bluish purple. Compounded of equal parts red and blue, purple comes in shades that are difficult to assign to one color or the other. When attempting to identify plants with purplish flowers, also consult section III, Pink to Red Flowers. White flowers tinged with blue or lavender are covered in section I, White Flowers. Brownish flowers tending toward maroon or purple are covered in section V, Green or Brown Flowers. The following species from other sections may have bluish or purplish flowers.

Subalpine mariposa lily, *plate 14*
Lyall's mariposa lily, *plate 14*
Mountain ladyslipper, *plate 16*
Western red baneberry, *plate 18*
Drummond's anemone, *plate 18*
Western pasqueflower, *plate 18*
Alpine smelowskia, *plate 19*
Alpine collomia, *plate 23*
Varileaf phacelia, *plate 23*
Yerba buena, *plate 23*
Dwarf mountain daisy, *plate 25*
Bracted lousewort, *plate 29*
Purple saxifrage, *plate 33*
Spreading phlox, *plate 34*
Magenta paintbrush, *plate 35*
Foxglove, *plate 35*
Lewis' monkeyflower, *plate 35*
Elephant's head, *plate 36*
Birdsbeak lousewort, *plate 36*
Edible thistle, *plate 36*
Western bronze bells, *plate 42*
Small-flowered twisted stalk, *plate 42*
Clustered ladyslipper, *plate 42*
Giant helleborine, *plate 42*
Wild ginger, *plate 43*
Brown's peony, *plate 43*
Youth-on-age, *plate 43*

PLATE 37

LILY FAMILY (LILIACEAE): 6 TEPALS

Common camas, *Camassia quamash.* Flrs 1½"–2" diam, pale blue to deep violet, occas white, gen slightly irreg, in long-bracted raceme. Lvs grasslike. Ht 12"–24". Grassy places, mdws, lowl–subalp s BC to Cal, e to RM. Spr–early sum. Leichtlin's camas, *C. leichtlinii,* similar but flrs more oft reg and/or white, inflor bracts short.

IRIS FAMILY (IRIDAE): 6 TEPALS

Blue-eyed grass, *Sisyrinchium idahoense.* Flrs ½"–1½" diam, tepals abruptly slender, pointed. Lvs grasslike, 2 forming spathe below inflor. Ht 4"–20". Moist places, lowl–mont, S Alas to Baja, e to n RM, e Can. Spr–midsum.

BUTTERCUP FAMILY (RANUNCULACEAE): 5–7 PETAL-LIKE SEPALS

Monkshood, *Aconitum columbianum.* Flrs occas white or greenish, upper sepal hoodlike, 2 tiny petals inside hood. Lvs palmately lobed, toothed, 2"–8" wide. Ht 18"–60". Moist places, lowl–subalp, Alas to Cal, e to RM, cen US. Sum.

Cut-leaf anemone (pasqueflower), *Pulsatilla patens.* Flrs blue to purple, rarely white, ca 1½"–3" diam, hairy outside. Lvs white haired, finely dissected, mostly basal (appearing after earliest flrs), but 2–3 in whorl below flr. Ht to ca 12". Mont–subalp slopes, E CMtns to Cas; Alas to Wn; e to RM, cen and s US. Sum. Cf western pasqueflower, plate 18.

Oregon (blue) anemone, *Anemone oregana.* Flrs gen blue, also pink or white, gen with 35–100 stamens, to 1½" diam, hairless. Lvs compound, 1 basal, 3 in whorl below flr. Ht 4"–12". Moist woods, brush, E Cas, n Wn to CRGorge, also sw Wn, e Ore. Spr–early sum. Lyall's anemone, *A. lyallii,* very similar but flr gen white, fewer than 35 stamens. Cf Columbia windflower, plate 18.

Rockslide (large-flowered) larkspur, *Delphinium glareosum.* Flrs irreg, 5 sepals, upper spurred, 4 smaller, deeply notched blue petals; raceme hairy, ca ½ length of stem. Lvs fleshy, deeply 5- to 7-lobed, petioles progressively smaller upward on stem so that blades tend to be clumped near mid-stem. Ht to 12". Talus, rocky ridges, alp–subalp, OMtns, E Cas, cen Wn, Ore Cas. Sum. One of 9 very similar spp in our mtns. Pale larkspur, *D. glaucum,* ht 40"–80", has basal lvs 6"–8" wide (smaller on stem), hairless stems with powdery bloom. Menzies' larkspur, *D. menziesii,* has deep blue sepals, pale blue or white petals, most of its lvs on stem. Upland larkspur, *D. lineapetalum,* has a few 2- to 4-lobed, mostly basal lvs.

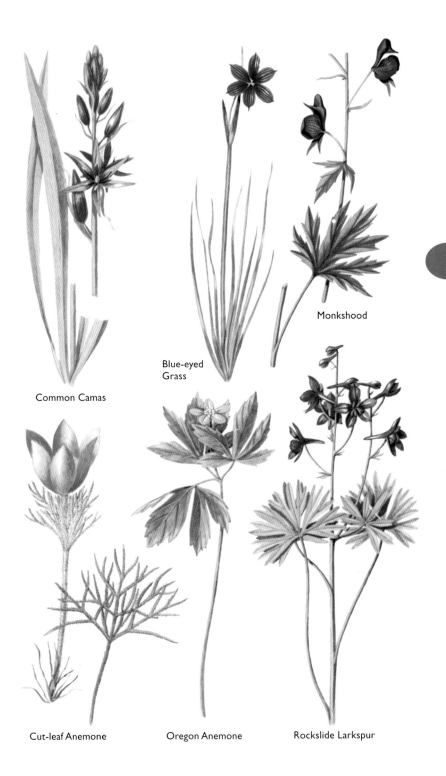

Common Camas

Blue-eyed
Grass

Monkshood

Cut-leaf Anemone

Oregon Anemone

Rockslide Larkspur

PLATE 38

PEA FAMILY (FABACEAE): FLOWERS IRREGULAR, 5 PETALS

Nuttall's pea, *Lathyrus nevadensis* sbsp *lanceolatus.* Flrs blue, white, pink, or purple, L to ca ½", gen 17 or fewer per inflor. Lvs pinnate, with 8–14 lflets, ending in forked tendril. Ht to 32". Open woods, grassland, s BC to Cal, e to Idaho. Spr-sum.

Broadleaf lupine, *Lupinus arcticus.* Flrs irreg, in long dense racemes. Lvs palmately compound, lflets gen 7–9, L usu 1¼"–2⅜". Plant usu hairy, stems branched. Ht to 40". Com, open places, lowl-subalp in all our mtns, Alas to Cal, e to Cas. Sum. Bigleaf lupine, *L. burkei,* best recognized through much of our range by unbranched stem, lvs usu with 9–13 lflets up to 4" long.

Alpine lupine, *Lupinus lepidus* var *lobbii.* Flrs irreg, in short, dense racemes. Lvs palmately compound, 6–8 lflets silky haired, L ⅝". Ht 3"–4", mat forming. Rocky alp slopes, BC to s Cal, e to Idaho, Nev. Sum. Other varieties of this sp occur from lowl to subalp in our region.

American vetch, *Vicia americana.* Flrs irreg, sweetpealike, 4–8 per stalk from lf axil. Lvs pinnately compound, gen with 8–12 lflets, usu ending in branched tendril. Plant trailing or climbing. Roadsides, open places, in all our mtns; widespread in N Amer. Late spr–sum.

VIOLET FAMILY (VIOLACEAE): FLOWERS IRREGULAR, 5 PETALS, 5 SEPALS

Early blue (hook) violet, *Viola adunca.* Flrs lilac or white with purple lines, to ¾" wide, with prominent spur, white-haired side petals. Lvs ovate or heart shaped, scalloped, long petioled, stipules oft slenderly toothed. Ht to 4". Moist mdws, woods, open places, lowl-subalp, in all our mtns, but esp E Cas; widespread in N Amer. Spr-sum.

Marsh violet, *Viola palustris.* Flrs lilac or white with blue lines, 1 per short stalk. Lvs rounded or heart shaped, to 1⅜" wide. Lvs and flrs both rise directly from rhizome. Ht 3"–6". Bogs, marshes, wet mdws, BC to Cal, e to RM, Atl; Europe. Spr-sum.

Flett's violet, *Viola flettii.* Flrs purple and yellow. Lvs kidney shaped, fleshy, finely scalloped or toothed, ca ½"–1½" wide. Ht 1"–6". Rocky places, high el, OMtns. Sum.

Nuttall's Pea

Broadleaf Lupine

Bigleaf Lupine

Alpine Lupine

American Vetch

Early Blue Violet

Marsh Violet

Flett's Violet

PLATE 39

GENTIAN FAMILY (GENTIANACEAE): 4- TO 5-LOBED FLOWERS
Explorer's (mountain, bog, pleated) gentian, *Gentiana calycosa.* Flr L 1"–1⅝", vaselike, 5-lobed, rarely yellowish, with 2- to 4-toothed pleats between corolla lobes, gen 1 per stem, occas 3 in inflor. Lf L to 1", ovate, opp, 7–9 pairs on stem. Ht 2"–12". Gen subalp-alp mdws, streamsides, BC to Cal, e to RM. Late sum–fall. Northern gentian, *G. amarella,* has several flrs in crowded inflor, ea flr 4- to 5-lobed, without pleats.

Hiker's gentian, *Gentianopsis simplex.* Flr solitary, with 4 corolla lobes oft spreading to form cross. Lvs opp, lancelike, 3–6 pairs on single stem. Ht 2"–8". Mtn bogs, mdws, Ore Cas to SNev. Sum.

PHLOX FAMILY (POLEMONIACEAE): 5-LOBED FLOWERS
Elegant sky pilot, *Polemonium elegans.* Flrs funnel shaped with flaring corolla lobes, in terminal head. Lvs pinnate, gen basal, lflets tiny, rounded. Plant sticky and strongly ill-smelling. Ht 2"–4". Rocky alp slopes, Cas, BC to Wn, OMtns. Sum.

Showy Jacob's ladder, *Polemonium californicum.* Flrs bell shaped, in headlike inflor, ill-smelling. Lvs pinnate, basal and on stem, 11–25 lflets elliptic, L to 1½". Inflor sticky but herbage otherwise hairless or nearly so. Ht gen 12"–20". Gen rocky places, mid el, Cas, Wn to Cal, e to Mont, Nev. Late spring–sum. *P. pulcherrimum* var *pulcherrimum* is a compact version found at high el in all our mtns.

WATERLEAF FAMILY (HYDROPHYLLACEAE): 5 PETALS, 5 SEPALS
Silky (alpine) phacelia, *Phacelia sericea.* Flrs ca ¼" diam, stamens longer than petals, in spikelike inflor. Lvs pinnately lobed, fernlike, L 1"–4", silky haired (except in Ore). Ht 4"–24". Various habitats, mid-high el, s BC to Cal, e to RM. Sum. Cf varileaf phacelia, plate 23.

BORAGE FAMILY (BORAGINACEAE): 5 SEPALS, 5-LOBED
Jessica's stickseed, *Hackelia micrantha.* Flrs ca ¼" diam, in open, branched inflor. Lvs lancelike, long petioled below, sessile above. Stems hairy. Ht 12"–40". Open places, Cas to SNev, e to RM. Sum.

Panicled bluebells (lungwort), *Mertensia paniculata.* Flrs tubular, nodding, in loose clusters. Lvs ovate, stem lf L 2"–3", short petioled, with slender, pointed tip; basal lvs, when present, heart shaped, long petioled. Ht to 5'. Moist places, Alas, Can, s to RM, Cas, OMtns, s Ore. Sum. Broad-leaved bluebells, *M. platyphylla,* has single stems; lowl streamsides, W Cas. Oregon bluebells, *M. bella,* has bell-shaped flrs; Cas, cen Ore–Cal. Fringed lungwort, *M. ciliata,* has hairy sepals, sessile upper-stem lvs; cen Ore–Cal.

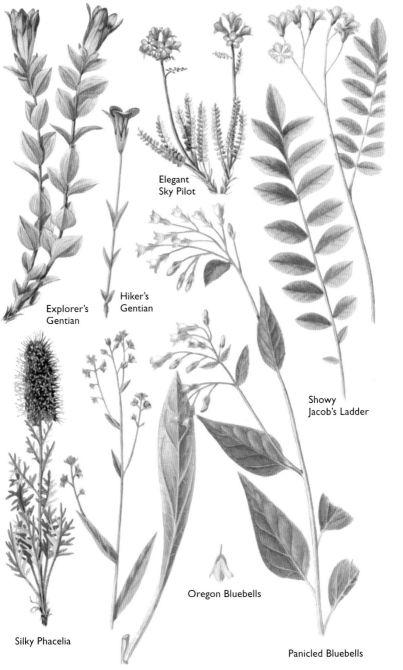

Elegant
Sky Pilot

Explorer's
Gentian

Hiker's
Gentian

Showy
Jacob's Ladder

Silky Phacelia

Oregon Bluebells

Panicled Bluebells

Jessica's Stickseed

PLATE 40

MINT FAMILY (LAMIACEAE): FLOWERS IRREGULAR

Mountain pennyroyal (coyote mint), *Monardella odoratissima.* Flrs occas white, L ca ½", in dense head, cupped by membranous bracts. Lvs opp, lancelike, L to 1¼". Ht 6"–20". Dry woods, rocky places, E Cas, Wn to SNev, also e Wn and n Idaho s to Ariz and NMex. Sum.

Selfheal, *Prunella vulgaris.* Flr L to ¾", 2-lipped, upper lip hoodlike, lower 3-lobed in short, dense spikes. Lvs opp, lancelike to ovate, toothed, petioled. Ht 4"–20". Moist places, lowl-mont, widespread in N Amer; Europe. Sum.

Cooley's hedgenettle, *Stachys chamissonis.* Flr L ½"–1", 2-lipped, upper lip hoodlike, lower longer, 3-lobed, droopy, in whorls on upper stem. Lvs opp, narrowly ovate or triangular, toothed, petioled, hairy on both sides, L 2½"–6". Stems 4-sided, bristly. Ht 24"–60". Damp places, BC to s Ore, Cas to coast. Sum.

FIGWORT FAMILY (SCROPHULARIACEAE): FLOWERS IRREGULAR

Large-flowered blue-eyed mary, *Collinsia grandiflora.* Flr L ca ¾", corolla attached at right angle to calyx, in whorls on upper stem. Lvs opp, ovate to spoon shaped, toothed on lower stem, narrower and entire above. Stem simple or branched. Ht 4"–16". Moist places, lowl-mont, BC to n Cal, W Cas to coast. Sum.

Small-flowered blue-eyed mary, *Collinsia parviflora.* Flrs like those of above sp, but L only ca ¼". Lvs opp, oblong to nearly round on lower stem, L 2"–4", short petioled; upper lvs lancelike, sessile. Stem simple or branched. Ht 2"–16". Moist places, BC s to Cal, Ariz; e to Colo, e Can, n US. Spr.

Davidson's penstemon, *Penstemon davidsonii.* Flr L to 1½", 2-lipped, hairy at base of lower lip, 1 per stalk. Lf L to ¾", oval, oft toothed, petioled. Stems woody at base. Ht 2"–6", mat forming. Rocky places, mont-alp, BC to Cal. Sum.

Small-flowered penstemon, *Penstemon procerus.* Flr L ca ½", 2-lipped, whorled. Lvs entire; lower ones ovate, petioled, L to 4"; upper ones lancelike, mostly sessile, L to 3". Plant singly stemmed. Ht 6"–12", mat forming. Moist places, mid-high el, in all our mtns, s to Cal and Nev. Sum. Cascade penstemon, *P. serrulatus,* similar but flr L ¾"–1", plant taller with several stems, larger toothed lvs.

Cusick's speedwell, *Veronica cusickii.* Flrs 4-petaled, ± irreg, ca ½" diam. Lvs oval, opp, shiny, L to 1". Ht 2"–8". Com, moist mdws, talus, stream banks, subalp, Wn Cas, OMtns, s to SNev, e to RM. Sum. Alpine speedwell, *V. wormskjoldii,* very similar but lvs gen oblong, not crowded on stem.

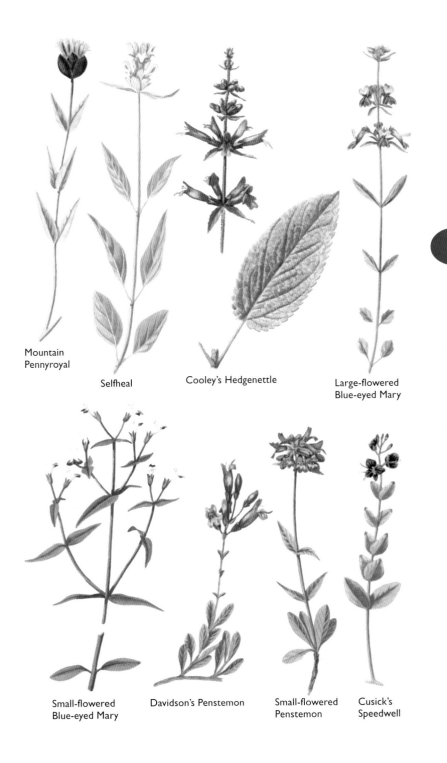

Mountain
Pennyroyal

Selfheal

Cooley's Hedgenettle

Large-flowered
Blue-eyed Mary

Small-flowered
Blue-eyed Mary

Davidson's Penstemon

Small-flowered
Penstemon

Cusick's
Speedwell

PLATE 41

BLADDERWORT FAMILY (LENTIBULARIACEAE): FLOWERS IRREGULAR, 5-LOBED

Common butterwort, *Pinguicula vulgaris.* Flrs 2-lipped, spurred, L to 1", 1 per stem. Lvs basal, ± spoon shaped, short petioled, succulent, slimy above, L 1"–2". Ht 2"–6". Bogs, wet places in mtns, Alas to n Cal, e to e Can, ne US; Eurasia. Spr-sum.

BELLFLOWER FAMILY (CAMPANULACEAE): 5-LOBED FLOWERS

Bluebells of Scotland (roundleaf bellflower, harebell, bluebell), *Campanula rotundifolia.* Flrs bell shaped, L ca ¾", lobes barely spreading. Lvs both basal and alt; basal ones round or heart shaped, long petioled, toothed; alt lvs linear, entire. Ht 4"–32". Many places, lowl-subalp, in all our mtns; widespread in n hemis. Sum. Parry's bellflower, *C. parryi,* similar but basal lvs spoon shaped, short petioled. Rough harebell, *C. scabrella,* covered with downy hairs.

Piper's harebell, *Campanula piperi.* Flrs dish-shaped, ca 1" diam. Lvs all ± spoon shaped, sharply toothed. Stems unbranched. Ht to 4". Rocky places, subalp-alp, OMtns only. Sum.

Scouler's harebell, *Campanula scouleri.* Flrs tubular with flaring lobes longer than tube, style exceeding upper corolla rim. Lvs toothed, + round and long petioled at base, + oval and shorter petioled on stem. Ht 4"–16". Woods, rocky places below 4,000', W CMtns–Cas to coast, Alas to n Cal. Sum.

Alaska bellflower, *Campanula lasiocarpa.* Flrs funnel shaped, calyx woolly, with toothed, lancelike segm. Lvs mostly basal, spoon shaped, sharply toothed. Ht 2"–6". Alp in all our mtns, Alas s to Wn; Asia. Sum.

ASTER OR SUNFLOWER FAMILY (ASTERACEAE): FLOWERS IN COMPOSITE HEADS

Alpine aster, *Oreostemma alpigenum.* Flr head daisylike, 1 per stem, rays lavender to violet. Lvs entire, mostly basal, linear to spoon shaped; stem lvs few, smaller. Ht 2"–6". Subalp-alp, OMtns, Cas, Wn to Cal, e to n RM. Sum.

Cascade aster, *Eucephalus ledophyllus.* Flr heads daisylike, gen several per stem, with 6–21 blue or pink rays. Lvs lancelike to elliptic, sessile, + gray-cottony beneath, scalelike on lower stem. Ht gen 12"–24". Open woods, mdws, mont-subalp, Cas, BC to Cal. Midsum-fall. Leafy aster, *Symphyotrichum cusickii,* has purple or blue rays, long petioled, spoonlike lvs on lower stem.

Wandering daisy (fleabane), *Erigeron peregrinus.* Flr heads with 30–80 blue, lavender, or pink rays, gen 1 or few per stem. Lower lvs spoonlike, long petioled; upper ones smaller, sessile, linear to ovate. Ht 12"–30"; alp plants oft less than 8" tall. Com, mdws, moist places, mont-alp, in all our mtns; widespread in mtns of w N Amer. Sum. One of numerous very similar spp in our range.

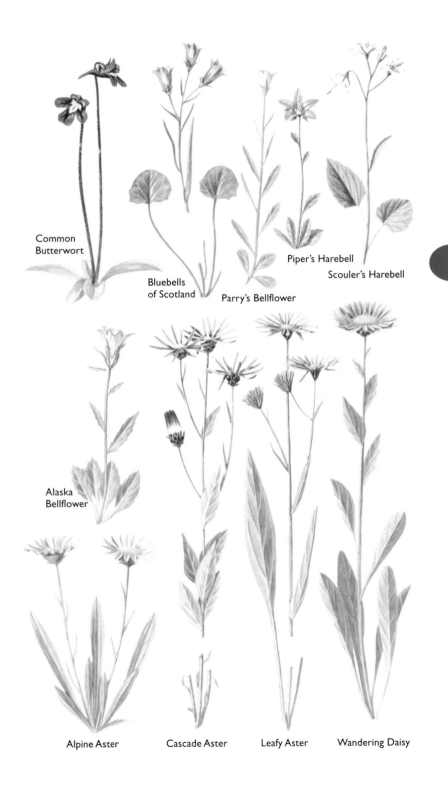

Common
Butterwort

Bluebells
of Scotland

Parry's Bellflower

Piper's Harebell

Scouler's Harebell

Alaska
Bellflower

Alpine Aster

Cascade Aster

Leafy Aster

Wandering Daisy

V. Green or Brown Flowers

This section includes flowers that are conspicuously green or brown, at least in part. The green may tend toward yellow or white, the brown toward maroon or purple. The following species may also have greenish or brownish flowers.

Clasping-leaved twisted stalk, *plate 15*
Sticky tofieldia, *plate 15*
Corn-lily, *plate 15*
Elegant death-camas, *plate 15*
Mountain ladyslipper, *plate 16*
Roundleaf bog orchid, *plate 16*
Lady's tresses, *plate 16*
False bugbane, *plate 18*
Globeflower, *plate 18*
White-veined wintergreen, *plate 22*
One-sided wintergreen, *plate 22*
Sweet-scented bedstraw, *plate 24*
Sibbaldia, *plate 27*
Rosy twisted stalk, *plate 31*
Spotted coralroot, *plate 31*
Monkshood, *plate 37*

PLATE 42

LILY FAMILY (LILIACEAE): 6 TEPALS

Checker (chocolate) lily, *Fritillaria affinis* var *affinis.* Flrs nodding, L ¾"–1½", mottled green (or yellow) and brown (or purple). Lvs both scattered on upper stem and in 1–2 whorls. Ht 6"–40". Forest, grassy places, lowl-mont, BC to Cal, e to Idaho. Spr-sum.

Western bronze bells, *Stenanthium occidentale.* Flrs greenish bronze or purplish green, nodding, in loose raceme. Lvs basal, grasslike, L 4"–12". Ht 4–20". Moist places, gen subalp-alp, in all our mtns s to Cal, e to RM. Sum.

Small-flowered twisted stalk, *Streptopus streptopoides.* Flrs greenish, oft purple tinged, tepals spreading. Lvs ovate, sessile, L to 2¼". Ht 4"–8". Mid-mtn forest, Alas to OMtns and Wn Cas, e to Idaho. Sum. Cf clasping-leaved twisted stalk, plate 15, and rosy twisted stalk, plate 31.

Green false-hellebore, *Veratrum viride.* Flrs greenish, in drooping, tasseled panicle. Lvs clasping, L 6"–14", 3"–6" wide. Ht 3'–7'. Wet places, lowl-subalp, Alas to n Ore, e to RM and e Can. Sum. Cf corn-lily, plate 15.

ORCHID FAMILY (ORCHIDACEAE): FLOWERS IRREGULAR

Clustered ladyslipper, *Cypripedium fasciculatum.* Flrs ca ½" wide, sepals and 2 petals brownish purple, lip pouchlike, pale green mottled with purple. Lvs 2, opp, ovate, L 2"–6". Stem hairy, 2"–8" tall. Open forest, s BC to Cal, E Cas to n RM. Sum. Cf mountain ladyslipper, plate 16.

Giant helleborine (stream orchid), *Epipactis gigantea.* Flrs to 1½" wide; 3 green, lancelike sepals; 2 pink or purplish lancelike petals; 3rd petal tonguelike, pinkish, purple-streaked at base. Lvs broadly lancelike, L 2"–8". Ht 12"–36". Moist-wet places, gen lowl-mont, s BC to Mex, e to RM. Spr-sum.

Heartleaf twayblade, *Listera cordata.* Flrs greenish or brownish, small, orchidlike, with forked lower lip, gen 5–16 in raceme. Lvs 2, opp, heart shaped. Ht to 10". Gen damp/wet places, Alas s to Cal and NMex, e to e Can, se US; Greenland. Sum. Western twayblade, *L. convallarioides,* similar but flr lip merely notched, not deeply forked, lvs ovate. Northwestern twayblade, *L. caurina,* also similar but lower lip wedge shaped and neither notched nor forked.

NETTLE FAMILY (URTICACEAE): NO PETALS, 4 SEPALS

Stinging nettle, *Urtica dioica.* Flrs small, greenish, in stringy inflor from lf axils. Lvs lancelike to ovate, opp, petioled, toothed. Stems 3'–7' tall, smooth or hairy. Lvs and sometimes stems covered with stinging hairs; avoid contact! Moist places, N Amer, Eurasia. Spr-sum.

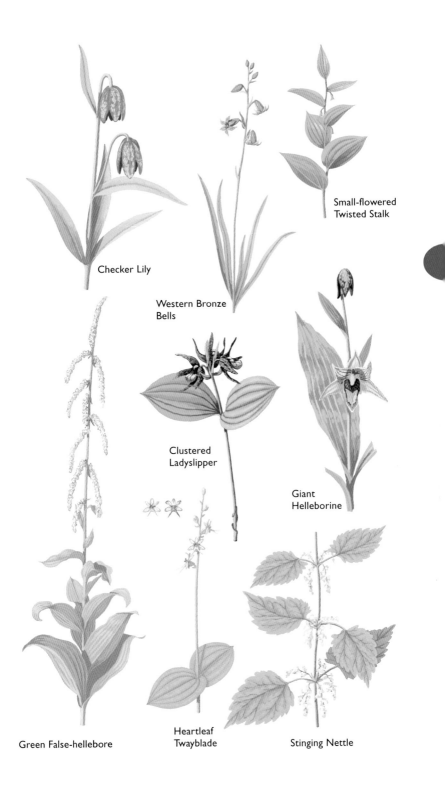

Checker Lily

Western Bronze Bells

Small-flowered Twisted Stalk

Clustered Ladyslipper

Giant Helleborine

Green False-hellebore

Heartleaf Twayblade

Stinging Nettle

PLATE 43

BIRTHWORT FAMILY (ARISTOLOCHIACEAE): 3-LOBED FLOWERS, NO PETALS

Wild ginger, *Asarum caudatum.* Flrs brownish or occas greenish, calyx bowl-shaped with very long, slender sepals. Lvs heart- or kidney-shaped, in pairs. Stems trailing, mat forming. Moist, shady woods, lowl-mont, BC to Cal, e to Idaho, Mont. Spr-sum.

BUCKWHEAT FAMILY (POLYGONACEAE): NO PETALS, 4 SEPALS

Mountain- (alpine) sorrel, *Oxyria digyna.* Flrs greenish to reddish, small, in slender panicles. Lvs green or reddish, heart- or kidney-shaped, long petioled, gen basal. Ht gen 4"–16". Moist, rocky places, subalp-alp, mtns of n hemis. Sum.

PEONY FAMILY (PAEONIACEAE): 5 PETALS, 5 SEPALS

Brown's (western) peony, *Paeonia brownii.* Flrs green and brown to maroon, 1"–1½" diam. Lvs 3-divided 2**x**, ultimate segm lobed, blade L to 2½", smooth, fleshy-leathery, waxy blue-green. Ht 8"–24". Pine forest, E Cas, Wn to Cal, e to Idaho, Wyo, Utah. Late spr–early sum.

BUTTERCUP FAMILY (RANUNCULACEAE): NO PETALS, 4–5 SEPALS

Western meadowrue, *Thalictrum occidentale.* Flrs small, in panicles, greenish white (M flrs) or purplish (F flrs). Lvs compound, divided in 3s, ultimate segm round. Young plants dk purplish. Ht to 40". Moist woods, BC s to n Cal, e to RM states. Late spr–midsum.

SAXIFRAGE FAMILY (SAXIFRAGACEAE): 4–5 PETALS

Brewer's mitrewort, *Mitella breweri.* Flrs greenish yellow, feathery, 20–60 in raceme. Lvs basal, 1½"–3½" diam, heart- or kidney-shaped, shiny green, 7- to 11-lobed, toothed. Flr stems lfless, ht 4"–16". Moist places, gen in mtns, BC s in Cas and OMtns to Cal, e to n RM. Spr-sum. Naked mitrewort, *M. nuda,* similar but lvs small, hairy. Three-toothed mitrewort, *M. caulescens,* has lvs on stems. Oval-leaved mitrewort, *M. ovalis,* has narrower, white-haired lvs.

Fringecup, *Tellima grandiflora.* Flrs with fringelike greenish to reddish petals, gen 10–35 in 1-sided racemes. Lvs mostly basal, also 1–3 on stem, coarse haired, 5- to 7-lobed, scalloped or toothed. Ht to 32". Moist places, lowl–low mtn, s Alas to cen Cal, gen W Cas to coast in Ore and Wn. Spr-sum.

Youth-on-age, *Tolmiea menziesii.* Flrs tiny, bristly, green and brown, tubular calyx, 4 threadlike petals, in raceme 4"–12" long. Lvs hairy, toothed, lobed, reduced upward on stem. Ht to 32". Moist places, Alas to Cal, W CMtns and Cas to coast. Spr-sum.

HEATH FAMILY (ERICACEAE): 5-LOBED COROLLA

Pinedrops, *Pterospora andromedea.* Flrs urn shaped, nodding, gen pale yellowish brown, also pink or white, 40–60 in spirelike raceme. Lvs bractlike. Stems rose to reddish or yellowish brown, ht 12"–40", sticky, persisting as dry stalks. Forest, Alas to Cal, s in RM to NMex, e to Atl. Sum.

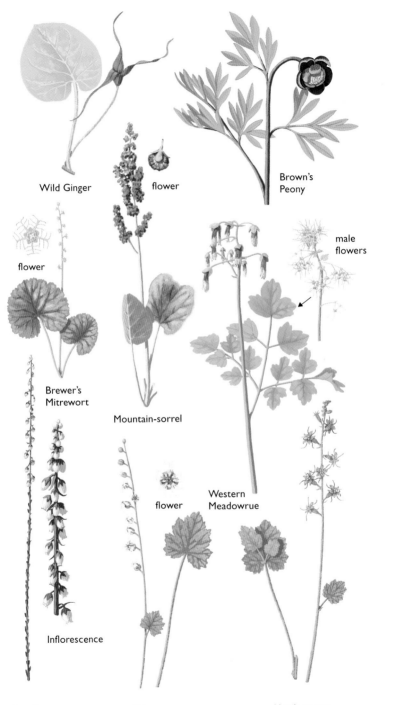

Wild Ginger

flower

Brown's Peony

flower

Brewer's Mitrewort

Mountain-sorrel

male flowers

Inflorescence

flower

Western Meadowrue

Pinedrops

Fringecup

Youth-on-age

6

shrubs

A shrub is a woody plant less than 15 feet tall with more than one main stem. Some trees, however, may be decidedly shrubby, especially in harsh environments where conditions inhibit normal growth. Moreover, some shrubs may exceed 15 feet in height or have one short, trunklike stem. Well over 100 species of shrubs occur within our range. These include erect shrubs, some large and treelike; prostrate or mat-forming plants; woody vines; and a few species, such as twinflower and bunchberry dogwood, which are herblike in general appearance but have more or less woody stems. Subshrubs are included with wildflowers in chapter 5, Flowering Plants. Plants that are typically treelike and only occasionally shrubby in our region are included among the trees in chapter 7.

While herbaceous plants are usually conspicuous only when in flower, shrubs catch our attention year-round. Some species have showy flowers or fruits, but these aids to identification may not always be present. Many other species have inconspicuous fruits and flowers that, even when they are present, may be of little help to an untrained observer. It is important, then, when attempting to identify shrubs, to pay particular attention to the stems and leaves.

The great majority of shrubs occurring in our region are illustrated in the following pages. The chief exceptions include members of the larger genera, such as *Ribes* (currants and gooseberries) and *Salix* (willows), which are represented by only about a half-dozen species each. In both cases, species often may be distinguished largely or solely on the basis of rather obscure, technical differences.

Among the trees, the following species are sometimes shrubby. Elfinwood (prostrate timberline trees): lodgepole pine, whitebark pine, subalpine fir, Engelmann spruce, mountain hemlock, yellow-cedar. Broadleaf trees: Pacific willow, water birch (see paper birch), golden chinquapin, Oregon oak, western crabapple, cascara, buckthorn.

Scientific names conform to those in *USDA Plant Database* (U.S. Department of Agriculture, Natural Resources Conservation Service; 2002; version 3.5; *http://plants.usda.gov;* National Plant Data Center). The common names, with some exceptions, are from the same source.

For information on the organization and use of the species descriptions and illustrations, as well as for a list of the abbreviations used in the accounts, see the Introduction. See also chapter 5, Flowering Plants, for a glossary and illustrations of plant terms.

PLATE 44

CYPRESS FAMILY (CUPRESSACEAE)

Common (dwarf) juniper, *Juniperus communis.* Prostrate evergreen shrub, mat forming. Lvs awl shaped, with shallow white channels, in whorls of 3, numerous on stems. Fruit a dk blue berrylike cone with whitish bloom. Bark scaly, gray-brown. Rocky places, subalp-alp, Alas to Cal, e to Atl; Eurasia. Cf junipers, plate 58.

WILLOW FAMILY (SALICACEAE)

Willows, *Salix* spp. Prostrate decid shrubs to trees. Lvs simple, alt, decid, short petioled, linear to oval or obovate, toothed or entire, smooth, hairy, or covered with powdery bloom on 1 or both sides. Flrs tiny, in erect M and F catkins on different plants. Nearly 24 spp in our mtns from BC to n Cal, most easily recognized as willows but notoriously difficult to separate by species. Following spp are com and + representative. Snow willow, *S. nivalis,* one of 3 similar, prostrate, mat-forming, timberline shrubs in our mtns. Undergreen willow, *S. commutata,* a com shrub, ht 3'-9', of wet places below timberline. Scouler's willow, *S. scouleriana,* a com shrub or small tree, ht 3'-35'±, along streams at low-mid el throughout the region. Also cf Pacific willow, plate 59.

BIRCH FAMILY (BETULACEAE)

Bog (swamp) birch, *Betula glandulosa.* Decid shrub, ht gen to 10'. Lvs oval, L ca ¾", scalloped or toothed, thick and leathery. Bark reddish brown with white spots, smooth on trunk, sticky and warty on branches. Wet places, lowl-mont, Alas to Cal, e to RM, ne US, e Can. Cf paper birch, plate 59.

Sitka (slide) alder, *Alnus sinuata.* Decid shrub, ht gen 10'-15'. Lvs ovate, with sharply pointed but not spiny tip, L to 4", double toothed. Catkins borne after lvs in sum. Fruit, clusters of 3-6 woody cones, L ca ½". Very com, moist places, avalanche tracks, in all our mtns, Alas to n Cal, e to Idaho. Mountain alder, *A. incana,* similar but lvs have rounded, ± blunt, or only slightly pointed tip and catkins appear in spring before lvs; E CMtns–Cas. Cf red alder, plate 59.

California hazelnut, *Corylus cornuta* var *californica.* Decid shrub, ht gen 3'-12'. Lvs ovate to heart shaped, coarsely toothed, ± hairy on both surfaces and pale beneath. Catkins yellow, borne before lvs. Fruit a hard-shelled edible nut in leafy cover. Com, lowl–low mont, BC to Cal, e to Idaho.

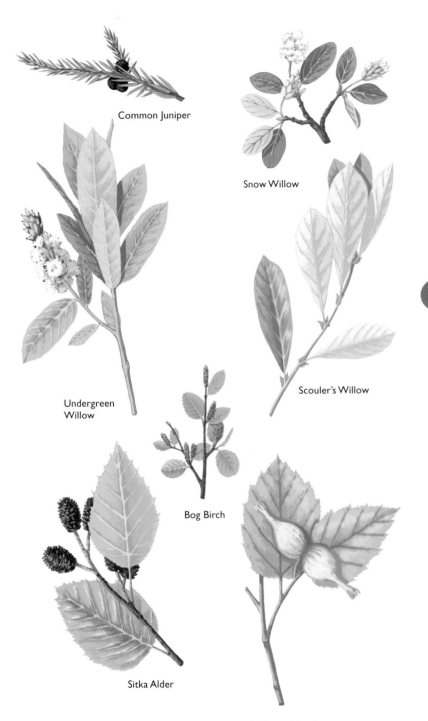

Common Juniper

Snow Willow

Undergreen
Willow

Scouler's Willow

Bog Birch

Sitka Alder

California Hazelnut

PLATE 45

BARBERRY FAMILY (BERBERIDACEAE)

Cascade Oregon-grape, *Mahonia nervosa.* Low, spreading evergreen shrub, ht gen 4"–12", with perst bud scales on stems. Lvs pinnately compound, L oft 12"–20", with 9–19 dull green, palmately veined, spiny-toothed, leathery lflets. Flrs in erect racemes. Fruit a sour blue berry with powdery bloom, in grapelike clusters. Gen open woods, Vanc I e to Cas, s to Cal. Tall Oregon-grape, *M. aquifolium,* very similar but taller (ht 3'–6'), with only 5–9 pinnately veined lflets. Creeping Oregon-grape, *M. repens,* is also a low, spreading shrub, but with 5–7 pinnately veined lflets; E Cas only.

HYDRANGEA FAMILY (HYDRANGEACEAE)

Mock orange, *Philadelphus lewisii.* Decid shrub, ht ca 5'–15'. Lvs ovate to oval, entire or minutely toothed, smooth or hairy, L ca 1"–4", with 3 main veins. Flrs fragrant, white, ca 1" diam. Streamsides, talus, cliffs, rocky places, gen low-mid el, BC to n Cal, e to Idaho, Mont.

CURRANT OR GOOSEBERRY FAMILY (GROSSULARIACEAE)

Gooseberries and currants, *Ribes* spp. Decid shrubs. Gooseberries have prickly fruits and stems; currants are without prickles; otherwise, the two are similar. More than 24 spp in our range. The following spp are com and representative.

Stink currant, *Ribes bracteosum.* Erect, oft straggly shrubs, ht to 10'. Lvs deeply 5- to 7-lobed, ill-smelling, 2"–8" wide, ½ as long, with yellow resin glands beneath. Flrs saucer shaped, greenish, in erect racemes with leafy bracts. Fruit a rough blk berry, in erect clusters 4"–8" long. Alas to n Cal, gen in and w of Cas.

Gummy gooseberry, *Ribes lobbii.* Shrub, ht 3'–6½', with 3-spined nodes on downy, not bristly, stems. Lvs 3- to 5-lobed, toothed, less than 1¼" wide, sticky haired beneath. Flr L ca 1", with sharply reflexed red sepals ca 2**x** as long as petals. Fruit a bristly, sticky, ± palatable purple berry. Moist places, lowl-mont, BC to Cal, mostly E Cas.

Sticky currant, *Ribes viscosissimum.* Erect or spreading, oft straggly shrub, ht to ca 6'. Lvs 3- to 5-lobed, 1"–3" wide, glandular, gen hairless except occas on veins. Flrs tubular, greenish white tinged with pink, gen 6–12 in ± erect raceme with large bracts, sticky haired throughout. Fruit a blk, sticky-haired berry. Various habitats, lowl-subalp, mostly E Cas, BC to Cal; e to RM.

Red-flowering currant, *Ribes sanguineum.* Erect shrub, ht 3'–10'. Lvs 3- to 5-lobed, double toothed, densely hairy beneath, 1¼"–3¼" wide. Flrs tubular, in showy racemes. Fruit an unpalatable blk berry with whitish bloom. Various habitats, lowl–low mont, BC to Cal, coast to E Cas in Wn and Ore.

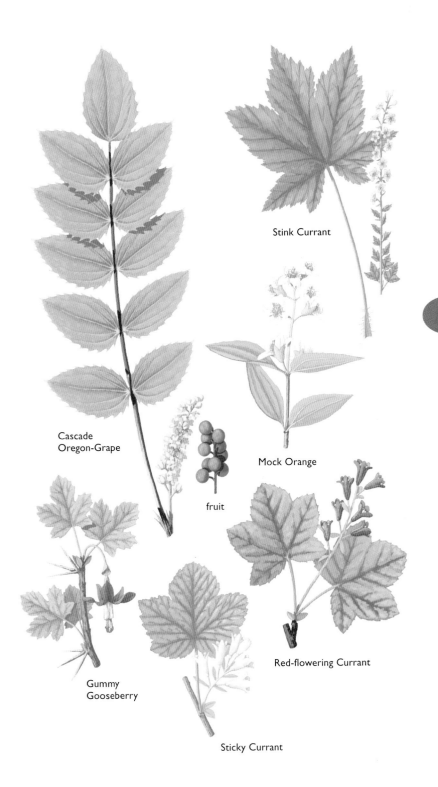

Stink Currant

Cascade
Oregon-Grape

fruit

Mock Orange

Gummy
Gooseberry

Red-flowering Currant

Sticky Currant

PLATE 46

ROSE FAMILY (ROSACEAE)

Western serviceberry, *Amelanchier alnifolia.* Spreading or erect shrub or small tree, ht gen 3'–16'. Lvs alt, decid, petioled, oval to oblong or wedge shaped, usu toothed toward tip, L ¾"–2", ± silky to hairless beneath. Flrs fragrant, white, ca 1" diam, 3–20 in short, erect racemes. Fruit an unpalatable reddish or blk berry. Open woods, rocky places, lowl–subalp, Alas s to Cal and NMex, e to mid US.

Black hawthorn, *Crataegus douglasii.* Decid shrub or small tree, ht gen 3'–13'. Branches armed with sharp thorns usu L ca ¾". Lvs oval to wedge shaped, petioled, blade L to 3", with sharp teeth or toothed and lobed at tip. Flrs white, ca ½" diam. Fruit small, dk purple "apples." Bark brown or gray, rough. In mtns, gen near water at low el, Alas to Cal, e to mid US and e Can.

Mountain-avens, *Dryas octopetala.* Prostrate, mat-forming evergreen shrub. Lf L ca 1", narrowly lancelike to oblong, deep green and wrinkled above, hairy and glandular beneath, margins scalloped and rolled under. Flrs cream or white, 1" diam, with 7–8 petals. Fruit a showy head of plumed seeds. Gravel bars, talus, alp ridges, mdws, mont-alp, Alas to Wn Cas, e to e Can, ne US, s in RM to Colo, also ne Ore.

Indian plum, *Oemleria cerasiformis.* Decid shrub, ht 5'–16'. Lf blade L 2"–5", entire, oblanceolate to elliptic, hairless above, paler and oft hairy beneath. Flrs small, greenish white, 5–10 per raceme from lf axils, fragrant. Fruit a bitter blue-blk berry. Bark purplish brown. Stream banks, woods, BC to Cal, W Cas to coast.

Olympic rockmat, *Petrophytum hendersonii.* Matted evergreen shrublet. Lf L ¼"–¾", + spoon shaped, entire, tufted, ± hairy. Flrs tiny, in dense spikelike racemes above lvs. Cliffs, talus, mid-high el, OMtns.

Creambush (ocean spray), *Holodiscus discolor.* Decid shrub, ht 1½'–10'. Lf L 1½"–3", shallowly lobed or toothed, hairy beneath. Flrs white, tiny, numerous in loose panicles 4"–7" long. Rocky places, open forest, lowl–low mont, BC to Cal, e to w Mont, Idaho, ne Ore.

Pacific ninebark, *Physocarpus capitatus.* Spreading to erect decid shrub, ht gen 6½'–13'. Lf blade 3- to 5-lobed, L 1"–4", doubly toothed, gen hairy beneath. Flrs ca ¾" diam, in corymbs terminating leafy twigs. Flrs replaced by reddish seed husks in sum. Bark peeling. Damp places, lowl–low mont, Alas to Cal, Cas to coast; n Idaho.

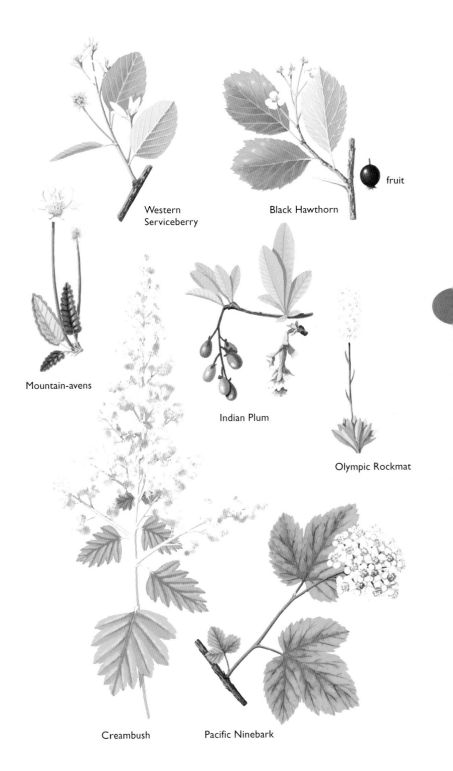

Western Serviceberry

Black Hawthorn

fruit

Mountain-avens

Indian Plum

Olympic Rockmat

Creambush

Pacific Ninebark

PLATE 47

ROSE FAMILY (ROSACEAE)

Shrubby cinquefoil, *Dasiphora floribunda.* Spreading to erect shrub, ht gen 4"–40". Lvs pinnate, usu with 5 lflets, L ca to ¾", entire, silky haired. Flrs to 1" diam, yellow, showy, single in lf axils or in branched inflor. Bark reddish brown, shreddy. Rocky places, in our range mostly subalp, Alas to Cal, e to RM, e Can, ne US; Eurasia.

Bitter cherry, *Prunus emarginata* var *emarginata.* Multistemmed decid shrub, ht gen 3'–13'. Lf blades ± elliptic or oblong, L 1¼"–3", margins finely toothed or scalloped, smooth to rather hairy. Flrs ca ¼" diam, white, 5–10 in loose inflor. Fruit a bitter, red to almost blk cherry. Bark dk brown to reddish purple. Moist woods, streamsides, mainly in Cas, BC to Cal, e to RM. *P. e.* var *mollis,* gen a tree to 50' tall, occurs mainly w of Cas from s BC to s Ore.

Common chokecherry, *Prunus virginiana.* Decid shrub or small tree, ht to 20'. Lf blades ± elliptic or oblong, L 2"–4", fine-toothed, paler and downy or hairless beneath, with 2 knobby glands on petiole. Flrs in spikelike racemes, L gen 3"–5". Fruit a puckery red to blk cherry, numerous in grapelike clusters. Low-mid el in our mtns; widespread in US and s Can.

Antelope (bitter) brush, *Purshia tridentata.* Decid shrub, ht gen 3'–6'. Lvs gen in fascicles, wedge shaped, 3-toothed at tip, L to ¾", greenish above, densely gray-haired beneath, margins ± curled under. Flrs solitary, yellow, calyx sticky haired. Fruit a downy "nutlet." Sagebrush steppe and ponderosa pine forest, E Cas, BC to Cal; widespread e to RM, s to NMex.

Nootka rose, *Rosa nutkana.* Decid shrub, ht to gen 3'–6', with thorns below ea lf. Lvs pinnate, usu with 5–9 oval or ovate toothed lflets, sticky haired beneath, lf axis sticky, oft prickly. Flrs to 3½" diam, gen solitary, with perst sepals. Fruit a rosehip crowned with sepals. Moist, gen wooded places, usu mont, Alas to Cal, C to RM. Baldhip rose, *R. gymnocarpa,* ± similar but plant and flr (to 1" diam) both smaller, stems prickly, rosehip without sepals.

Red raspberry, *Rubus idaeus.* Decid shrub, ht gen to 6½'. Branches bristly and spiny, spines stout, straight. Lvs compound, 3–5 lflets doubly toothed, gray-woolly beneath. Flrs white, less than ¾" diam, with petals shorter than sepals, in short, sticky, bristly racemes. Fruit a red raspberry. Widespread in N Amer and Eurasia. Blackcap raspberry, *R. leucodermis,* has hooked spines and ± blk berries.

Thimbleberry, *Rubus parviflorus.* Erect, unarmed decid shrub, ht to 10'. Lvs 4"–8" wide, palmate, gen 5-lobed, double toothed, velvety above and beneath. Flrs white, to 2" diam. Fruit a bland, rather dry red raspberry. Very com, open places and woods, lowl-subalp, Alas to s Cal, e to RM.

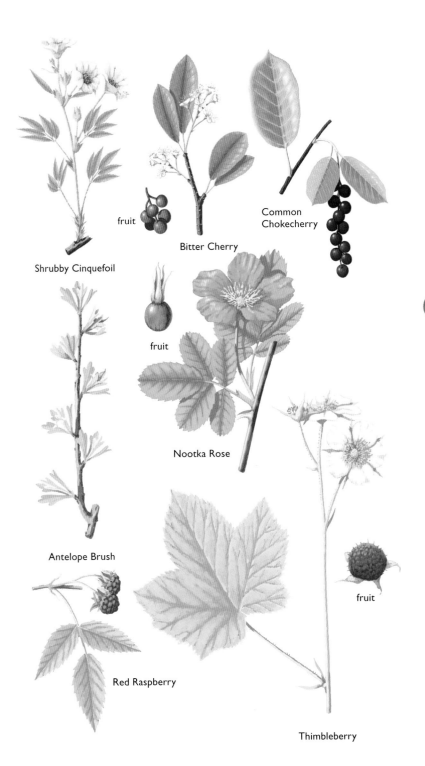

Shrubby Cinquefoil

fruit

Bitter Cherry

Common
Chokecherry

fruit

Nootka Rose

Antelope Brush

Red Raspberry

fruit

Thimbleberry

PLATE 48

ROSE FAMILY (ROSACEAE)

Salmonberry, *Rubus spectabilis.* Decid shrub, ht to 16'. Stems erect, weakly armed when young, unarmed with age. Lvs 3-compound, toothed. Flrs ca 1" diam, rosy pink, showy, usu solitary. Fruit salmon orange to red, sweet, bland. Moist places, lowl–mid-mtn, Alas to nw Cal, Cas to coast.

Pacific blackberry, *Rubus ursinus.* Trailing decid shrub. Branches spined. Lvs 3-compound or simple and 3-lobed, lflets ± oval, toothed, downy. Flrs white or pale pink. Fruit a choice blackberry. Lowl-mont, BC to n Cal, e to Idaho.

Subalpine spiraea, *Spiraea splendens.* Decid shrub, ht 8"–40". Lvs ± oval, L to 1½", tips blunt or rounded and toothed. Flrs small, pink to red, numerous in dense, flat-topped inflor. Moist open places, rocky slopes, low-high mtns, BC to Cal, e to n RM. Douglas spiraea, *S. douglasii,* similar but inflor pyramidal; lowl.

Sitka mountain-ash, *Sorbus sitchensis.* Decid shrub, ht to 13' in our region. Lvs pinnate with 7–11 elliptic to oblong lflets with blunt or rounded tips, oft red-haired midvein and marginal teeth gen confined to upper ½–¾ of lflet. Flrs small, creamy, numerous in flat-topped inflor. Fruit a red berry with bluish cast from waxy bloom. Open, gen moist places, mont-subalp, Alas to n Cal, e to n RM. Cascade mountain-ash, *S. scopulina,* very similar but lflets narrower, pointed at tip, oft white-haired along midvein, finely toothed entire length, berries without waxy bloom.

STAFF-TREE FAMILY (CELASTRACEAE)

Oregon boxleaf, *Paxistima myrsinite.* Evergreen shrub, ht gen 8"–24". Lvs opp, leathery, ± oblong or lancelike, toothed, hairless, L ca 1". Flrs maroon, flat, 4-petaled. Gen open places at mid el in mtns, BC to Cal, e to RM.

PEA FAMILY (FABACEAE)

Scotch broom, *Cytisus scoparius.* Decid shrub, ht to 10' tall. Branches numerous, green, broomlike, strongly angled. Lvs compound near base of branches, simple above. Flrs irreg, sweetpealike, yellow, L ca ¾", ± covering plant. Fruit a flattened pod. Com, roadsides, waste places, BC to Cal; introduced from Europe.

SUMAC FAMILY (ANACARDIACEAE)

Poison-oak, *Toxicodendron diversiloba.* Erect decid shrub, ht to 6'. Lvs compound, 3 lflets gen toothed, lobed. Flrs greenish white, in axillary panicles. Fruit a white or brownish berry. Dry woods, open places, entirely w of Cas crest at low el, sw Wn to Baja. Poison-ivy, *T. radicans,* similar, twining vine on grnd or tree trunks, found sparingly at low el, E Cas of Wn and Ore. Both cause contact dermatitis in most people.

CROWBERRY FAMILY (EMPETRACEAE)

Crowberry, *Empetrum nigrum.* Spreading evergreen shrub, ht to 6". Branches ± woolly. Lvs needlelike, alt and whorled in 4s, L ca ¼", sticky haired, grooved beneath. Flrs obscure, pinkish or purplish, 3-sepaled, no petals. Fruit a + bitter blk berry. Peat bogs, rocky places, Alas to n Cal, Cas to coast.

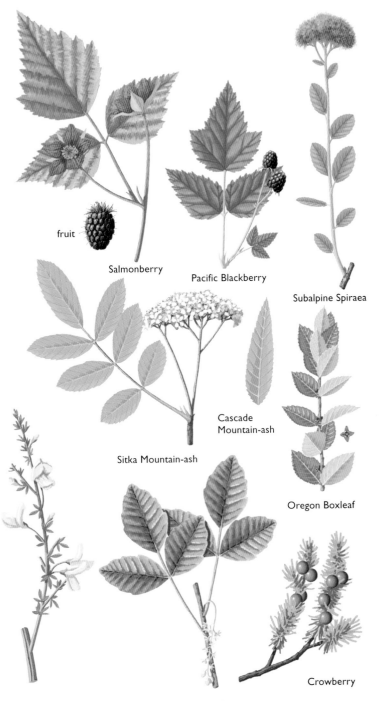

fruit

Salmonberry

Pacific Blackberry

Subalpine Spiraea

Cascade
Mountain-ash

Sitka Mountain-ash

Oregon Boxleaf

Scotch Broom

Poison-oak

Crowberry

PLATE 49

MAPLE FAMILY (ACERACEAE)

Vine maple, *Acer circinatum.* Decid shrub or small tree, ht 3'–26'. Lvs 2"–6" wide, palmately 7- to 9-lobed, double toothed, red or yellow in fall. Flrs white, red sepaled, in loose inflor. Fruit a double samara. Com, lowl-subalp, Alas to n Cal, E Cas to coast.

Douglas' maple, *Acer glabrum* var *douglasii.* Decid shrub or small tree, ht to 25'. Lvs 1"–3" wide, palmate, 3- to 5-lobed, red in fall. Flrs yellow, in panicle. Fruit a double samara. Moist places, lowl-mont, BC to Cal, e to Idaho and Mont.

BUCKTHORN FAMILY (RHAMNACEAE)

Snow bush, *Ceanothus cordulatus.* Spreading evergreen shrub, ht 3'–6½'. Stiff spiny twigs. Lvs ovate or elliptic, ± entire, L to ¾", 3-veined, hairless or downy, green with bloom above, gray-green beneath. Flrs small, white, fragrant, in dense inflor. Bark smooth, whitish. Dry forest openings, mid-high el, Cas, s Ore and Cal, throughout Cal.

Deer brush, *Ceanothus integerrimus.* Decid shrub, ht 3'–13'. Branches green or yellow; twigs smooth or hairy, flexible. Lf blades thin, oblong to ovate, entire, 3-veined, L to 2¾", pale green and downy to smooth above, paler and usu downy beneath. Flrs white (pink or blue), fragrant, sticky, in dense inflor. Dry mont places, E Cas, Wn to Cal, s to Baja, e to NMex.

Alderleaf buckthorn, *Rhamnus alnifolia.* Erect decid shrub, ht to 5'. Lf blades ± oval, toothed, thin, bright green, L ca 2½", with 5–7 pairs of parallel veins. Flrs without petals, greenish, 2–5 in stalkless umbels. Wet, brushy places, E Cas s to Cal, e to Atl.

Mahala mat, *Ceanothus prostratus.* Prostrate evergreen shrub, mat forming. Lvs thick and fleshy, sharp toothed, L to 1", pale glossy green above, finely haired beneath. Flrs tiny, blue, in umbel-like inflor. Dry forest floor, E Cas, Wn to Cal.

Redstem ceanothus (Oregon tea-tree), *Ceanothus sanguineus.* Erect decid shrub, ht 5'–10'. Twigs flexible, smooth, reddish. Lf blades ± oval, L to 4", nearly hairless, rarely shiny or sticky above, with small glandular teeth and decid stipules. Flrs white, fragrant, in compound inflor 4"–8" long. Dry open places in mtns, Cas, BC to Cal, e to Idaho and Mont. Tobacco brush (mountain balm, greasewood, sticky laurel), *C. velutinus,* similar but lvs evergreen, varnished and sticky above, stipules tiny and perst.

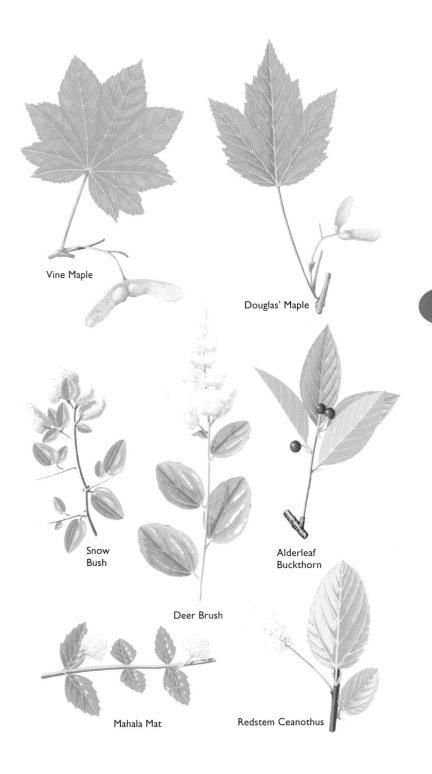

Vine Maple

Douglas' Maple

Snow
Bush

Deer Brush

Alderleaf
Buckthorn

Mahala Mat

Redstem Ceanothus

PLATE 50

GINSENG FAMILY (ARALIACEAE)

Devil's club, *Oplopanax horridus.* Decid shrub, ht 3'–10', with stems, petioles and lf veins densely armed with yellowish spines to ⅜" long. Lf blades palmately 7- to 9-lobed, 4"–14" wide, toothed, long petioled. Flrs small, greenish white, in headlike umbels borne in inflor to 10" long. Fruit a bright red berry. Moist woods, streamsides, Alas s along coast and in mtns to s Ore, e to e Can, Mich.

DOGWOOD FAMILY (CORNACEAE)

Bunchberry dogwood, *Cornus canadensis.* Low, trailing evergreen shrublet, ht 2"–8". Lvs ovate or elliptic, L to 3", 4–7 in whorl below inflor. Flrs tiny, greenish, in head surrounded by 4 showy, gen white, petal-like bracts. Fruit, red berries in tight clusters. Com, moist woods, Alas to Cal and NMex, e to e Can, ne US; Greenland, Asia.

Red-osier dogwood, *Cornus sericea.* Decid shrub, ht 6½'–20', with some rooting lower stems. Lf blades ± oval, entire, L to 4¾", ± hairy above, hairy or with powdery bloom beneath. Flrs tiny, white or bluish, in dense inflor. Bark reddish. Moist thickets, widespread in N Amer.

SILKTASSEL FAMILY (GARRYACEAE)

Fremont's silktassel, *Garrya fremontii.* Erect evergreen shrub, ht 4'–10'. Lvs opp, elliptic to ovate or oblong, L to 3½", entire, shiny yellow-green above, paler beneath, oft hairy when young. Flrs in tassel-like catkins. Woodland and brush, W Cas, Ore to Cal.

FIGWORT FAMILY (SCROPHULARIACEAE)

Shrubby penstemon, *Penstemon fruticosus.* Decid shrub, ht 6"–16". Branches ascending from woody base. Lvs variable, ± elliptic or oval, entire or toothed, opp. Flrs lavender, bluish, purplish, occas white, 2-lipped, L 1"–2", very showy. Fruit a capsule. Lowl-subalp, mostly E Cas, BC to Ore, e to Mont, Wyo.

ASTER OR SUNFLOWER FAMILY (ASTERACEAE)

Big sagebrush, *Artemisia tridentata.* Erect evergreen shrub, ht gen ½'–6½'. Lvs wedge shaped, 3-toothed at tip, gray-green with matted hairs above and beneath, alt, oft in fascicles. Flr heads with disk flrs only, numerous in large, loose inflor. E CMtns–Cas, BC to Cal; widespread in w US, BC to Mex.

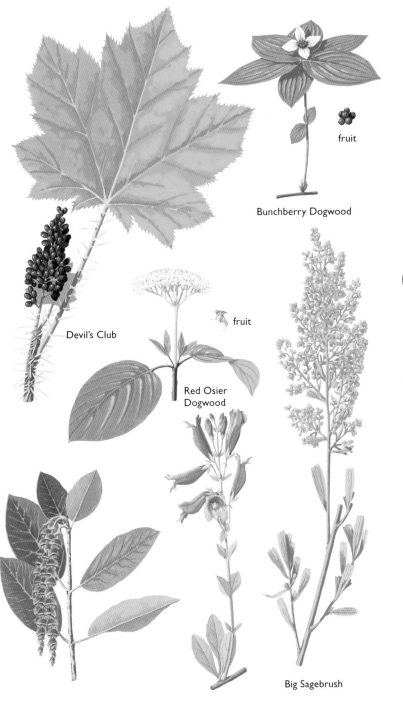

Bunchberry Dogwood

fruit

Devil's Club

fruit

Red Osier
Dogwood

Big Sagebrush

Fremont's Silktassel

Shrubby Penstemon

PLATE 51

HEAT FAMILY (ERICACEAE)

Pinemat manzanita, *Arctostaphylos nevadensis.* Evergreen prostrate shrub, ht to 8". Lvs oblong to spoon shaped, sharply tipped, L to 1½", thick and leathery. Flrs white, occas pink, L ca ¼", in short racemes. Fruit a smooth, dk brown berry. Bark reddish brown, peeling in strips. Dry woods, openings, Wn Cas to Cal, also ne Ore.

Kinnickinnick, *Arctostaphylos uva-ursi.* Evergreen prostrate shrub, ht to 6". Lvs spoon shaped or ovate, L to 1", rounded or blunt at tip, thick and leathery. Flrs white or pinkish, L ca ¼", in short racemes. Fruit a red berry. Bark reddish brown, shredding. Dry woods, openings, Alas to Cal, e to RM and e US.

Greenleaf manzanita, *Arctostaphylos patula.* Erect evergreen shrub, ht 3'–7'. Lvs ovate to ± round, L to 1¾", hairless, entire. Flrs pinkish, L ca ¼", in dense panicles. Fruit a smooth, dk brown berry. Bark reddish brown, peeling. Gen dry forest, E Cas, s Wn to Cal, W Cas Ore and Cal; Cal mtns, e to RM.

White mountain-heather, *Cassiope mertensiana.* Mat-forming evergreen shrub, ht to 12". Lvs broadly lancelike, tiny, in 4 rows flattened to stems, rounded on back. Flrs white, 1 per stalk. Com, open areas, subalp-alp, Alas to Cal, e to RM. Four-angled mountain-heather, *C. tetragona,* very similar but lvs grooved on back; Alas to NCas. Alaska mountain-heather, *Harrimanella stelleriana,* similar but lvs alt, not flattened against stem; Alas s to Mt. Rainier.

Copper bush, *Elliottia pyroliflorus.* Erect decid shrub, ht 2'–7'. Lvs spoon shaped, L 1"–2", sharply tipped, entire, pale green, hairless, occas with bloom. Flrs copper colored, to 1¼" diam. Bark peeling. Moist places, mont-subalp, Alas to n Ore, Cas to coast.

Salal, *Gaultheria shallon.* Creeping or erect evergreen shrub, ht gen 4"–80". Lvs thick, leathery, ovate, toothed, gen glossy, L 2"–5". Flrs bell shaped, white or pink, in sticky-haired inflor. Fruit a sweet, pungent blk "berry." Com, forest, lowl-mont, E Cas to coast, BC to Cal.

Alpine wintergreen, *Gaultheria humifusa.* Prostrate evergreen shrublet, ht scarcely 1¼". Lvs ± oval or round, L to ¾", entire or toothed. Flrs white, bell shaped, calyx hairless. Fruit reddish. Subalp-alp, in all our mtns s to n Cal, e to RM. Slender wintergreen, *G. ovatifolia,* similar but lvs larger and calyx red-hairy.

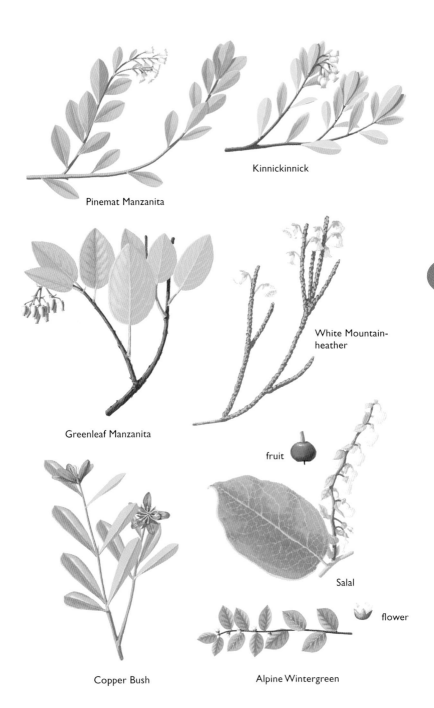

Pinemat Manzanita

Kinnickinnick

Greenleaf Manzanita

White Mountain-
heather

Copper Bush

Salal

fruit

Alpine Wintergreen

flower

PLATE 52

HEATH FAMILY (ERICACEAE)

Mountain labrador-tea, *Ledum glandulosum.* Erect evergreen shrub, ht to ca 6½'. Lvs ovate to elliptic, L to 2", dk green and smooth above, paler, mealy, and/or finely haired beneath. Flrs white. Moist, shady places, BC to Cal, e to RM. Bog labrador-tea, *L. groenlandicum,* similar but lvs gen narrower and rusty-haired beneath.

Fool's huckleberry (menziesia), *Menziesia ferruginea.* Straggling decid shrub, ht 1½'–6½'. Lvs elliptic to obovate, L 1½"–2½", blue-green and oft sticky above, whitish beneath, finely haired on both sides, alt but in whorl-like groups. Flrs copper colored, urn shaped, with sticky calyx. Fruit a 4- to 5-celled capsule. Com, moist places, lowl-subalp, Alas to Cal, e to RM.

Red mountain-heather, *Phyllodoce empetriformis.* Dwarf evergreen shrub, ht 4"–16". Lvs needlelike, L ca ½", numerous on stems. Flrs pink, bell shaped, L ca ¼", single in lf axils near stem tips. Fruit a 5-celled capsule. Open places, gen subalp, Alas to Cal, e to RM. Brewer's mountain-heather, *P. breweri,* with stamens extending beyond corolla, replaces this sp s of Mt. Shasta.

Alpine-laurel (western swamp laurel), *Kalmia microphylla.* Low, spreading evergreen shrub, ht to 6". Lvs opp, dk green above, gray and downy beneath, ± oblong or elliptic, gen L to ¾". Flrs pink, saucer shaped, few in inflor. Wet mdws, bogs, low el to subalp-alp, Alas to Cal, e to RM.

Yellow mountain-heather, *Phyllodoce glanduliflora.* Evergreen shrub, ht to 12". Lvs needlelike, L ca ¼", numerous on stems. Flrs yellow to greenish white, urn shaped, sticky-haired. Open places, gen subalp-alp, Alas to Ore, e to Can RM.

Pacific rhododendron, *Rhododendron macrophyllum.* Evergreen, occas treelike shrub, ht to 15'+. Lvs leathery, oblong-elliptic, L to 8". Flrs white to rose purple, L ca 1½", tubular to bell shaped with flaring lobes, in dense, rounded, terminal inflor. Very showy. Drier woods, coastal forest, W Cas to coast, BC to nw Cal.

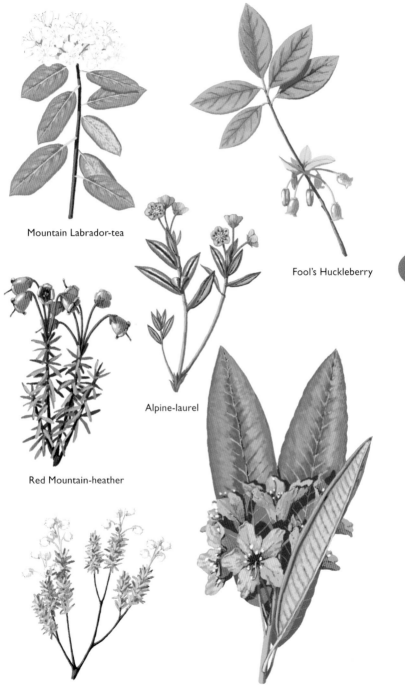

Mountain Labrador-tea

Fool's Huckleberry

Alpine-laurel

Red Mountain-heather

Yellow Mountain-heather

Pacific Rhododendron

PLATE 53

HEATH FAMILY (ERICACEAE)

Cascade azalea (white rhododendron), *Rhododendron albiflorum.* Decid shrub, ht ca 3'–6½'. Twigs sticky haired. Lvs + oval, dk green above, paler beneath, rusty-haired when young. Flrs white, ca ¾" diam, in axillary inflor. Moist places, mont-subalp, BC to Ore, e to Mont.

Western azalea, *Rhododendron occidentale.* Decid shrub, ht 3'–16'. Lvs elliptic to obovate, L 1"–4", entire, slightly hairy. Flrs white, oft tinged pink or yellow at throat, L ca 1½", 5–20 in terminal inflor. Moist places, low-mid el, Cas, s Ore to Cal mtns.

Oval-leaved blueberry, *Vaccinium ovalifolium.* Decid shrub, ht to 48". Lvs + elliptic, entire or minutely toothed, L to 2⅜", dk green and slightly waxy above, paler beneath. Flrs urn shaped, bronzy pink, sharply constricted at mouth, with pedicels straight, swollen just below flr. Fruit a choice, blue to blk berry ca ¼" diam. Moist forest, lowl-mont, Alas to nw Ore, Cas to coast.

Cascade blueberry, *Vaccinium deliciosum.* Low, oft matted decid shrub, ht gen 6"–12". Twigs greenish brown, circular in cross section. Lvs obovate, L ⅝"–2⅜", thick, finely toothed above base, with powdery bloom beneath. Flrs pinkish, nearly spherical. Fruit a choice blue to blk berry with bloom. Mont-alp, but esp subalp mdws, BC to n Ore, Cas to coast. Dwarf blueberry, *V. caespitosum,* similar but lvs lack bloom beneath and flrs tubular.

Thinleaf blueberry, *Vaccinium membranaceum.* Decid shrub, ht 3'–10'. Twigs slightly angled in cross section. Lvs ovate or oval, slender-pointed, L 1"–2", toothed, bright green above, paler and sticky or with bloom beneath. Flrs yellowish pink, urn shaped. Fruit an extremely choice purplish berry. Com, open places, mont-subalp, BC to Cal, e to RM.

Evergreen huckleberry, *Vaccinium ovatum.* Evergreen shrub, ht 1½'–13'. Twigs hairy, branches very lfy. Lvs oval to ovate, leathery, glossy dk green above, sharply toothed. Flrs pink or white. Fruit a sweet purple or blk berry. Coastal forest, lowl-low mont, W Cas to coast, BC to Cal.

Red huckleberry, *Vaccinium parvifolium.* Open-branched decid shrub, ht gen 3'–6'. Branches green, angled in cross section. Lvs oval to ± round, thin, entire, pale green, L to 1". Flrs reddish or greenish. Fruit a red berry. Forest, esp on logs and stumps, lowl-low mont, BC to Cal, W Cas to coast.

Grouseberry (whortleberry), *Vaccinium scoparium.* Mat-forming decid shrub, ht 4"–12". Branches numerous, broomlike. Lvs + ovate, gen smooth, finely toothed, L ca ½". Flrs pink. Fruit a sweet, bright red berry. Woods, open places, subalp-alp. Mostly E Cas, s BC to Cal; e to RM, SDak. Dwarf bilberry, *V. myrtillus,* similar but branches few and not broomlike.

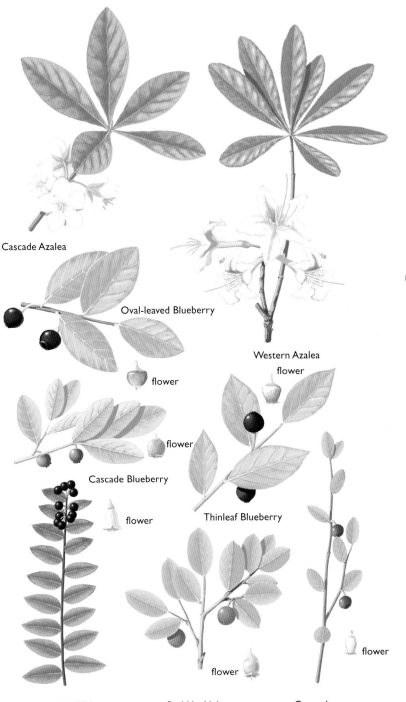

Cascade Azalea

Oval-leaved Blueberry

flower

Western Azalea
flower

flower

Cascade Blueberry

flower

Thinleaf Blueberry

flower

flower

Evergreen Huckleberry   Red Huckleberry   Grouseberry

PLATE 54

HONEYSUCKLE FAMILY (CAPRIFOLIACEAE)

Twinflower, *Linnaea borealis.* Creeping, herblike, evergreen shrublet with erect flr stalks to 4" tall. Lvs opp, ± oval, L to 1", with a few shallow teeth or entire. Flrs pink, 2 on erect, forked stalk. Moist woods, N Amer s to Cal, Ariz, NMex, e to W Vir.

Orange (trumpet, northwest) honeysuckle, *Lonicera ciliosa.* Trailing or twining woody decid vine with stems to 20' long. Lvs opp, upper pair perfoliate, ± oval, entire, with waxy bloom beneath. Flrs orange, funnel shaped, L to 1¾". Woods, thickets, low-mid el, s BC to n Cal, e to w Mont. Purple honeysuckle, *L. hispidula,* also a woody vine but flrs pink to purple and some lvs have united stipules.

Blue elderberry, *Sambucus nigra.* Decid shrub occas treelike, ht gen 6½'–13'. Lvs opp, long petioled, pinnate, with 5–11 lancelike or elliptic, toothed, oft asymmetrical lflets to 6" long. Flrs white or creamy, small, numerous in flat-topped inflor. Fruit a dk blue berry with whitish bloom. Open areas, lowl-mont, BC s to Mex, e to RM.

Black twinberry (honeysuckle), *Lonicera involucrata.* Erect decid shrub, ht 3'–13'. Lvs opp, oval to spoon shaped, L 2"–5", abruptly pointed at tip. Flrs yellow, occas tinged red, tubular, L ca 1", in 2s from lf axils. Fruit a pair of blk berries. Widespread in mtns of w N Amer. Utah honeysuckle, *L. utahensis,* similar but lvs rounded at tip and berries red, ± united at base. Double honeysuckle, *L.conjugalis,* has broadly elliptic to ovate lvs and pairs of red-purple flrs.

Coast red elderberry, *Sambucus racemosa* var *arborescens.* Large, occas treelike decid shrub, ht 10'–20'. Lvs like those of blue elderberry. Flrs creamy white, in pyramidal inflor. Fruit a red berry without powdery bloom. Moist woods, open places. BC to Cal, e to Atl. Black elderberry, *S. r.* var *melanocarpa,* similar to blue elderberry but fruit lacks bloom.

Common snowberry, *Symphoricarpos albus.* Erect decid shrub, ht gen 3'–6½'. Lvs opp, blade L gen ⅜"–2", ± elliptic, entire or toothed, smooth above, smooth or sparsely hairy beneath. Flrs bell shaped, hairy inside, pinkish. Fruit a white berry, oft persisting after lvs. Woods, thickets, open areas, lowl-mont, widespread in N Amer. Western snowberry, *S. occidentalis,* has style longer than petals. Mountain snowberry, *S. oreophilus,* has funnel-shaped flrs. Creeping snowberry, *S. mollis,* is a trailing shrub.

Moosewood viburnum (high-bush cranberry, squashberry), *Viburnum edule.* Straggling decid shrub, ht 1½'–8'. Lvs opp, blade L 2"–3", gen 3-lobed and palmately veined. Flrs white, few per inflor. Fruit a smooth, sour, edible red berry. Moist places, Alas to e Can, s to n Ore and Colo. Snowball, *V. opulus,* has inflor with outer fls much larger than inner ones. Oval-leaved viburnum, *V. ellipticum,* has oval-toothed lvs.

Twinflower

Orange Honeysuckle

fruit

Black Twinberry

Blue Elderberry

fruit

Common
Snowberry

fruit

fruit

Coast Red Elderberry

Moosewood Viburnum

trees

A tree is often defined as a woody plant at least 15 feet tall, usually with a single trunk at least several inches thick and a well-developed crown of branches. This section includes only those native plants that characteristically occur as trees in our region. Woody plants that are normally shrubs, becoming treelike in certain favored places, are discussed in chapter 6, Shrubs. These include Scouler's willow, Sitka alder, California hazelnut, black hawthorn, osoberry, vine maple, Douglas' maple, red-osier dogwood, blue elderberry, and coast red elderberry.

Roughly two-thirds of the more than forty species of trees found in our mountains are conifers, which overwhelmingly dominate the forests. Although several broadleaf trees occur regularly in these forests, they form a distinctly minor element except where logging or fire has removed the conifers. Conifers have needlelike or scalelike leaves and bear naked seeds in cones. Native conifers in the region belong to either the pine family or the cypress family. Members of the pine family—pines, larches, true firs, Douglas-fir, hemlocks, and spruces—have needlelike leaves and woody cones with conspicuous scales. Members of the cypress family—incense-cedar, western red cedar, Alaska yellow-cedar, and junipers— usually have overlapping, scale-shaped leaves. The single exception in our region is common juniper, a shrub that has awl-shaped leaves. Junipers have fleshy, berrylike cones; other members of the cypress family have small, few-scaled, woody cones.

Broadleaf trees have true flowers and bear their seeds in a fleshy capsule, called an ovary, at the base of each flower. Most broadleaf trees in our region are deciduous, losing their leaves each autumn; a few are evergreen, retaining their leaves through the winters. Evergreens, it should be noted, lose their leaves, but not all at one time. Most broadleaf trees in the region have tiny, inconspicuous flowers, which may be borne singly or, more commonly, in elongated inflorescences called catkins.

Catkins consist entirely of either male or female flowers. Some trees, such as red alder, bear catkins of both sexes on the same plant; others, such as willows, bear male and female catkins on different plants. In identifying broadleaf trees, it is important to attend to leaves, flowers, and fruit (see figures 5 through 8 in chapter 5, Flowering Plants).

For information on the organization and use of the species descriptions and illustrations, as well as for a list of the abbreviations used in the accounts, see the Introduction. Scientific names conform to those in *USDA Plant Database* (U.S. Department of Agriculture, Natural Resources Conservation Service; 2002; version 3.5; *http://plants.usda.gov;* National Plant Data Center). The common names, with some exceptions, are from the same source.

PLATE 55

PINE FAMILY (PINACEAE)

Lodgepole pine, *Pinus contorta.* Evergreen conif, ht gen 30'–90', 1'–3' diam, with slender, pyramidal crown. Needles 2 per bundle, L 1¼"–2½", deep or yellow green, oft curved. Cone L 1½"–2½", oft perst on branches. Bark orange brown to dk gray, flaky. Poor or disturbed sites, all forest zones, in all our mtns but Vanc I; widespread in w N Amer. Shore pine, *P. contorta* var *contorta,* gen 25'–30' tall, with rounded crown and crooked branches; low el, W CMtns, also along coast s to Cal.

Ponderosa (western yellow) pine, *Pinus ponderosa.* Evergreen conif, ht gen 150'–180', 3'–4' diam, with irreg crown. Needles 3 per bundle, L ca 4½"–10", yellow green. Cone L 3"–5½", ea scale ending in out-turned prickle. Bark reddish or golden brown, in large scaly plates; dk brown and furrowed on young trees. E CMtns–Cas s to Cal; W Cas, s Ore to Cal; widespread in w US s to Mex. Jeffrey pine, *P. jeffreyi,* very similar but cones larger, with inturned prickles; Cal Cas s in SNev to s Cal.

Knobcone pine, *Pinus attenuata.* Evergreen conif, ht gen 30'–80', 1'–2' diam, with sparse, irreg crown. Needles 3 per bundle, L 3"–7", yellow green. Cone L 3¼"–6", in perst whorls on branches. Bark dk gray, fissured; smooth on young trees. Rare and local on poor soils and rocky sites in mtns of s Ore and Cal.

Whitebark pine, *Pinus albicaulis.* Dwarfed or ± contorted evergreen tree, ht gen 20'–50', 1'–2' diam, or sprawling shrub near timberline. Needles 5 per bundle, L usu 1½"–2¾", dull green, clustered at branchlet tips. Cones deep red to purple, L 1½"–3¼", perst on branches. Bark whitish gray, ± smooth. Subalp forest, CMtns–Cas s to SNev, e to RM.

Sugar pine, *Pinus lambertiana.* Evergreen conif, ht gen 175'–200', 3'–5' diam, with irreg crown of long, spreading branches. Needles 5 per bundle, L 2¾"–4", blue-green. Cone L 11"–18", without prickles. Bark brown or gray, furrowed on trunk, smooth on branches. Cas, cen Ore to Cal and Baja.

Western white (silver) pine, *Pinus monticola.* Evergreen conif, ht gen 100'–175', 3'–5' diam, with narrow crown. Needles 5 per bundle, L 2"–4", blue-green. Cone L 5"–9", without prickles. Bark gray, thin, checked. All forest zones, esp W Cas, s BC to cen Cal, e to Idaho.

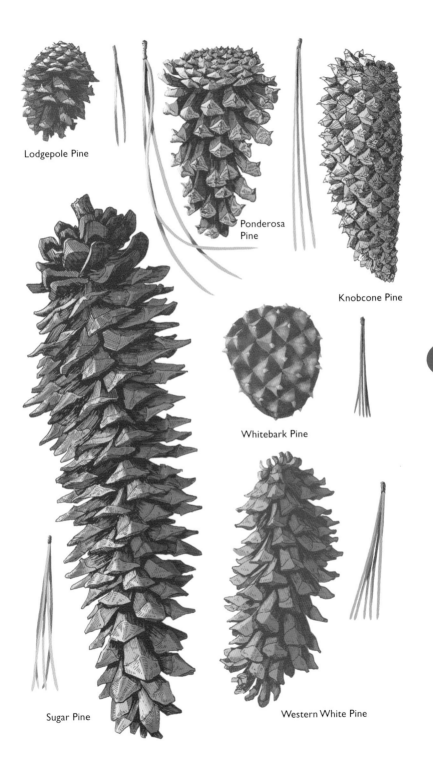

Lodgepole Pine

Ponderosa Pine

Knobcone Pine

Whitebark Pine

Sugar Pine

Western White Pine

PLATE 56

PINE FAMILY (PINACEAE)

Grand (lowland) fir, *Abies grandis.* Evergreen conif, ht to 290', 1½'–3½' diam, with slender, pointed crown. Needle L 1¼"–2", flat, horizontal in 2 ranks, blunt or notched at tips, twisted at base, shiny dk green above, 2 silver lines beneath. Cones yellow green to green, L ca 2"–4", erect on upper branches. Bark grayish to light brown, smooth or shallowly ridged. All forest zones, mostly in lowl, s BC to Cal.

White fir, *Abies concolor.* Evergreen conif, ht to 225'–260', 1½'–4' diam, with slender, pointed crown. Needle L 1½"–2¾", flat, twisted at base, blunt or pointed at tip, gen spreading in 2 ranks but upturned on cone-bearing branches, blue-green with 2 silvery lines on both sides. Cones yellow to greenish purple, L 3"–5", erect on upper branches. Bark dk gray or brownish, furrowed. Cas, Ore to Cal; widespread in w US s to Mex.

Silver (Cascades, lovely) fir, *Abies amabilis.* Evergreen conif, ht to 230', 2'–4' diam, with spirelike crown of drooping branches. Needle L ¾"–1½", flat, mostly notched at tip, shiny dk green and grooved above, striking silver and ridged beneath, crowded on stem, longer ones horizontal, shorter ones brushed forward. Cones gen dk purple, L 3"–6", erect on upper branches. Bark gray, usu smooth. All forest zones, W CMtns–Cas, higher el, E CMtns–Cas, se Alas to n Cal.

Noble fir, *Abies procera.* Evergreen conif, ht to 230', 2½'–4' diam, with tapering, rounded crown and short horizontal branches. Needle L 1"–1½", plump, blue-green with whitish lines above and below, grooved above, notched or pointed at tip, brushed up and crowded on branchlets. Cone L 4½"–7", with papery bracts extending beyond scales, erect on upper branches. Bark gray-brown, readily flaking. Cas, cen Wn to s Ore; rare in n Cal.

Red fir, *Abies magnifica,* and **Shasta fir,** *A. m.* var *shastensis.* Evergreen conifs, ht gen 60'–120', 1'–4' diam, with open, tapering crown rounded at tip. Needle L ¾"–1½", 4-sided, gen spreading in 2 ranks, blue-green with whitish lines. Cone L 6"–8", erect on upper branches, with bracts either inconspicuous (red fir) or extending beyond scale tips (Shasta fir). Bark cinnamon red, deeply furrowed. Cas, cen Ore s to Mt. Shasta (Shasta fir); Mt. Shasta s in SNev (red fir).

Subalpine (alpine) fir, *Abies lasiocarpa.* Evergreen conif, ht gen 50'–100', 1'–2½' diam, with slender, spirelike crown and short horizontal branches extending to base of tree, or prostrate shrub near timberline. Needle L 1"–1¾", gen upturned, dk green with white lines on both sides. Cones dk purple, L 2¼"–4", erect on upper branches. Bark gray, furrowed. Gen subalp forest, Alas s to s Ore, in RM to Ariz, e OMtns but not Vanc I.

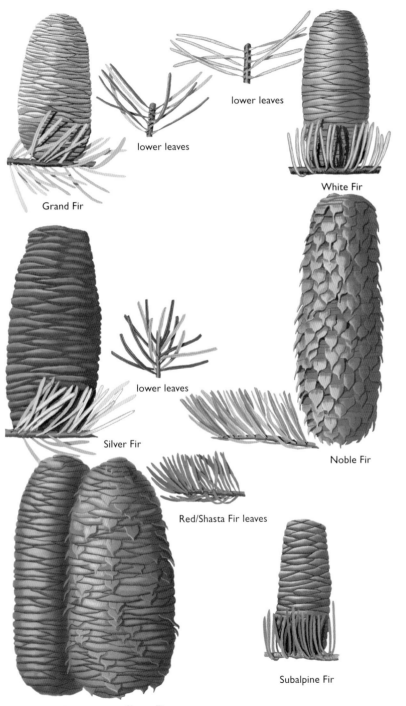

lower leaves

lower leaves

Grand Fir

White Fir

lower leaves

Silver Fir

Noble Fir

Red/Shasta Fir leaves

Red Fir

Shasta Fir

Subalpine Fir

PLATE 57

PINE FAMILY (PINACEAE)

Sitka spruce, *Picea sitchensis.* Evergreen conif, ht to 230', gen 3'–8' (to 16') diam, with open, conical crown. Needle L to 1", pale to bluish green, stiff, sharp, flattened above, keeled beneath, on all sides of a twig from perst woody pegs. Cones tan, L 2"–3½", with papery scales. Bark grayish brown or purple-scaly; smooth and gray on young trees. Coast and lowl-mtns, Alas to nw Cal, e to Wn Cas.

Engelmann spruce, *Picea engelmannii.* Evergreen conif, ht to 160', 1'–3' diam, with narrow, pointed crown of short branches. Needle L to 1", 4-sided, stiff, sharp, dk green, on all sides of a twig from perst woody pegs. Cone L 1½"–2½", tan, with papery scales. Bark brownish or reddish, scaly. All forest zones, mostly E CMtns–Cas, BC to s Ore; rare in n Cal; also RM s to Ariz, NMex.

Western hemlock, *Tsuga heterophylla.* Evergreen conif, ht gen 100'–160', 3'–5' diam, with narrow crown and drooping leader. Needle L to ¾", flat, rounded at tip, very short stalked, spreading in 2 rows, dk green with 2 white lines beneath, forming flat sprays. Cone L to 1", hanging from twig ends. Bark brown, furrowed and cross-ridged. Low-mid el forests, W CMtns–Cas to coast, locally E CMtns, Cas s to Wn, s to cen Ore in Cas, to Cal along coast, n to Alas.

Mountain hemlock, *Tsuga mertensiana.* Evergreen conif, ht gen 30'–100', 1'–3' diam, with conical crown and drooping leader; or a sprawling shrub near timberline. Needle L to ¾", curved, ½-round to nearly 4-sided, on all sides of twig, blue-green with white lines on both sides. Cone L 1"–3", purplish to brown. Bark dk, purplish- or reddish-scaly, furrowed; young twigs hairy. Gen subalp in all our mtns, Alas to Cal, also n RM.

Alpine (subalpine) larch, *Larix lyalli.* Decid conif, ht gen 30'–50', 1' diam, with short branches and irreg crown. Needle L gen 1"–1⅛", clustered on spur twigs and at cone bases or in spirals on leader twigs, 4-sided, stiff, pale blue-green, gold in autumn. Cone L to 2", upright, with hairy, purplish scales and bracts extending well beyond scales. Bark thin, brown, scaly. Subalp, E Cas, BC to cen Wn, also n RM.

Western larch, *Larix occidentalis.* Decid conif, ht to 260', 1½"–3' diam, with narrow, conical crown. Needle L to 1¾", 3-sided, pale green, gold in autumn, clustered on spur twigs and at cone bases or in spirals on leader twigs. Cone L to 1½", erect, with hairy scales and slender, pointed bracts extending beyond scales. Bark cinnamon brown, scaly, becoming furrowed and plated. E Cas, BC to n Ore, also n RM.

Douglas-fir, *Pseudotsuga menziesii.* Evergreen conif, ht to 290', 2'–8' diam, with compact, conical crown. Needle L to 1¾", flattened, roundly tipped, twisted at base, yellow-green to dk or blue-green, on all sides of twigs. Cone L 2"–3½", pale brown, with 3-pointed bracts extending beyond scales. Bark dk brown, corky, furrowed. In all but highest forest zones, BC s in all our mtns to Cal, e to RM.

needle
cross section

Sitka Spruce

Engelmann Spruce

needle cross section

Western Hemlock

Mountain Hemlock

Alpine Larch

Western Larch

Douglas-fir

PLATE 58

CYPRESS FAMILY (CUPRESSACEAE)

Western red cedar, *Thuja plicata.* Evergreen conif, ht gen 150'–200', 2'–10' diam, with conical crown, downswept, spraylike branches, deeply fluted and buttressed trunk. Lvs scalelike, L to ½", shiny green, in alt pairs tightly pressed to stems, the lateral pair keeled. Cone L ca ½", erect on curved stalks, in clusters, with 10–12 sharply pointed scales. Bark cinnamon red, fibrous, shreddy. Low-mid el forests, W CMtns–Cas to coast, Alas to nw Cal; also E CMtns–Cas in BC and Wn; e to n RM.

Alaska yellow-cedar, *Chamaecyparis nootkatensis.* Evergreen conif, ht gen 65'–130', 2'–3' diam, with droopy branches and leader and shaggy foliage; or a prostrate shrub at timberline. Lvs scalelike, sharp, L ca ¼", bluish green, in alt pairs loosely pressed to stems. Cones spherical, ½" diam, erect with 4 or 6 rounded, pointed scales. Bark gray, fibrous, shreddy. All our mtns, upper mont–subalp, Alas to n Cal.

Incense-cedar, *Calocedrus decurrens.* Evergreen conif, ht gen 60'–150', 3'–4' diam, with columnar crown ± rounded at apex. Lvs scalelike, L to ½", shiny green, in alt overlapping pairs tightly pressed to stems, lateral pair keeled. Cones oblong, L to 1", hanging from twig ends, with 6 opp woody scales. Bark cinnamon red, deeply furrowed, fibrous, shreddy. Mont forest, Cas from Mt. Hood s to Cal, Cal mtns to Baja.

Western juniper, *Juniperus occidentalis.* Evergreen conif, ht gen 13'–30', 1'–3' diam, with short, thick trunk, open crown of spreading branches, oft twisted and gnarled. Lvs scalelike, tiny, mostly in 3s, ea with glandular dot, tightly pressed to stems, gray-green. Cones berrylike, ca ¼" diam, soft and juicy, blue-blk with whitish bloom. Bark cinnamon red, fibrous, shreddy. Ponderosa Pine zone and lower, E Cas, Ore to Cal; e Wn to Cal, e to Idaho, Nev.

Rocky mountain juniper, *Juniperus scopulorum.* Evergreen conif, ht to ca 30', 1½" diam, with short, oft divided trunk and rounded, bushy crown. Lvs scalelike, pointed, tiny, in alt overlapping pairs, forming 4-sided twigs. Cones berrylike, ¼" diam, soft and juicy, sweetish, bright blue with whitish bloom. Bark brown or reddish brown, fibrous, shreddy. Local in e OMtns, E Cas, Wn, elsewhere; BC and w US e to mid US and s to Mex. Baker cypress, *Cupressus bakerii,* an open, conical tree to 100' tall, with small, gray-green, scalelike lvs in alt pairs, with glandular dot exuding resin. Rare and local on rocky or poor soils in mtns of s Ore, n Cal.

YEW FAMILY (TAXACEAE)

Pacific (western) yew, *Taxus brevifolia.* Evergreen tree or large shrub, ht gen 16'–30', 2' diam, with rounded crown. Lvs needlelike, flat, sharply tipped, dk green above, pale green with 2 white lines beneath, spreading in 2 ranks. Seed brown, 1 borne in ea scarlet gelatinous cup resembling a berry. Bark purplish brown, thin, smooth, with papery scales. Lowl-mont forests, oft in shaded, moist places, se Alas to cen Cal, also se BC and Idaho.

Western Red Cedar

Alaska Yellow-cedar

Incense-cedar

Western Juniper

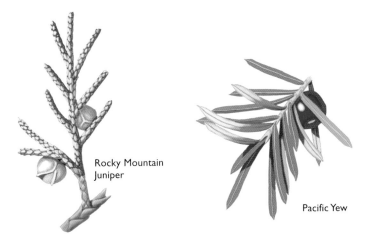

Rocky Mountain
Juniper

Pacific Yew

PLATE 59

WILLOW FAMILY (SALICACEAE)

Quaking (trembling) aspen, *Populus tremuloides.* Decid broadleaf tree, ht gen to 50', 1'–1½' diam, with narrow, open crown. Lf L 1¼"–3", nearly as wide, with short, pointed tip, shiny green above, dull below, yellow in fall, the margins toothed, on flat, twisted petiole. Flrs brownish catkins, M and F on separate trees. Fruit a small, conical capsule. Bark pale gray to white, gen smooth, with blk, warty blisters. Moist places, E CMtns–Cas s to Cal; widespread in Can and in n and w US.

Black cottonwood, *Populus balsamifera* spp *trichocarpa.* Decid broadleaf tree, ht gen 60'–125', 24' diam, with open crown. Lvs long petioled, broadly ovate with rounded base and pointed tip, blade L 2"–8", 1¼"–4¾" wide, margins wavy or toothed, dk green above, whitish, oft with rusty veins beneath, yellow in fall. Flrs purplish catkins, M and F on separate trees. Fruit ca ¼" diam, round, hairy, 3-parted capsule. Bark dk gray, furrowed. Moist places, s Alas to s Cal, e to RM.

Pacific willow, *Salix lucida* spp *lasiandra.* Decid tree or shrub, ht 6½'–40', 1' diam, with broad, irreg crown. Lvs narrowly lancelike, L mostly 2½"–6", ½"–1¼" wide, shiny green above, paler below, toothed, short petioled. Flrs ± erect catkins, L 1½"–4". Fruit reddish brown, hairless capsule, L ca ¼". Moist places, low-mid el, Alas to s Cal, NMex.

BIRCH FAMILY (BETULACEAE)

Red alder, *Alnus rubra.* Decid broadleaf tree, ht gen 30'–60', 1'–2' diam, with rounded crown. Lvs ovate to elliptic, L 3"–6", 2"–3" wide, dk green and ± hairless above, gray-green and rusty-haired beneath, margins double toothed and slightly curled under, veins parallel, straight. Flrs tiny, M yellowish, in catkins, F reddish, in woody cones. Bark pale gray or whitish, thin, ± smooth. Streamsides, damp places, low-mid el, W CMtns–Cas to coast, se Alas to Cal.

Paper birch, *Betula papyrifera.* Decid broadleaf tree, ht to 65', 1'–2' diam, with narrow, open crown. Lf blades ovate, L 2"–4", 1½"–2" wide, double toothed, smooth to hairy and dull dk green above, usu hairy and yellow-green beneath, yellow in fall. Flrs tiny, M in droopy catkins, F in erect woody "cone." Bark chalky white with dk cross lines, thin, peeling, papery. Low el, Vanc I, CMtns, W Cas s to n Wn; widespread in n N Amer. Water birch, *B. occidentalis,* a droopy shrub or small tree to 25' tall, with shiny, dk brown bark; local, rare, streamsides, E Cas s to Cal.

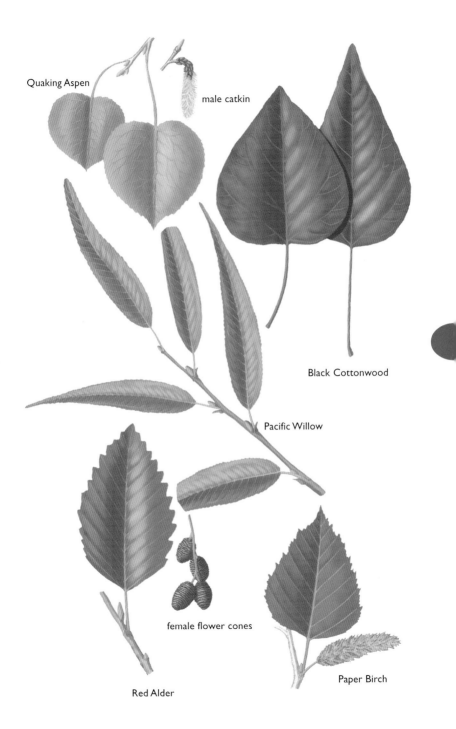

Quaking Aspen

male catkin

Black Cottonwood

Pacific Willow

female flower cones

Red Alder

Paper Birch

PLATE 60

BEECH FAMILY (FAGACEAE)

Golden (giant) chinquapin, *Chrysolepis chrysophylla.* Evergreen broadleaf tree, ht gen 20'–80', with straight trunk and spreading crown; or a large shrub. Lvs lancelike or oblong, L ca 2"–5", ½"–1½" wide, leathery, shiny dk green above, golden-scaly beneath, margins entire, slightly curled under. Flrs tiny, white, in erect catkins near twig tips. Fruit a spiny bur. Bark reddish brown, deeply furrowed. Cas, Ore–Cal; n to sw Wn, s in mtns of Cal.

Oregon (white, garry) oak, *Quercus garryana.* Decid broadleaf tree, ht gen 30'–70', 1'–2½' diam, with rounded, spreading crown; occas shrubby. Lvs ± oblong, deeply lobed, leathery, shiny dk green above, pale and gen hairy beneath. Fruit an acorn, L to 1½". Bark gray, furrowed or scaly. Low el, oft with ponderosa pine, Cas, s Wn to Cal; s in SNev, w of Cas, BC to Cal.

Black (Kellogg) oak, *Quercus kelloggii.* Decid broadleaf tree, ht gen 30'–80', 1'–3' diam, with large branches and broad, irreg crown. Lvs + oblong, deeply lobed, ea lobe with bristly teeth, shiny dk green above, paler and oft hairy beneath. Fruit an acorn, L to 1½". Bark dk brown, thick, furrowed. Low-mid el forests, with ponderosa pine, Cas, cen Ore s through SNev.

ROSE FAMILY (ROSACEAE)

Western (Pacific, Oregon) crabapple, *Malus fusca.* Decid broadleaf tree or shrub, ht 10'–40', diam to 1'. Lvs ovate, elliptic, or lancelike, blade L 1½"–3½", ¾"–1½" wide, occas 3-lobed at tip, shiny green above, paler and hairy beneath, orange or red in fall, margins toothed. Flrs to 1" diam, white or pink. Fruit a sour yellow or red apple to ¾" diam. Bark gray, ± smooth. Mostly along coast, but in mtns to about 2,500', se Alas to n Cal, CMtns–Cas to coast.

fruit

Golden Chinquapin

Oregon Oak

Black Oak

Western Crabapple

PLATE 61

MAPLE FAMILY (ACERACEAE)

Bigleaf (broadleaf, Oregon) maple, *Acer macrophyllum.* Decid broadleaf tree, ht to 100', 1'–2½' diam, with broad, rounded crown. Lvs opp, deeply 5-lobed, L and width 4"–12", shiny green above, paler and hairy below, yellow in fall, with small lobes and teeth on margins, petiole L to 10". Flrs fragrant, ¼" diam, yellow, in drooping inflor at twig ends. Fruit a brown, double samara (see Glossary in chapter 5, Flowering Plants), with stiff yellow hairs. Bark dk gray, furrowed. Moist places, low-mid el in all our mtns, BC to Cal. Cf shrubby maples, plate 49.

BUCKTHORN FAMILY (RHAMNACEAE)

Cascara buckthorn (cascara sagrada), *Rhamnus purshiana.* Small decid broadleaf tree or large shrub, ht to 35', 1' diam, with rounded crown. Lvs elliptic, finely toothed, blade L 2"–6", 1"–2½" wide, parallel veined, dull green and ± hairless above, paler and slightly hairy below, yellow in fall. Flrs bell shaped, greenish, ca ¼" diam. Fruit a small red to blk, sweet, juicy "berry." Bark gray or brown, + fissured and scaly, thin. Coast and lower mtns, BC to n Cal, also n RM.

HEATH FAMILY (ERICACEAE)

Madrone (madrona, arbutus), *Arbutus menziesii.* Evergreen broadleaf tree, ht gen 20'–80', 1'–4' diam. Lvs elliptic, thick and leathery, glossy green above, L 3"–6". Flrs urn shaped, creamy to pink, in branched inflor. Fruit a small, mealy red or orange "berry." Bark cinnamon red, very thin and smooth, peeling off in strips. Dry sites in forest, lowl–low mont, W CMtns–Cas, s BC to Cal.

OLIVE FAMILY (OLEACEAE)

Oregon ash, *Fraxinus latifolia.* Decid broadleaf tree, ht to 80', 2'–3' diam, with slender trunk and narrow crown. Lvs opp, pinnately compound, L 5"–14", with gen 5–7 lflets, ea 3"–6" long, obovate, pale green above, hairy below, yellow or brown in fall. Flrs tiny, greenish, in small inflor. Fruit a brown samara, L ca 1½". Bark dk gray or brown, furrowed. Locally along streams, low-mid el, Cas, s Wn to Cal, w to coast, s to cen Cal.

DOGWOOD FAMILY (CORNACEAE)

Pacific (western flowering) dogwood, *Cornus nuttallii.* Decid broadleaf tree, ht to 60', 2' diam, with narrow to rounded crown. Lvs opp, elliptic, L 2½"–4½", shiny green above, paler and woolly beneath, reddish in fall, with ± wavy margins. Flrs tiny, greenish, set amid 4–7 large, showy, white, petal-like bracts. Fruit elliptic, L ½", mealy, bitter. Bark brown, scaly. Moist places, low-mid el, sw BC to s Cal.

Bigleaf Maple

fruit

Cascara Buckthorn

Madrone

flower

fruit

Orgeon Ash

Pacific Dogwood

PART III

Animals

insects

Insects are one of the many kinds of invertebrates with segmented bodies and jointed appendages—*arthropods*—found in our region. Some of the other arthropods include spiders, crabs, and scorpions. Insects are distinguished by having three body parts—a head, thorax, and abdomen—and six legs. Like the rest of the arthropods, they have an exoskeleton, which they must shed in order to grow. Insects generally are small, ranging from microscopic to 3–4 inches long, although a few may get as large as 6 inches. They are the most successful animal life on earth, with a huge number of species and staggering numbers of individuals. A mountain meadow may host several hundred species of insects and tens of thousands of individuals. There are more than 10,000 identified insect species in the forests and mountains of the Pacific Northwest, and each year new ones are found. A single Douglas-fir tree was found to host more than 300 species of insects.

Insects are crucial components of the ecology of the world, and many species of flowering plants have evolved dependencies on insects for reproduction. The elaborate flowering structures of plants are designed to attract insects and transfer pollen to the insect, ensuring cross-fertilization as the insects travel from flower to flower. Many species of animals also depend on insects, as a primary or secondary source of food. Mammals as large as bears eat insects at certain times. The abundant insect life in the northern hemisphere represents a high-protein food source that draws migrating terrestrial birds to nest here. Outbreaks of large numbers of insects, such as bark beetles, can alter the composition of forests by selectively killing or weakening certain tree species, making way for other species to flourish.

The life cycle of many insects includes a larval stage, which is often very different, both in structure and life habits, from the adult stage. For example, beetles' larva stage is a soft-bodied, white, wormlike form that in some species eats the inner layer of bark of trees, burrowing channels in the inner bark, which damages or kills the host tree. The adult form of the beetle is hard bodied and flies from tree to tree seeking a mate. The change from larval stage to adult stage is one of the amazing transitions in nature, often involving a complete structural rearrangement of the animals' bodies in a relatively short amount of time.

Some families of insects, such as bees, termites, and ants, form large social colonies that have regimented social systems in which members are divided into roles for the colony, such as worker, drone, and queen. Some insects have shown other complex behaviors, such as defending territories and migrating. This is quite remarkable, considering that the brain of an insect is very small, often no bigger than the period at the end of this sentence.

The many species of insects can be overwhelming. The insect species included in this chapter are those that are both very common and relatively easy to identify. In some cases, a representative genus is described because it is typical of the many species. A few non-insect arthropods commonly encountered are also included. For ease in identification, butterflies comprise a separate chapter, chapter 9.

Insects are identified by their color, shape, size, and arrangement of wings. The length of antennae and of legs are good field marks as well.

PLATE 62

SOLDIER BEETLE FAMILY (CANTHARIDAE)
Solider beetle, *Podabrus* spp, *Cantharis* spp. L ½"–¾". Long, narrow beetle, antennae about ½ body length. Thorax oft red or yellowish, elytra with yellow or reddish mark near end. Oft perched on flwrs or lvs in flower mdws, avalanche slopes, lowl–subalp, in all our mtns.

LADY BUG FAMILY (COCCINELLIDAE)
Lady bug beetle, *Cycloneda* spp. Small oval beetle, L ¼". Red, orange, or yellowish, blk head and thorax, oft with white marks and blk spots. Occas in large masses on trees in fall. Mdws, lowl–alp, in all our mtns.

METALLIC WOOD BORER FAMILY (BUPRESTIDAE)
Golden jewel beetle, *Buprestis* spp. L ½"–¾". Shiny metallic green, oft with yellow or reddish lines. Oft found on hot summer days on sunny tree trunks, lowl–mont, Cas.

GROUND BEETLE FAMILY (CARABIDAE)
Ground beetle, *Pterostichus lama*. L 1"–1¼". Constriction between thorax and abdm. Elytra lined and shiny blk. Nocturnal. Conif forests, fallen trees, under bark, lowl–mont, in all our mtns.

Long-faced carabid, *Scaphinotus angusticollis*. L ¾"–1¼". Stout; long, slender head and thorax. Long legs. Dull blk, oft with greenish or bluish hue on elytra, margins of elytra oft greenish. Adults forage at night. Rotting wood, lowl–mont, occas alp, in all our mtns.

LONG HORNED BEETLE FAMILY (CERAMBYCIDAE)
Banded alder borer, *Rosalina funebris*. L 1"–1¼". Slender, long blk- and gray-banded elytra, blk- and white-banded antennae longer than body. Thorax gray with blk spot. Alder forests, lowl, in all our mtns.

Pine sawyer, *Ergates spiculatus*. L 1¾"–2¼". Large beetle, brown overall, long, curving antennae. Nocturnal, oft flies into camp lights. Burned areas in ponderosa pine, Douglas-fir forests, lowl–mont, E Cas, occas W Cas.

CLICK BEETLE FAMILY (ELATERIDAE)
Western eyed click beetle, *Alaus melanops*. L 1"–1½". Dull blk with scattered small white dots on elytra; 2 distinctive blk spots with white borders on thorax. Rotting wood, stumps, logs, lowl–mont, in all our mtns.

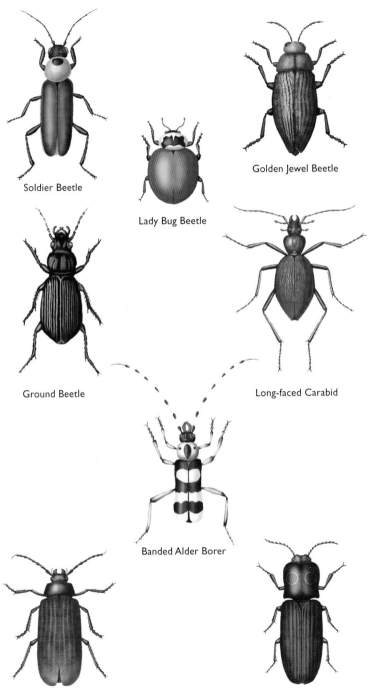

Soldier Beetle

Lady Bug Beetle

Golden Jewel Beetle

Ground Beetle

Long-faced Carabid

Banded Alder Borer

Pine Sawyer

Western Eyed Click Beetle

PLATE 63

CENTIPEDE FAMILY (LITHOBIIDAE)

Red centipede, *Lithobius* spp. L ½"–1¼". Reddish brown, sometimes partly translucent, 21–23 segm, single pair of legs from each segm. Antennae oft curled. Under logs, in leaf litter, old stumps, lowl-mont, in all our mtns.

SOW BUG FAMILY (ONISIDAE)

Sow bug, *Oniscus asellus.* L ¼"–½" Gray to brown, many overlapping plates, noticeable antennae, 7 pairs of legs. Under logs, in leaf litter, rotten wood, lowl-mont, W Cas, OMtns. Pill bug, *Armadillidium vulgare,* similar to sow bug, dker gray, rolls itself completely into a ball when disturbed. Under logs, damp areas, campgrounds, lowl, W Cas, OMtns.

MILLIPEDE FAMILY (XESTODESMIDAE)

Yellow-spotted millipede, *Harpaphe haydeniana.* L 1½"–3". Blk, 20 segm, yellow or red spots along side near feet, feet in pairs from each segm. On grnd in leaf litter, older forests, lowl-mont, W Cas, OMtns.

HOVER FLY FAMILY (SYRPHIDAE)

Hover fly, *Syrphus* spp. L ⅜". Boldly patterned, slender, beelike with blk and yellow abdm, large eyes cover most of head, antennae shorter than head, hovers in flight, oft over flwrs. Mdws, clearings, lowl-alp, in all our mtn; throughout N Amer.

HORSE FLY FAMILY (TABANIDAE)

Horse fly, *Hybomitra* spp. L ¾"–1¼". Large, blk, iridescent multicolored eyes. Abdm light brown with alternating blk bands. Only F bites. Near water, mont-alp, in all our mtns.

Deer fly, *Chrysops* spp. L ⅜"–⅝". Blk with greenish markings on thorax and abdm. Eyes iridescent yellow or green, wings clear with brown markings. Only F bites. In forested marshy areas, mont-subalp, in all our mtns; throughout N Amer.

WATERSTRIDER FAMILY (GERRIDAE)

Waterstrider, *Aquarius remigis.* L ½"–¾". Blk, front legs small, mid legs long, fine-haired. Distinctive, walks on water surface. Pools in streams and rivers, ponds and lakes, com, lowl-mont, in all our mtns; widespread.

CRANE FLY FAMILY (TIPULIDAE)

Crane fly, *Tipula* spp, *Holorusia* spp. L ⅜"–2½". Mosquito-like, long, fragile legs, V-shaped groove on top of thorax. Abun in moist, forested areas, lowl-subalp, in all our mtns; widespread throughout N Amer.

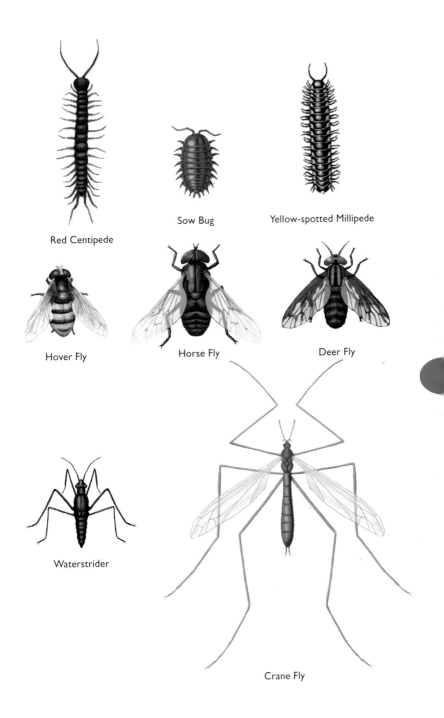

Red Centipede

Sow Bug

Yellow-spotted Millipede

Hover Fly

Horse Fly

Deer Fly

Waterstrider

Crane Fly

PLATE 64

DARNER FAMILY (AESHNIDAE)

Blue darner, *Aeshna* spp. L 2"–2¼". Diagonal stripes on thorax, blue and blk patterns on abdm. Several spp. Blue-eyed darner, *A. multicolor,* blue thorax stripes, pale blue eyes. Paddle tailed darner, *A. palmate,* yellow thorax stripes, blue eyes, white face, blue spotted abdm with blk rings. Ponds and lakes, lowl–subalp, in all our mtns.

Green darner, *Anax junicus.* L 2"–2¼". Green thorax, abdm with dk stripe on top, pale blue or gray to violet sides. Ponds and lakes, lowl–mont, in all our mtns.

POND DAMSEL FAMILY (COENAGRIONIDAE)

Bluet, *Enallagma* spp. L 1"–1¼". Small, very skinny, thorax blue with blk stripes, abdm blue with blk rings. Wings clear or with small blk markings near end. Several spp. Ponds and lakes, mont–subalp, in all our mtns.

SKIMMER FAMILY (LIBELLULIDAE)

Meadowhawk, *Sympetrum* spp. L 1¼"–1¾". Distinctive red abdm, wings with red tinge or small red section. Wet mdws, mont, in all our mtns. Striped meadowhawk, *S. pallipes,* pale stripes on side of brown thorax; lakes and ponds, low–mont, Cas. Cardinal meadowhawk, *S. illotum,* stout red body with 2 white diagonal lines at wingbase; red head and red or yellow legs, red wing veins; forested mdw edges, lowl, Cas.

Eight-spotted skimmer, *Libellula forensis.* L 1¾"–2". Large and stout, powder blue with blk head. Distinctive blk and light blue markings on wings. Ponds and lakes with wetland edges or abun vegetation, lowl–mont, Cas.

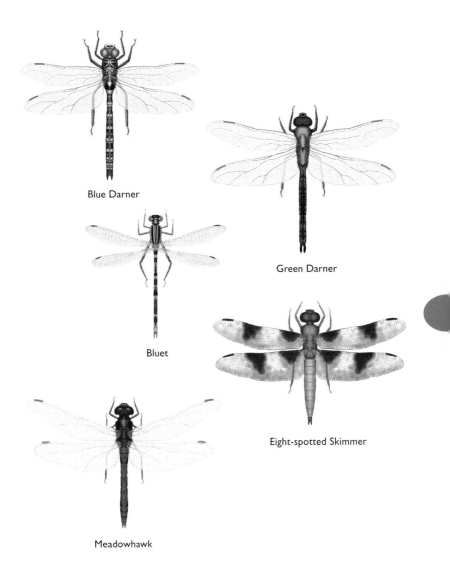

Blue Darner

Green Darner

Bluet

Eight-spotted Skimmer

Meadowhawk

PLATE 65

STREAM MAYFLY FAMILY (HEPTAGENIIDAE)

Mayfly, *Rhithrogena* spp. L ¼"–⅜". Long winged, oft holds body in upward curl, oft with 2 longish "tails" that equal or exceed length of abdm. Adults oft in groups, flying with up-and-down pattern. Larva aquatic, L ¼"–½", three "tails" and legs all pointing forward, external gills on abdm. Com under rocks in mtn streams, lakes, lowl-mont, in all our mtns.

NORTHERN CADDISFLIES FAMILY (LIMNEPHILIDAE)

Caddisfly, *Chyranda* spp. L ¼"–⅞". Adult mothlike, soft brown or patterned wings; distinctive long antennae. Larva aquatic, L ¼"–¾", covers abdm with case made of pebbles, leaves, or sticks. Head oval, thorax oft hairy, blk legs. Streams and lakes, lowl-subalp, in all our mtns.

CRICKET FAMILY (GRYLLIDAE)

Field cricket, *Gryllus* spp. L ½"–1". Shiny blk, reddish brown, antennae longer than body, legs spiky-hairy, with 2 tail-like extensions in rear longer than head and thorax combined. Males rub wing covers to make familiar cricket call in late sum, fall. Open forests, drier areas, lowl, E and S Cas, W Cas on south-facing slopes.

Hump-backed cricket, *Cyphoderris monstrosa.* L 1"–1½". Brown, blk, or dk greenish, long antennae, horny plate covering ⅓ of abdm. On grnd in forest litter, perches in lower trees to sing; pine, mtn hemlock forest, lowl-mont, BC, Wn, Ore Cas, mostly e of Cas crest.

GRASSHOPPER FAMILY (ACRIDIDAE)

Alpine grasshopper, *Melanoplus alpinus.* L 1¼"–2½". Head and thorax gray with cream underbody. Legs blk above, cream under, chevron markings along sides. Mdws, subalp-alp, Cas.

STINK BUG FAMILY (PENTATOMIDAE)

Stink bug, *Banasa* spp, *Euschistus* spp. L ½"–¾". Distinctive shield shape, upper wings colored and hard, lower wings membranous. Various colors, green and brown. Com along sunny decid forest shrub edges, lowl-mont, in all our mtns.

DAMPWOOD TERMITE FAMILY (RHINOTERMITIDAE)

Pacific dampwood termite, *Zootermopsis angusticollis.* L 1". Reproductive adult with wings 2✕ as long as body. Slow, awkward flier, head larger than thorax, whole body reddish brown. Soldier and worker forms found in rotting wood, L ¾", large head, light brown, long blk mandibles. Forest, lowl-mont, in all our mtns.

GIANT STONEFLY FAMILY (PTERONARCIDAE)

Salmonfly, *Pteronarcys californica,* L 1¼"–1⅝". Adult brown–reddish gray, long wings with prominent veins. Abdm clearly segm, poor flier, often skip and flutter. Larva aquatic, L ¾"–1½", 2 long "tails" at tip of abdm, com under rocks in mtn streams, lowl-mont, in all our mtns.

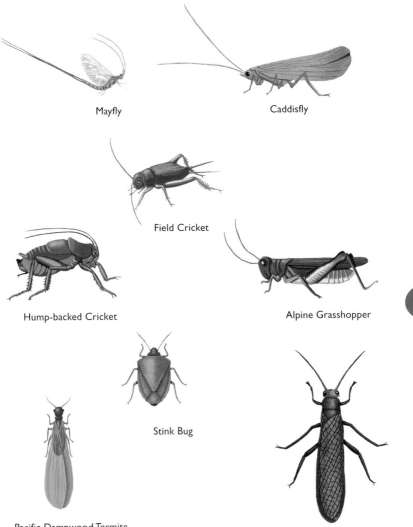

Mayfly

Caddisfly

Field Cricket

Hump-backed Cricket

Alpine Grasshopper

Stink Bug

Pacific Dampwood Termite

Salmonfly

PLATE 66

SPIDER WASP FAMILY (POMPILIDAE)

Spider wasp, *Anoplius* spp. L ½"–¾". Metallic blue to blk. Long hind legs dangle as it flies. Oft with orange spot or band on abdm. Oft runs on grnd searching for spiders. Several genera. On bare grnd, trails, sparse grassy mdws, subalp–alp, in all our mtns.

SOLITARY HUNTING WASP FAMILY (SPECIDIAE)

Thread-waisted wasp (mud dauber), *Ammophila* spp, *Sceliphron* spp. L ⅝"–2⅛". Mostly blk with yellow bands and markings on abdm. Abdm separated from thorax by narrow waist. Long hind legs dangle in flt. Streams/lakeshores in mud, lowl–alp, in all our mtns; widespread.

PARASITIC WASP FAMILY (ICHNEUMONIDAE)

Giant ichneumon, *Megarrhyssa* spp. L 1⅜"–3". Body blk with yellow-white banding on abdm, ovipositor longer than body, long reddish-brown legs dangle in flt. Oft seen on stumps, rotting logs, lowl–mont, widespread.

HORNET FAMILY (VESPIDAE)

Baldfaced hornet, *Vespula maculata.* L ⅝"–¾". Mostly blk, white-yellow head with black eye; thorax with white-yellow markings, abdm blk with white-yellow stripes on rear 3 segms. Nests large orbs of paper, in trees or shrubs. Painful sting. Forest edges, lowl–mont, widespread. Yellow jacket, *Vespula* spp, dk head with bold yellow stripes on thorax and abdm, nest oft undergrnd; forests, rocky areas, lowl–mont, in all our mtns; com and widespread.

SWEAT BEE FAMILY (HALICTIDAE)

Virescent green metallic bee, *Agapostemon* spp. L ⅜"–½". Small, compact, head and thorax metallic green, adbm hairy, ringed blk and yellow, legs blk. Undergrnd nests in sandy soils. Mdws and avalanche corridors, oft found in flowers, lowl–mont, in all our mtns; widespread.

BEE FAMILY (APIDAE)

Bumblebee, *Bombis* spp. L ⅜"–¾". Robust, hairy, variable blk and yellow striping, face and head typically blk, thorax oft blk between wings. Slow moving, oft seen on flrs. Mdws and flowered areas, lowl–alp, in all our mtns; widespread.

ANT FAMILY (FORMICIDAE)

Carpenter ant, *Camponotus modoc.* L ½"–1". Large, blk, with slightly hairy abdm. Queens and breeding males have wings, oft in swarms in summer; workers wingless. Piles of sawdust indicate this sp. Serious house pest. Stumps, dead trees, decaying wood, lowl–mont, forests, in all our mtns, widespread BC to Cal.

Western thatch ant, *Formica obscuripes.* L ⅛". Small, reddish, with blk head. Makes distinctive mound nests, oft 2'–3' tall. Dry, well-drained areas, woods, fields, mdws, lowl–mont, in all our mtns.

Spider Wasp

Thread-waisted Wasp

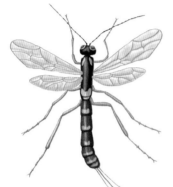

Giant Ichneumon

Baldfaced Hornet

Virescent Green Metallic Bee

Bumblebee

Carpenter Ant

Western Thatch
Ant

butterflies

Butterflies, scaly-winged insects of the order Lepidoptera, are given a separate chapter in this book from the other insects in chapter 8, for ease of identification. They are divided into two major groups: true butterflies and skippers. Skippers are typically small, rather drab, mothlike butterflies with triangular wings and stout, hairy bodies. Though quite common, skippers on the whole are difficult to separate by species unless one is thoroughly familiar with their anatomy and behavior. They are represented in this chapter by only a few fairly common, more or less typical, examples.

Butterflies, like all insects, have bodies composed of three segmented sections: head, thorax, and abdomen. In adults, the head includes two club-shaped antennae, two compound eyes, two sensory organs, or *palpi,* one on each side of the mouth, and a long, coiled, tubular proboscis for sipping flower nectar or other liquids. The thorax is the stout middle section of the body. It consists of three segments, each bearing a pair of five-jointed legs. In addition, the middle and rear segments each bear a pair of wings. The abdomen is the slender rear portion of the body. It consists of eleven segments, not all of which may be visible to the unaided eye. Butterflies breathe through *spiracles,* a series of minute openings located along the body. Attached to the end of the abdomen are the genitals: the ovipositor of the female and the claspers of the male.

Butterfly wings are membranous and densely coated with overlapping scales that come off as "dust" when the insect is carelessly handled. The scales determine the color and pattern of the wings either by pigmentation or light refraction. Some scales are modified into hairs. In male butterflies, certain scales may also secrete *pheromones,* distinctly scented chemicals that probably play an important role in mate recognition and courtship.

After mating, female butterflies lay their eggs either singly or in rows or clusters, usually on the plants that will serve as food for the hatched larvae. The eggs of most species hatch within a few days. Certain species, however, overwinter in egg form, with the larvae emerging the following spring.

Butterfly larvae are caterpillars. They are smooth skinned, though often adorned with hairs, bristles, or horns. Caterpillars possess simple eyes, powerful mandibles for chewing vegetation, spinnerets for producing silky thread used to attach themselves to plants or to join leaves into shelters, three pairs of legs near the front, and five pairs of prolegs farther back.

As a caterpillar grows, it molts several times, reaching full size in a few days to several months, depending on the species. During the final molt, it transforms into a pupa by developing a hard, mummylike case called a *chrysalis*. During the pupal stage, which also may last from a few days to several months, the caterpillar undergoes a radical anatomical reorganization, losing its jaws and wormlike body as it becomes an adult. Although various species may overwinter as eggs, larvae, or adults, most do so as pupae, emerging as adults in the spring.

The creature we normally think of as a butterfly is the adult insect. Upon emergence, its wings and legs are completely folded and shrunken, but they quickly expand as fluid is pumped throughout the body. While the role of the caterpillar is to eat and grow, that of the adult is reproduction. Its distinctive colors and patterns are probably important in mate recognition. The ability to fly allows the insects to track one another down over relatively large areas and assists the female in dispersing her eggs. Many species have elaborate courtship rituals featuring flight displays and other distinctive behavior. Copulation often lasts several hours, and fertilization is internal.

In warm regions, most species produce several broods a year. At the other extreme, certain arctic and alpine species may require two years to produce a single brood, and adults may therefore be abroad in only alternating years.

Each species has a limited flight period, during which most or all adults are abroad. The flight period for each species is fairly constant from year to year but may vary according to locale and weather. A long, cold winter can delay emergence of butterflies in the spring, and a mild winter followed by warmer weather can hasten their appearance. A cool, damp summer, as often occurs in our mountains, can inhibit a year's flight entirely.

As a rule, the butterfly season begins in April or May on the west side of the Cascades and ends in September or October. On the warmer, drier east side of the range, the season begins a month earlier and ends a month later. May and June are the best months for finding butterflies at lower elevations. July and August are best for seeking butterflies in the high country.

The most important factor influencing the distribution of butterflies is the presence of suitable food plants. The larvae of most butterfly species are limited to one plant or to a group of closely related plants. Some species tolerate a wider variety but still have certain preferences. Adult butterflies also prefer certain nectar plants but are generally less finicky. In their pursuit of nectar, butterflies perform the important function of cross-pollinating plants. Indeed, some plant species depend primarily on certain butterflies. Some adult butterflies, however, rarely visit flowers but instead relish such delicacies as tree sap, rotten fruit, dung, and aphid honeydew. Since most butterflies are rather weak fliers, they normally occur only in the vicinity of both larval and adult food plants.

Butterfly habitats must also have adequate sunlight, moisture sources, suitable terrain for courtship, and appropriate conditions for overwintering eggs, larvae, pupae, or adults. In the mountains, such places include subalpine parklands and the open pine forests of the eastern Coast Mountains and Cascades. Relatively few butterflies inhabit the shady conifer forests of the coastal region, where wildflowers and sunlight are both less common.

There are about 700 species of butterflies in North America north of Mexico, of which more than 130 occur in our mountains. The majority, however, are difficult to separate by species without collecting specimens for in-hand inspection. To discourage this practice simply for the purpose of identifying a species, this chapter focuses on only those species that are sufficiently large or distinct to allow identification "on the wing," as it were. The several groups of small or otherwise indistinct butterflies are therefore represented by only one or two common and rather typical species. Because careless handling will result in a butterfly's death, the casual observer, to whom this chapter is directed, should be content to identify difficult species by genus or family alone. If one wishes to pursue butterflies as a serious hobby, several excellent field guides are listed in Selected References at the back of this book. No collecting, however, is allowed in national or provincial parks without special permit.

The term *food* as used in the species descriptions refers to larval food. The flight period for each species is given in months and refers to the appearance of adults throughout the species' given range. The actual flight period at any given locale, however, may well be shorter than that indicated. As a rule, butterflies appear earlier in the flight period at lower elevations and on the west side of the Coast Mountains–Cascade crest; later they appear at higher elevations and east of the mountains. The flight period will also vary from year to year and place to place, depending on local conditions.

Scientific and common names conform to the North American Butterfly Association prescriptive checklist 1995. For general information on the organization and use of the species descriptions and illustrations, as well as for a list of the abbreviations used in the accounts, see the Introduction.

PLATE 67

SWALLOWTAIL FAMILY (PAPILIONIDAE)

Clodius parnassian, *Parnassius clodius.* WS 2½"–3". Gray- and blk-checked white wings with red spots on HW only. Food mainly bleeding heart. Forest, mdws, lowl-subalp, se Alas to cen Cal, e to RM states. June–mid-Sept. Phoebus parnassian, *P. phoebus,* very similar but red spots on *both* FW and HW.

Anise swallowtail, *Papilio zelicaon.* WS 2½"–3". Broad yellow midwing band. Food parsley family. All habitats but dense forest, lowl-alp, BC to Baja, e to mid US. May-Sept.

Short-tailed black swallowtail, *Papilio indra.* WS 2"–3½". Narrow yellow band on mostly blk wings. Food parsley family. Many habitats, lowl-subalp, widespread in w N Amer. Apr-Aug.

Western tiger swallowtail, *Papilio rutulus.* WS 2¾"–4". Esp large size, blk-striped yellow wings with 1 "tail" at tip of ea HW. Food various hardwoods. Moist, wooded places, BC to Baja, e to RM and just beyond. May-Sept. Two-tailed tiger swallowtail, *P. multicaudatus,* very similar but larger, with 2 "tails" on ea HW; lower E Cas only.

Pale tiger swallowtail, *Papilio eurymedon.* WS 3"–3¾". Blk stripes on white or creamy ground color. Food alders, chokecherry, creambush, *Ceanothus.* Forest streams, brush, lowl-subalp, BC and Mont s to Baja and NMex. May-Aug.

BRUSH-FOOTED BUTTERFLY FAMILY (NYMPHALIDAE)

Monarch, *Danaus plexippus.* WS 3½"–4". Large, bright burnt-orange wing with blk veins and blk margins with white dots. Food milkweeds. Uncom in our range, esp w of CMtns–Cas, widespread in N Amer. June-Sept.

Lorquin's admiral, *Limenitis lorquini.* WS 2¼"–2¾". Blk wings with white midwing band and orange FW tips. Food willows, cottonwoods, other hardwoods. Open places, streamsides, cen BC, Albta, s to Baja, Idaho, ne Nev. Feb-Oct.

Mourning cloak, *Nymphalis antiopa.* WS 3"–3½". Chocolate brown with yellow wing margins. Food willows, cottonwoods, other hardwoods. Open woods, forest openings, widespread in n hemis; also S Amer. Year-round.

Ciodius Parnassian

Phoebus Parnassian

Anise Swallowtail

Short-tailed Black Swallowtail

Western Tiger Swallowtail

Pale Tiger Swallowtail

Monarch

upperside

underside

Lorquin's Admiral

Mourning Cloak

PLATE 68

WHITE BUTTERFLY FAMILY (PIERIDAE)

Pine white, *Neophasia menapia.* WS ca 1¾". Blk leading edge and white-spotted blk tip on FW; F's HW oft dk lined above, M's HW dk lined only beneath, F's orange- or red-lined beneath. Food conifs. Forest, s BC, Albta, s to s Cal, NMex, e to mid US. Apr–Aug.

Margined white, *Pieris marginalis.* WS ca 1½". Wings ± clear white above, creamy to yellowlsh beneath with or without dk veins. Food mustard family. Forest, woods, clearings, lowl–subalp, Alas to e Can, ne US, s to Ariz, n Cal; in our region mostly W CMtns–Cas. Several other similar whites in our area; difficult to distinguish in flight. Apr–Aug.

Sara's orange-tip, *Anthocharis sara.* WS ca 1½". Bright orange FW tips; F occas yellow above. Food mustard family. Forest clearings, mdws, woods, se Alas to Baja, e to RM. Apr–Aug.

Alfalfa (orange) sulphur, *Colias eurytheme.* WS 1½"–2⅜". Orange wings with blk borders. Food pea family. Open places, low-high el, widespread in N Amer. Apr–Sept.

Western sulphur, *Colias occidentalis.* Both sexes similar to above sp but lemon-yellow above. Food pea family. Mdws, clearings, low-high el, se Alas to SNev, in and w of W CMtns–Cas (only sulphur on Vanc I). Difficult to distinguish from several other very similar sulphurs in our range. June–Aug.

SATYR SUBFAMILY (SATYRINAE)

Ochre (northwest) ringlet, *Coenonympha tullia.* WS 1"–2". Clear, buffy yellow to ochre color above. Food grasses. Mdws, forest clearings, other grassy places, s BC to Ore, n Nev, Idaho; more com, E Cas. May–Sept.

Large wood nymph, *Cercyonis pegala.* WS 2"–2⅞". Large; 1–2 large eyespots on brown FW. Food grasses. Wet, grassy places, pine-oak woodlands and pine forest, lower E Cas, BC, Wn, n Ore, E and W Cas, s Ore, Cal; widespread in N Amer but gen absent from Northwest Coast and Gulf Coast. Other wood nymphs in our range much smaller. June–Sept.

Alpines, *Erebia* spp. WS 1¼"–2". Above, dk brown wings with russet or orange band surrounding small dk eyespots. Food grasses. Mdws, clearings, gen subalp–alp, all our mtns but Vanc I. June–Aug. Vidler's alpine, *E. vidleri,* has broad, irreg orange bands above, checked wing fringes and grayish HW band beneath. Common alpine, *E. epipsodea,* very similar but has smooth russet bands above; lacks checked wing fringes and gray HW band beneath; only alpine s of Snoqualmie Pass, Wn.

Chryxus arctic, *Oeneis chryxus.* WS 1¾"–2". Above, tan with 2–3 eyespots; beneath, broad dk band across HW. Food grasses. Mdws, forest clearings, subalp–alp, in all our mtns, Alas s to Wn; in RM s to NMex. June–Aug. Nevada arctic, *O. nevadensis,* very similar but larger (WS 2"–2½"), lacks *broad* dk band across HW beneath. Melissa's arctic, *O. melissa,* smaller (WS ±1¼"), gen lacks eyespots, smoky gray to dull tan; BC, N Cas.

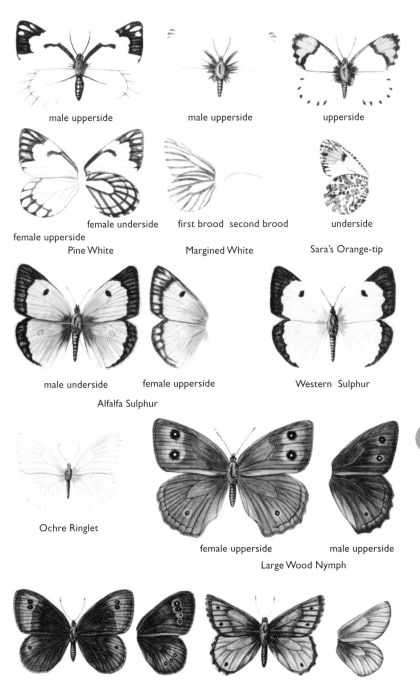

male upperside

male upperside

upperside

female underside

first brood second brood

underside

female upperside

Pine White

Margined White

Sara's Orange-tip

male underside

female upperside

Western Sulphur

Alfalfa Sulphur

Ochre Ringlet

female upperside

male upperside

Large Wood Nymph

Vidler's Alpine

Common Alpine

Chryxus Arctic

Melissa's Arctic

PLATE 69

BRUSH-FOOTED BUTTERFLY FAMILY (NYMPHALIDAE)

Large fritillaries, *Speyeria* spp. WS 1⅝"–3". Orange wings (yellow only in great spangled fritillary, *S. cybele)* with blk spots, bars, and chevrons; large, oft silver orbs beneath; relatively large (cf small fritillaries below). Mormon fritillary, *S. mormonia,* and Hydaspe fritillary, *S. hydaspe,* both with black wing margins enclosing white spots. 8 spp in our range, all very similar and + variable in appearance. With some practice, 3 spp can gen be distinguished in the field, but beginners will do well to identify these insects by genus alone. Food violets. Various habitats in all our mtns.

Small fritillaries, *Boloria* spp. WS 1⅛"–2". Smaller than above spp, but otherwise similar. 2 most common in our mtns—western meadow fritillary, *B. epithore,* arctic fritillary, *B. chariclea*—distinguished by underside of wings (see illustrations). Mdws, clearings, low-high el, in all our mtns.

Field crescent, *Phyciodes pulchellus.* WS ca 1¼". Above, wings blk with orange and yellow marks; beneath, orange FW, paler HW. Food asters. Open places, mid-high el, Alas, n Can, s to Cal, Mex, mid US. July-Aug. Northern crescent, *P. cocyta,* similar beneath, but above wings dk orange with dk marks and borders. Mylitta crescent, *P. mylitta,* lighter, brighter, more banded above, HW is white-banded, not yellow, beneath. Pale crescent, *P. pallidus* (not shown), of E Cas foothills, like mylitta crescent but larger (WS 1¼"–1¾") with large blk spot on lower margin of FW beneath.

Checkerspot, *Euphydryas* spp, *Chlosyne* spp. WS ca 1½". 9 spp in our region, all so similar and variable as to defy identification in the field. Recognizable as a group by numerous red, orange, and/or yellow checks on dk field.

Satyr anglewing, *Polygonia satyrus.* WS ca 2". Ragged wings, lack of white spots above, pale mottled brown beneath. Food stinging nettle. Various habitats, esp near water, BC to e Can, s in w US. Year-round. Similar spp are zephyr anglewing, *P. zephyrus* (mottled gray beneath), faun anglewing, *P. faunus* (mottled gray and dk brown beneath), oreas anglewing, *P. oreas* (very dk brown to nearly blk beneath).

Milbert's tortoiseshell, *Aglais milberti.* WS ca 2". Distinctive vertical, red-orange, and yellow bands. Food nettles. Most habitats, low-high el, n Can to s Cal, e US. Year-round.

California tortoiseshell, *Nymphalis californica.* WS ca 2". Broad, dk brown marginal bands across FW and RW. Food *Ceanothus,* other shrubs. Open areas, BC to Cal, e to mid US. Year-round.

Western painted lady, *Vanessa annabella.* WS 1¾"–2". Above, orange bar near FW tip, blue eyes along HW margin; beneath, 5 eyes along HW margin. Food mallows, nettles. CMtns–Cas crest to coast, BC to Baja. Painted lady, *V. cardui,* has white, not orange, bar near FW tip, black dots along HW. American painted lady, *V. virginiensis,* similar to *V. annabella* above, but beneath has 2 large eyes on HW, large pink area on FW.

Mormon Fritillary
Speyeria mormonia

LARGE FRITILLARIES

underside
Hydaspe Fritillary
Speyeria hydaspe

male

Great Spangled Fritillary
Speyeria cybele

upperside   W. Mdw. Fritillary   underside   und.   Arctic Fritillary   upperside
Field Crescent

Checkerspot

upperside   underside
Mylitta Crescent

upperside   underside
Northern Field Crescent

Satyr Anglewing

Milbert's Tortoiseshell

California
Tortoiseshell

upperside
W. Painted Lady

upperside
Painted Lady

underside
American Painted Lady

PLATE 70

METALMARK FAMILY (RIODINIDAE)

Mormon metalmark, *Apodemia mormo.* WS ¾"–1¼". Small; bright checkered pattern. Food wild buckwheats. Dry, open, rocky places, lower E Cas; widespread in w US s to Mex. July-Oct.

GOSSAMER WING BUTTERFLY FAMILY (LYCAENIDAE)

Blues, several genera. WS ca ½"–1"+. Tiny, active; M gen various shades of blue, F usu brown or coppery; both gen white or pale beneath. More than a dozen spp in our range, most very difficult to distinguish on the wing.

Coppers, several genera. WS ca ½"–1"+. Tiny, active; M gen coppery or gold above, F drabber; both white, gray, orange, tan, or brown beneath. About a dozen spp in our range, most difficult to distinguish on the wing.

Cedar hairstreak, *Mitoura grynea.* WS ⅞"–1". Dk gray-brown or rusty brown above, brown tinged with pink or lilac beneath, ± distinct, light band on FW and HW. Food western red cedar, incense-cedar. Forest, oft near cedars or junipers, BC to Baja, W CMtns–Cas to coast. May-June. Johnson's hairstreak, *M. johnsonii,* very similar but rarer, slightly larger, to 1½", not tinted with lilac or pink beneath. Several other hairstreaks in our range, most gen brown or coppery above; brown, gray, silvery, gold, or green beneath.

Western pine elfin, *Incisalia eryphon.* WS ¾"–1". Chocolate brown to orange-brown color above; gray and brown beneath, with bands of blk and white spots and chevrons. Food pines. Mtn forests and clearings, oft near pines, BC to Cal and NM; e to Albta, ne US. Apr-June. Brown elfin, *I. augustinus,* plain brown beneath. Moss's elfin, *I. mossi,* two-toned brown and gray beneath.

SKIPPER FAMILY (HESPERIIDAE)

Silver-spotted skipper, *Epargyreus clarus.* WS 1¾"–2⅜". Above, yellowish spots on FW; beneath, large silver spot on HW. Food legumes. Most habitats, low-mid el, BC to e Can, s to Baja, Florida. Apr-Aug.

Arctic skipper, *Carterocephalus palaemon.* WS ¾"–1¼". Small; brown and orange checkered pattern above, creamy spots on HW beneath. Food grasses. Forest clearings, subalp-alp mdws, Alas, Can, n US s to cen Cal, Wyo, ne US. May-July.

Alpine checkered skipper, *Pyrgus centaureae.* WS ⅞"–1¼". Dk brown wings checked with white spots above. Food unknown. Alp zone, CMtns, NCas; e to e Can, ne US. July. Common checkered skipper, *P. communis,* similar but not alp. Two-banded checkered skipper, *P. ruralis,* distinctly bluish.

Orange skippers, several genera. WS ca 1". At least 7 spp of small orange skippers in our range, most very similar and difficult to identify.

Northern cloudy-wing, *Thorbyes pylades.* WS ca 1½". Note 2 slim, triangular white bars on dark FW. Food pea family. Dry, open forest, E Cas; widespread in N Amer. May-July. One of nearly a dozen small to medium-sized dark skippers in our range.

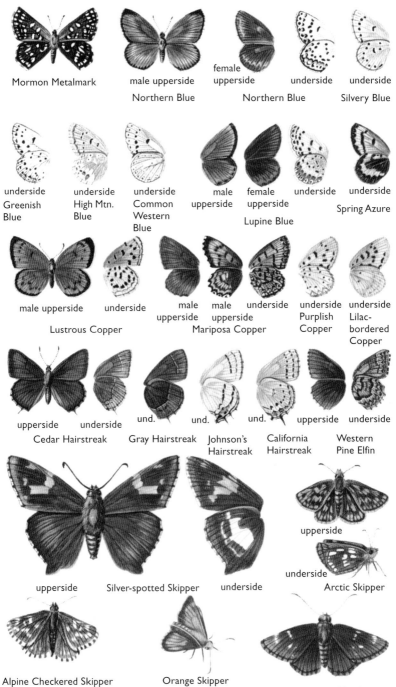

Mormon Metalmark

male upperside
Northern Blue

female upperside
Northern Blue

underside

underside
Silvery Blue

underside
Greenish Blue

underside
High Mtn. Blue

underside
Common Western Blue

male upperside

female upperside
Lupine Blue

underside

underside
Spring Azure

male upperside

underside
Lustrous Copper

male upperside

male upperside
Mariposa Copper

underside

underside
Purplish Copper

underside
Lilac-bordered Copper

upperside

underside
Cedar Hairstreak

und.
Gray Hairstreak

und.
Johnson's Hairstreak

und.
California Hairstreak

upperside

underside
Western Pine Elfin

upperside   Silver-spotted Skipper   underside

upperside

underside
Arctic Skipper

Alpine Checkered Skipper

Orange Skipper

Northern Cloudy-wing

10

trout and salmon

Fish are cold-blooded aquatic vertebrates with fins, gills, and, usually, scales. Most are covered as well with a slimy coating of mucus, which reduces water resistance and protects against disease and parasites. Fins are extensions of the skin supported by soft or spiny rays. There are typically two sets of paired fins and three unpaired fins.

Fish breathe by taking water in through the mouth and passing it out through the gill openings. In the passage the water flows over numerous gill filaments, which are richly endowed with blood vessels. Dissolved oxygen in the water thereby passes into the bloodstream, while dissolved carbon dioxide in the blood is released to the water.

Fish are able to see clearly for short distances and use their eyes for both navigation and orientation, as well as for spotting food. Internal ears—without external openings—serve to both transmit sound and maintain equilibrium. A special sense organ, the *lateral line,* consists of a series of minute pores extending from the gills to the base of the tail. It is sensitive both to temperature changes in the water and to vibrations from external objects, both moving and stationary.

Although a variety of species inhabits the lakes and streams of our mountains, this guide focuses on the popular sport fish of the family Salmonidae: Pacific salmon, trout, and char. For other species native to the mountain waters of our region, the reader is referred to the books listed in Selected References at the back of this book.

Salmonids, which are native to cold waters of the northern hemisphere, are characterized by a streamlined body, small round scales, soft-rayed fins, and a fatty, or *adipose,* fin. There are five species of Pacific salmon—pink, coho, chinook, sockeye, and chum—all native to our region. Our native trout are the rainbow and cutthroat. The Dolly Varden, though popularly considered a trout, is our only native char.

Species introduced to our region include the brook trout and lake trout (both chars), the brown trout, and the golden trout. Lake trout and golden trout, however, are present only in very limited numbers in a few widely scattered lakes or streams. Of these introduced species, the brook trout is by far the most common and widespread in our region, having been stocked in lakes and streams both in the Cascades and Olympics, as well as on Vancouver Island.

All the salmon and some populations of rainbow, cutthroat, and Dolly Varden are *anadromous,* or seagoing, spawning in fresh water but thereafter migrating to the ocean. Sea-run rainbow are called steelhead and normally attain a much larger size than nonmigratory rainbows. Pacific salmon spend the greater part of their lives—from one to several years, depending on the species—at sea and are therefore generally classed as marine fish. At the end of their sojourn, however, they return to their home streams to spawn, after which they die.

Spawning behavior is similar for all five species of Pacific salmon. Upon or after entering the home stream, the males change radically in appearance, turning from silvery to various shades and combinations of red, green, and brown and developing pronounced hooked jaws and, in some cases, a humped back. Changes in the female are subtler, usually involving only a degree of alteration in color and pattern.

The time of year for spawning varies with each species and, to a lesser degree, with different populations of the same species, although many salmon populations have a fall/winter spawning cycle and can be observed in rivers and streams at that time. Salmon stop feeding when they enter fresh water to spawn and thus are less likely to be caught by anglers. Sockeye are unique among Pacific salmon in moving to freshwater lakes before their journey to the sea. Landlocked populations of sockeye, known as kokanee or silver trout, spend their entire lives in fresh water and are often taken by anglers.

Trout are the principal sport fish in our mountain waters and the only ones the vast majority of anglers ever lay eyes on in the course of fishing. Rainbow trout, cutthroat trout, and brook trout are the species most commonly encountered. Dolly Varden are somewhat less common, particularly south of Washington. Relatively few anglers will hook brown, golden, or lake trout in our waters. Large steelhead runs in the major streams provide a popular fishery throughout the region.

Most high glacial lakes in our mountains had no fish whatsoever prior to artificial stocking. Generally deficient in nutrients and lacking suitable spawning areas, those lakes are today stocked annually with brook, cutthroat, and rainbow trout. Golden trout, brown trout, or lake trout may also be present in some lakes.

Like salmon, trout and char spawn in gravel riffles in streams. Fish in lakes commonly move to tributary streams at spawning time and back into the lakes thereafter. Unlike salmon, trout and char do not die after spawning. Steelhead that survive the ordeal even return to the ocean. Seagoing Dolly Varden swim to the sea each spring and return in late summer or fall to spawn in headwater streams. Rainbow, steelhead, and cutthroat spawn from winter through late spring, depending on the species and particular population.

Trout fry feed on zooplankton and aquatic insect larvae. Adults, depending on the species and opportunities, take a variety of aquatic invertebrates, as well as terrestrial insects, fish, amphibians, and salmon eggs. Trout occupy a position near the top of the food chain in our mountain waters. As adults, they are preyed upon mainly by humans, less commonly by minks, otters, bears, bald eagles, ospreys, and one another.

Our trout and salmon, which require clear, well-aerated, unpolluted water, are indicators of water quality. Waters that maintain healthy populations of these magnificent fish are in the main in good condition. Where salmon and trout populations have declined, water quality is suspect. The three principal threats to trout and salmon populations in our region are dam building, improper logging practices, and the release of toxic substances into the water. The last of these is a minor concern in the mountains but a major problem in the lowlands. Improper logging, however, is the chief destroyer of streams in the mountains. It results in stream siltation, destruction of spawning grounds, and possibly lethal changes in water chemistry and increases in water temperature. Losses of fish in some watersheds have been substantial as a result and are particularly regrettable because they are avoidable. Dam building has reduced or destroyed salmon runs, particularly in the upper Columbia River watershed, and locally has created detrimental changes in water flow, temperature, and chemistry.

Although most trout caught in our mountains are hatchery stock, there are still a few natives around. Among serious anglers, the philosophy of catch-and-release is widely practiced in the cases of large native trout. These fishermen keep the smaller fish for food but toss the big natives back for others or themselves to catch again. Undersized fish should be handled as little as possible to avoid injuring them.

The species descriptions in this chapter focus on gross characteristics that serve to distinguish *most* individuals of one species from those of another. In some cases in which the species may be very similar, more technical distinctions are cited. A great deal of variation in color and pattern exists among both individuals and populations of both salmon and trout. The descriptions provided are for typical specimens.

Both popular and scientific names conform to *A List of Common and Scientific Names of Fishes from the United States and Canada* (fifth edition, American Fisheries Society, Special Publication 20, 1991). Other names in use are given in parentheses following the preferred name for each species. For general information on the organization and use of the species descriptions and illustrations, as well as for a list of the abbreviations used in the accounts, see the Introduction.

PLATE 71

TROUT AND SALMON FAMILY (SALMONIDAE)

Pink (humpback) salmon, *Oncorhynchus gorbuscha*. L to 30", wt to 10 lbs. Smallest, most abun Pacific salmon. Spawning M has pronounced dk, humped back, red sides blotched with brown; spawning F troutlike, olive green on sides; both sexes silvery upon entering spawning stream; large oblong spots, largest as long as eye diam, on back and *both* lobes of caudal fin. Spawn odd-numbered years, June-Sept, Alas to Cal; also ne Asia.

Coho (silver) salmon, *Oncorhynchus kisutch*. L to 38", wt to 31 lbs. Spawning M bluish green on back and head, with bright red stripe on ea side; spawning F drabber; abun small blk spots on back, dorsal fin, and *upper lobe only* of caudal fin, plus white gums on lower jaw. Spawn Sept-Dec (occas later), Alas to Cal; also ne Asia.

Chinook (king) salmon, *Oncorhynchus tshawytscha*. L to 60", wt gen to ca 80 lbs. Largest Pacific salmon. Spawning M has slight hump; both sexes at that stage are dk olive green to maroon or nearly blk, without conspicuous stripes or blotches on sides. Spawn gen May-Sept, esp in major rivers, Alas to Cal; also ne Asia.

Sockeye salmon and kokanee, *Oncorhynchus nerka*. L to 33", wt to 15½ lbs. Spawning M bright red on back and sides, with green head and white belly; spawning F similar, darker on sides; no distinct spots on backs and fins; 28–40 *long, slender* gill rakers (which don't show unless gills are opened) on first gill arch (cf chum salmon). Landlocked sockeye or kokanee silvery in nonbreeding stage. Spawn Aug-Dec, streams tributary to lakes, Alas to Cal; also ne Asia. Fry migrate to lakes after hatch, spending 1–2 years before migrating to ocean.

Chum (dog) salmon, *Oncorhynchus keta*. L to 38", wt to 45 lbs. Spawning adults nearly blk on back, brick red on sides with vertical greenish bars or mottling; no distinct spots on back and fins; 19–26 *short, stout* gill rakers (not visible unless gills are opened) on first gill arch (cf sockeye salmon). Spawn Aug-Jan, Alas to Cal, Arctic coast e to Mackenzie R; also ne Asia.

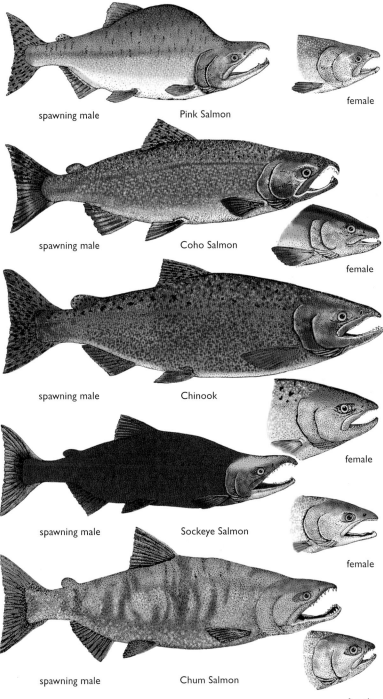

spawning male   Pink Salmon   female

spawning male   Coho Salmon   female

spawning male   Chinook   female

spawning male   Sockeye Salmon   female

spawning male   Chum Salmon   female

PLATE 72

TROUT AND SALMON FAMILY (SALMONIDAE)

Brown trout, *Salmo trutta.* L to 32½". Golden brown with dark spots surrounded by pale halos on sides of body. Secretive, wary, difficult to catch. Tolerates warmer waters (68°–75°F) than other trout. Native, n Europe; uncom and local, Cas.

Cutthroat trout, *Oncorhynchus clarki.* L gen to 19", occas larger. Both sea-run and nonmigratory populations in our range. Fresh sea-run fish bluish with silvery sides; nonmigratory fish gen green above, olive green on sides, silvery below, with pinkish sheen on gill covers. Numerous dk spots on back and sides, extending below lateral line; red-orange slash marks on underside of lower jaw (sometimes missing in sea-run fish). Lacks red side stripe or fins with colored borders; 150–180 scales in lateral line. Coastal fish spawn in smallest headwater streams, Alas to Cal; inland fish introduced to lakes and streams, Cas.

Rainbow trout and steelhead, *Oncorhynchus mykiss.* L gen to 30" (nonmigratory) or 45" (steelhead). Steelhead is the sea-run form of rainbow trout, both occurring throughout our range. Inland rainbows known as Kamloops trout in BC. Color variable, gen bluish or greenish on back and upper sides, usu with broad red lateral band on each side, plus numerous dk spots. Lacks red slashes beneath lower jaw; less than 150 scales in lateral line. Steelhead uniformly silver. Native, n Mex to Alas, e to Albta, Idaho, Nev; widely planted in mtn lakes and streams throughout our range. Steelhead runs in coastal streams Dec-Feb and Aug-Sept.

Brook trout (char), *Salvelinus fontinalis.* L gen 8"–16" in our area. Gen olive green with small greenish spots—some with red centers—surrounded by blue halos on sides of body; wavy marks on back and dorsal fin; white front margins on lower fins; caudal and lower fins gen pinkish. Native, e N Amer; widely planted in lakes and streams, Cas and OMtns; Cowichan drainage, Vanc I.

Dolly Varden, *Salvelinus malma.* L gen to 20". Both sea-run and nonmigratory populations in our range. Olive green with numerous creamy to red spots ca size of eye or slightly smaller. Spawning M has orange belly and red lower fins. Sea-run fish silvery with indistinct spots. Cold-water lakes and streams, Alas to n Cal, inland to RM; uncom s of Wn. Interior Dolly Varden, or bull trout, *S. confluentus,* similar in appearance; longer, broader head; local and uncom, Cas, Wn to n Cal.

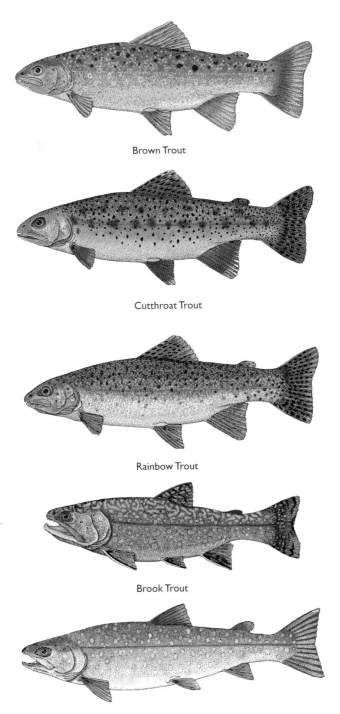

Brown Trout

Cutthroat Trout

Rainbow Trout

Brook Trout

Dolly Varden

II

amphibians

Amphibians occurring in our region include salamanders, tailed frogs, tree frogs, toads, and true frogs. All are partly aquatic, partly terrestrial vertebrates that regulate their body temperature through behavior. Such behavior includes spending a good deal of time in especially favored environments—in animal burrows, under rocks and logs, in the water—where changes in temperature and humidity are less pronounced than in the open. Frogs rarely venture far from water even as adults and may be seen abroad during the day along the margins of lakes and streams. Toads, tree frogs, and salamanders are more terrestrial, returning to water to spawn, but otherwise spending most of their time on land. Salamanders hole up in various damp retreats, emerging mainly at night for short periods during or after rains. Toads and tree frogs are chiefly nocturnal but may also be about during the day.

At higher elevations in the mountains, the spawning season begins early to midsummer and ends in the fall. During the remainder of the year, amphibians hibernate beneath the insulating blanket of snow. At lower elevations, however, the period of activity is longer.

Most amphibians have moist skin produced by a thin coating of mucus secreted from numerous glands. Toads also secrete a toxic milky fluid that repels some predators. By secreting mucus, terrestrial amphibians in a sense are able to carry the aquatic environment of their youth around with them. The mucus retards moisture loss and aids in respiration. (Though most amphibians possess lungs, all breathe to some extent through their skin.) The slippery coating may also assist them in eluding predators.

Amphibians begin life as larvae—i.e., tadpoles—equipped with gills and fins, as well as a streamlined shape, for successful existence in an aquatic environment. The larvae gradually transform into adults, losing gills and fins, developing lungs (in most cases) and limbs (which are absent in the larvae of frogs and toads, rudimentary in the larvae of salamanders).

Usually this transformation, or metamorphosis, occurs in a single season, but at high elevations two years may be required, with the larvae overwintering beneath the ice surface of frozen lakes. Some salamanders never transform into adults but grow in size and breed in the larval state.

Salamanders superficially resemble lizards but are readily distinguished by their smooth, moist, scaleless skin and clawless toes. Toads and frogs also have moist skin, which is smooth in frogs and warty in toads. Both have enlarged hind legs, webbed feet, and clawless toes.

Amphibians will eat almost any creature they can capture and swallow, including small vertebrates such as fish or tadpoles. In practice, however, their principal food is insects, worms, centipedes, spiders, and other invertebrates. They are preyed upon in turn by various birds and mammals and thus occupy a middle position in the food chain. The greatest threat to amphibians is human activity, particularly habitat destruction such as the draining of marshes and clear-cutting.

Because they are largely nocturnal and rather reclusive as a group, amphibians often go unseen even where they are abundant. Frequently they can be located only by lifting up logs, rocks, or loose bark to reveal their dens. If done carefully, this is a permissible activity that will not unduly disturb the animals. Further disturbance should be avoided, and when observation is complete the cover materials should be carefully replaced.

All but one of the eighteen species of amphibians found in our mountains are depicted in this chapter. The exception, a small salamander restricted to the Columbia River Gorge, is described briefly in the account of the western red-backed salamander.

Common and scientific names conform to *Scientific and Standard English Names of Amphibians and Reptiles of North America North of Mexico* (The Committee on Standard English and Scientific Names, 1997).

PLATE 73

NEWT FAMILY (SALAMANDRIDAE)

Rough-skinned newt, *Taricha granulosa.* L 5"–8½". Skin warty, not slimy, light brown to blk above, yellow or orange beneath, with or without black spots on belly. Breeding M has smooth skin. Only newt in our range. Ponds, lakes, slow-moving streams, adjacent forest, grassy places, se Alas s in W CMtns–Cas, Vanc I, OMtns to nw Cal.

MOLE SALAMANDER FAMILY (AMBYSTOMATIDAE)

Northwestern salamander, *Ambystoma gracile.* L 5½"–8". Brown above, with or without light flecks, light brown beneath, with conspicuous parotoid glands and thick tail. Moist places, beneath logs, rocks, near water, lowl-subalp, se Alas s in all our mtns to sw Ore, nw Cal.

Long-toed salamander, *Ambystoma macrodactylum.* L 4"–6". Dk brown to blk above, oft with lighter flecks and ± blotchy yellow or greenish stripe down back. Moist woods, mdws, near water, under logs, rocks, n BC s in all our mtns to Cal, e to RM.

Pacific giant salamander, *Dicamptodon tenebrus.* L 7"–12". Skin smooth, mottled brown or purplish above, paler beneath. Rivers, streams, moist forest under bark, rocks, logs, even walking or climbing about, extreme s BC s to cen Cal, also Idaho. Cope's giant salamander, *D. copei,* similar to larvae of Pacific giant salamander, but never transforms to adult; streams, OPen.

Torrent salamander, *Rhyacotriton olympicus.* L 3"–4½". Brown above, yellow-orange beneath, or mottled olive and brown above, yellow-green with blk mottling beneath. Cold, shady streams, seeps, springs in coastal forest, OMtns. Cascade torrent salamander, *R. cascadae,* found along W Cas of s Wn, Ore.

LUNGLESS SALAMANDER FAMILY (PLETHODONTIDAE)

Clouded salamander, *Aneides ferreus.* L 3"–5¼". Plain brown or mottled with green, gray, or copper above; whitish, or brown speckled with white, beneath. Coastal forest, oft near clearings under bark, Vanc I, w Ore (including Cas) s to nw Cal.

Oregon slender salamander, *Batrachoseps wrightii.* L 3¼"–4¼". Slim, short legged, wormlike; dk brown above with back stripe of gold or reddish blotches; blk spotted with white beneath. Coastal forest, Ore Cas, CRGorge to cen Ore.

Ensatina, *Ensatina eschscholtzii.* L 3"–6". Brown to nearly blk above; whitish or yellowish, with blk speckles, beneath; tail swollen, constricted at base. Forest, under rocks, logs, bark, W Cas to coast (Vanc I but not CMtns), extreme s BC to s Cal.

Rough-skinned Newt

parotoid glands

Northwestern Salamander

Long-toed Salamander

Pacific Giant Salamander

Torrent Salamander

Clouded Salamander

Oregon Slender Salamander

Ensatina

PLATE 74

LUNGLESS SALAMANDER FAMILY (PLETHODONTIDAE)

Dunn's salamander, *Plethodon dunni.* L 4"–6". Dk brown or blk above, with tan spots, white flecks, mottled yellowish or greenish stripe down back (not reaching tip of tail); dk gray-brown with yellowish spots beneath. Moist, shady rocks near water in coastal forest, W Cas in Ore, sw Ore to nw Cal.

Van Dyke's salamander, *Plethodon vandykei* sbsp *vandykei.* L 3¾"–5". Blk above with yellowish stripe down back and pale yellow throat; some individuals uniformly tan. Under rocks and logs near water, OMtns, W Cas of s Wn to coast.

Western red-backed salamander, *Plethodon vehiculum.* L 2¾"–4½". Dusky, speckled with white, on sides; back stripe gen reddish or tan, occas yellowish, distinct, extending to tip of tail; blue-gray beneath, flecked with yellow or orange. Moist places, low-mid el, W Cas to coast, extreme sw BC (including Vanc I), to s Ore. Larch Mountain salamander, *P. larselli,* similar but belly reddish, only in and near CR Gorge.

TAILED-FROG FAMILY (ASCAPHIDAE)

Tailed frog, *Ascaphus truei.* L 1"–2". Skin rough, gen olive or gray, occas dker, oft with blk stripe through eye; M with tail-like copulatory organ; pupils vertical; no external eardrum. Cold, swift streams, in all our mtns but Vanc I, s BC to nw Cal, e to Idaho, Mont.

TREE FROG FAMILY (HYLIDAE)

Pacific chorus frog (Pacific tree frog), *Pseudacris regilla.* L ¾"–2". Color variable and changeable; blk eyestripe and pale underside. Amid vegetation near water, low-high el, in all our mtns, s BC to Baja, e to Mont, Idaho, Nev.

TOAD FAMILY (BUFONIDAE)

Western toad, *Bufo boreas.* L 2½"–5". Gray to green with ± white stripe and many dk blotches. Forest, mdws, near water, lowl-subalp, in all our mtns, se Alas to Baja, Colo, Nev.

FROG FAMILY (RANIDAE)

Red-legged frog, *Rana aurora.* L 2"–3". Brownish or reddish above with blk flecks and blotches, red behind legs and on belly. Damp forest near water, sw BC to Baja, W Cas to coast. Spotted frog, *R. pretiosa,* very similar but dk spots oft have light centers, hind legs are shorter, skin has more warts.

Cascades frog, *Rana cascadae.* L 1¾"–2¼". Brown or olive above with distinct blk spots on back and legs; yellowish beneath. Moist mdws near water, mont-subalp, OMtns, Cas, Wn to Cal. Foothill yellow-legged frog, *R. boylei,* lacks distinct blk spots but is ± gray-mottled above and yellow beneath; W Cas, s Ore and Cal, w to coast, s to s Cal.

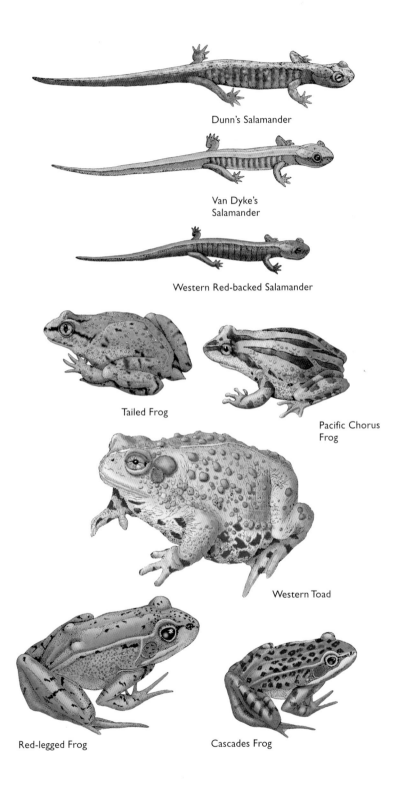

Dunn's Salamander

Van Dyke's
Salamander

Western Red-backed Salamander

Tailed Frog

Pacific Chorus
Frog

Western Toad

Red-legged Frog

Cascades Frog

12
reptiles

Reptiles are represented in our region by turtles, lizards, and snakes. The painted turtle and western pond turtle, confined largely to low-elevation ponds and slow-moving streams, are not included in this guide. Approximately six species of lizards and twelve species of snakes inhabit our mountains, and these are most numerous in the southern portion of the Cascade Range. The cool, humid climate of our northern mountains is particularly inhospitable to most reptiles. In western British Columbia and Washington, one is likely to encounter only two species of lizards (western fence lizard and northern alligator lizard) and four species of snakes (rubber boa, common garter snake, western terrestrial garter snake, and northwestern garter snake). Along the east slope of the Cascade Range, the number increases somewhat but still is not large. There is only one poisonous snake in our region, the northern Pacific rattlesnake, and it is absent from western Washington, much of western Oregon, and all but extreme south-central British Columbia.

Most reptiles hatch from hard- or leathery-shelled eggs that are buried in warm, sandy ground. Some garter snakes and rattlesnakes, however, are born live. In either case fertilization is internal, and the young are born fully active and alert.

Reptiles maintain remarkably constant body temperatures by moving back and forth between sunny and shady locations. During the morning hours, many snakes and lizards warm up by basking on rocks or open ground. At dusk they commonly seek out rocks, which retain the day's heat after sundown. In cool, cloudy weather, they may remain in their dens or burrows even during the day. Reptiles tend to be intolerant of cold weather, and our species either hibernate or at least temporarily den up during cold spells. The only reptiles apt to be found at high elevations in our region are garter snakes.

The appreciation of reptiles seems to be an acquired taste. The great majority of humankind has a deep-seated, time-honored, and ultimately irrational aversion to lizards and, in particular, snakes. Presumably, many readers share this feeling. On behalf of reptiles, however, it should be noted that many species boast patterns and colors whose beauty rivals that of birds, and all display modes of behavior that, precisely because they are alien to those of warm-blooded creatures such as ourselves, are just that much more interesting. Moreover, reptiles are voracious feeders upon insects, spiders, and other invertebrates and thus play an important role in keeping populations of those creatures in check. True, reptiles may also feed upon birds, amphibians, small mammals, and fish, but in this they are no different from any other predators. Finally, the great majority of reptiles are harmless to humans, and in our region only the northern Pacific rattle-snake poses a potential—and vastly overrated—threat. The rattlesnake is by nature retiring and, if unmolested, will quickly retreat upon encountering a human. Anyone tramping through rattlesnake country should feel fortunate even to get a glimpse of the animal. To actually get bitten requires either monumental bad luck or carelessness. Moreover, even if one sustains a bite, it is rarely fatal—despite popular notions to the contrary—to a normally healthy adult. Visitors who can learn to regard reptiles with an objective eye will find much to repay their attention.

Common and scientific names conform to *Scientific and Standard English Names of Amphibians and Reptiles of North America North of Mexico* (The Committee on Standard English and Scientific Names, 1997). For information on the use of the species descriptions and illustrations, as well as for a list of the abbreviations used in the accounts, see the Introduction.

PLATE 75

IGUANA FAMILY (IGUANIDAE)

Sagebrush lizard, *Sceloporus graciosus*. L 5"–6¼". Gray or brown above, with dker spots and bars and pale stripes down body; blue belly patches and throat patch in M; orange throat in F; rusty behind forelegs; no yellow or orange on back of legs; smaller scales than western fence lizard. Sagebrush, dry woods, lower E Cas of Wn, Cas of Ore and Cal; widespread in w US s to s Cal, e to RM.

Western fence lizard, *Sceloporus occidentalis*. L 6"–9¼". Brown, gray, or blk above with dker spots, bars, occas paler stripes; orange or yellow behind legs, blue belly patches, blue throat patch in M; scales larger, spinier than sagebrush lizard. Rocky places, low-high el, E Cas of Wn, Cas of Ore and Cal, local on OPen; Wn to Baja, e to Idaho, Utah.

ALLIGATOR LIZARD FAMILY (ANGUIDAE)

Northern alligator lizard, *Elgaria coerulea*. L 8¾"–13". Large, short legged, dark eyed; olive to bluish above with indistinct crossbars or blotches on back and tail. Moist woods to high el, s BC to Cal, e to n RM.

Southern alligator lizard, *Elgaria multicarinata*. L 10"–17". Similar to above sp, but eyes yellow, body rusty to yellowish above with distinct crossbars on back and tail. Moist places, woods and forest, Cas, Wn (E Cas only) to Cal, s to Baja.

SKINK FAMILY (SCINCIDAE)

Western skink, *Eumeces skiltonianus*. L 6½"–9¼". Boldly blk, cream, and brown striped; tail indistinctly striped in adults, blue in juveniles. Gen rocky places, Cas, Ore to Cal, lower E Cas in Wn.

Sagebrush Lizard

Western Fence Lizard

Northern Alligator Lizard

Southern Alligator Lizard

Western Skink

PLATE 76

BOA FAMILY (BOIDAE)

Rubber boa, *Charina bottae.* L 14"–29". Plain brown above, yellowish beneath, without pattern; scales small, smooth, shiny; tail ± shaped like head. Damp places, oft near water, in forest, also mdws, in all our mtns but Vanc I, s BC s to Cal, e to RM.

RACER FAMILY (COLUBRIDAE)

Racer, *Coluber constrictor.* L 22"–78". Plain olive or brown above, yellow beneath; slender, whiplike, large eyes. Dry forest, woods, Cas from Wn (E Cas only) to Cal; widespread in w US, s Can to Mex.

Sharp-tailed snake, *Contia tenuis.* L 8"–18". Rusty brown or gray above, grading to red near tail; distinct yellow and black crossbars beneath; tail sharply pointed. Forest, grassy places, oft near water, low-mid el, W Cas, mostly Ore to Cal (local in s Wn Cas), s along coast and in SNev to cen Cal.

Ringneck snake, *Diadophus punctatus.* L 12"–30". Olive or bluish above, red or yellow beneath and extending in ring around neck. Moist woods, Cas, Ore to Cal; also CR Gorge; widespread but spotty throughout US.

Common kingsnake, *Lampropeltis getula.* L 30"–82". Dk brown or blk rings alternating with pale yellow or white. Various habitats, Cas, s Ore to Cal; widespread in N Amer. California mountain kingsnake, *L. zonata,* with white and red bands bordered with blk, occurs locally in extreme s Wn Cas and in mtns of sw Ore and Cal, including Cas.

Striped whipsnake, *Masticophis taeniatus.* L 30"–72". Gray to olive above, with creamy stripe bisected by black line on ea side; whiplike. Dry woods, sagebrush, E Cas, Ore to Cal; e Wn and Idaho s to e Cal, Ariz, NMex, Mex.

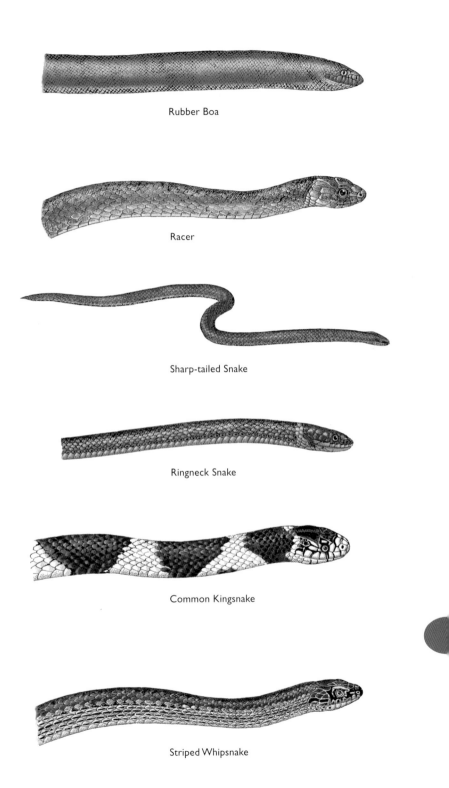

Rubber Boa

Racer

Sharp-tailed Snake

Ringneck Snake

Common Kingsnake

Striped Whipsnake

PLATE 77

RACER FAMILY (COLUBRIDAE)

Gopher snake, *Pituophis melanoleucus.* L 3'–8⅓'. Yellowish or creamy with blk spots and blotches. Grassland, brush, open woods, Cas, Wn (E Cas only) to Cal.

Common garter snake, *Thamnophis sirtalis.* L 18"–51". 3 sbspp: Puget Sound garter snake, *T. s.* sbsp *pickeringii,* similar to red-spotted but yellowish back stripe confined to only one scale row and top of head gen blk; wet places, sw CMtns, Vanc I, OMtns, W Cas of Wn. Red-spotted garter snake, *T. s.* sbsp *concinnus,* blk with yellowish stripe down back, reddish spots on sides and gen red on head, blk extending onto belly, lateral stripes oft obscured; damp places, W Cas of Ore, sw Wn and w Ore. Valley garter snake, *T. s.* sbsp *fitchi,* dk gray or brown with broad back stripe, no reddish side spots, blk on top of head; moist places, CMtns, Cas, BC to Cal, e to RM.

Western terrestrial garter snake, *Thamnophis elegans.* L 18"–57". 2 sbspp: wandering garter snake, *T. e.* sbsp *vagrans,* gray or olive above (occas blk near Puget Sound), with distinct yellowish or tan stripes and black spots between stripes; no reddish spots; moist places near water, lowl–subalp, CMtns, OMtns, Cas, BC to Ore; s in e Ore to Cal, e to RM. Mountain garter snake, *T. e.* sbsp *elegans,* blkish above, pale beneath, with yellow back stripe and pale yellow side stripes; no reddish spots; moist places near water, Cas, Ore to Cal; s in Cal mtns.

Northwestern garter snake, *Thamnophis ordinoides.* L 15"–26". Brown, greenish, bluish, or blk above, yellow beneath, with distinct red, yellow, or orange back stripe, lateral stripe occas obscure or absent. Moist mdws, thickets, low-mid el, W CMtns, Vanc I, OMtns, Cas to s Ore, also nw Cal.

VIPER FAMILY (VIPERIDAE)

Northern Pacific rattlesnake, *Crotalus viridis* sbsp *oreganus.* L 15"–62". Triangular head and rattles on tail; olive, gray, or brownish, with large dk brown or blk blotches. Dry brushy or rocky places, low-mid el, Cas, Wn to Cal, E Cas only in BC, Wn, n Ore; s to s Cal, e to Idaho.

Gopher Snake

Common (Puget Sound) Garter Snake

Western Terrestrial (Wandering) Garter Snake

Western Terrestrial (Mountain) Garter Snake

Northwestern Garter Snake

Northern Pacific Rattlesnake

13

birds

Birds attract our attention by their sheer numbers, variety, beauty, and bold, lively behavior. Mammals, reptiles, and amphibians are not only less numerous, both in species and absolute numbers, but are less obvious, tending more often to be reclusive or nocturnal. An observant visitor to the mountains can expect to encounter many species of birds but may not see a single mammal, reptile, or amphibian. To a greater degree than these other vertebrates, birds rely heavily on visual cues for choosing mates and recognizing members of their own species. As a result, most species have evolved distinctive, often striking plumages, which allow us to identify them with relative ease.

Feathers, which distinguish birds from all other animals, provide excellent insulation against cold and a smooth outer surface to reduce air resistance during flight and—through various types of pigmentation and structure—to aid in recognition and courtship. Flight is made possible by the specialized flight feathers of the wings, as well as by other anatomical features, such as hollow bones and enlarged breast bones to which the relatively huge flight muscles are attached.

Flight provides birds a degree of mobility denied to other terrestrial vertebrates. As a result, birds are able to move rapidly into newly available habitats and to avoid shortages of food or water—as well as other problems—by utilizing different, often widely separated habitats during different seasons of the year. More than half the species nesting in our mountains during the summer migrate southward in the fall and winter, heading to the southern United States or even South America, depending on the species. Many other species simply move downslope to spend the winter in the milder climes of the lowlands. A small number of species spends the entire year in the mountains.

The best places to look for birds are near water and along habitat boundaries. For example, far more species will be seen along the margins of the forest than deep within its interior. As a matter of fact, dense conifer forests, contrary to popular belief, support relatively few species of birds compared to adjacent meadows, brush, and woodlands, where food is available in greater variety. Moreover, observing the birds that do live in the forest is often difficult because many species spend the greater part of their time foraging high in the trees. The best times to look for birds other than owls, which are largely nocturnal, are shortly after dawn, when activity is at its daily maximum, and near dusk, when activity increases after a midday hiatus. Few birds may be in evidence in the afternoon.

Approximately 120 species of birds are depicted in this guide, including all the common nesting species. Omitted for reasons of space are uncommon or rare visitors, migrants, and casual nesters, which even experienced birders are unlikely to encounter. This guide, however, is not intended for serious birders, who will be able to recognize virtually all these species without recourse to a field guide, but for the casual observer who wants to identify the birds seen on the trail or in camp.

Birds are grouped on the plates by family, though for entirely practical reasons the taxonomic order preferred by most ornithologists is not strictly followed. If male and female differ greatly in appearance, usually both are shown. If the difference is minor, the showier of the two (nearly always the male) is shown, and the female's plumage is described in the species description. Several species either occur in more than one color phase or exhibit markedly different plumages during different times of the year. Such species are shown only in the plumages they most commonly exhibit during their sojourn in our mountains. Finally, birds, like people, exhibit individual differences, and their markings and colors may seem to change somewhat according to available light. Such variations should be considered when your specimens do not exactly match the illustrations, which depict typical individuals seen at close range in a direct, bright light.

Common and scientific names conform to the *Checklist of North American Birds* (seventh edition, American Ornithologists Union, 1998). For information on the use of the species descriptions and illustrations, as well as for a list of the abbreviations used in the accounts, see the Introduction.

PLATE 78

LOON FAMILY (GAVIIDAE)
Common loon, *Gavia immer.* L 28"–36". Ducklike, with long, pointed bill; rides low in water; neck and legs droop in flt. Uncom sum res, lakes, Vanc I, CMtns, Cas s to n Cal; breeds Alas e to Iceland, s to n US.

WATERFOWL FAMILY (ANATIDAE)
Barrow's goldeneye, *Bucephala islandica.* L 16½"–20". M has white crescent on head; F's head brown with white collar. Uncom sum res, lakes and streams, CMtns, Cas s to Cal; breeds Alas, n Can, s in mtns to US; win along coasts; Eurasia.

Harlequin duck, *Histrionicus histrionicus.* L 14½"–21". M has rusty sides, harlequin pattern; F has 3 white spots on head. Uncom-rare sum res, mtn streams in all our mtns; breeds Alas, n Can, s in mtns to US; win along coasts; ne Asia, Greenland.

Common merganser, *Mergus merganser.* L 22"–27". M has white body, green head; F has rusty head and crest; both have narrow, hooked, serrated bill. Com sum res, lakes and streams, in all our mtns; Alas, n Can s in mtns to s US; win along coasts; Eurasia.

PLOVER FAMILY (CHARADRIIDAE)
Killdeer, *Charadrius vociferus.* L 9"–11". Has 2 blk breast bands, reddish rump. Nests on ground. Fairly com to rare sum res or vis, open places near water, in all our mtns s to Cal; Can to cen Mex and Caribbean, also Peru.

SANDPIPER FAMILY (SCOLOPACIDAE)
Common snipe, *Gallinago gallinago.* L ca 11". Extremely long bill, white belly, zigzag flt. Uncom sum res, wet mdws, bogs, mtn marshes, in all our mtns, BC to Cal; N Amer and Eurasia.

Spotted sandpiper, *Actitis macularia.* L 7"–8". Round blk spots on white breast; bobbing walk; smaller than snipe, with much shorter bill. Com sum res, mtn lakes and streams in all our mtns, BC to Cal; Alas, Can to US; win s US to S Amer.

KINGFISHER FAMILY (ALCEDINIDAE)
Belted kingfisher, *Ceryle alcyon.* L 11"–14½". Large, crested head; long, pointed bill; broad, gray breastband; F has rusty breastband. Com sum res near water, in all our mtns; N Amer s to s US; win s to cen Amer.

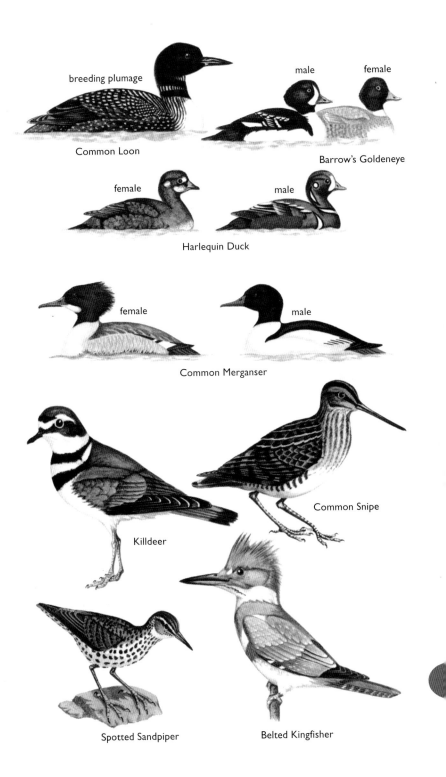

breeding plumage

Common Loon

male female

Barrow's Goldeneye

female male

Harlequin Duck

female male

Common Merganser

Killdeer

Common Snipe

Spotted Sandpiper

Belted Kingfisher

PLATE 79

HAWK FAMILY (ACCIPITRIDAE)

Northern goshawk, *Accipiter gentilis.* L 20"–26". Gray back; light, barred breast; barred tail; young are brown with spotted breast. Uncom-rare res, forest, in all our mtns s to Cal; Eurasia, N Amer.

Cooper's hawk, *Accipiter cooperii.* L 14"–20". Contrasting rusty-barred breast and gray back. Com to rare sum res, forest and decid woods, esp near clearings, in all our mtns s to Cal. Sharp-shinned hawk, *A. striatus,* very similar but smaller and tip of tail notched, not rounded as in Cooper's hawk.

Red-tailed hawk, *Buteo jamaicensis.* L 19"–25". Gen seen soaring. Clear rusty tail is diagnostic. Some birds dker than shown. Com sum res, in all our mtns s to Cal; widespread in N Amer s to Panama. Ferruginous hawk, *B. regalis,* white beneath except for rusty legs; vis or rare res in our mtns. Rough-legged hawk, *B. lagopus,* has white tail with blk band near tip; migr.

Swainson's hawk, *Buteo swainsoni.* L 19"–22". Gen seen soaring. From below, note white wing linings with dker flt feathers, white tail (dk forms—not shown here—lack white wing linings, have narrowly banded tails). Uncom-rare sum res and vis, Wn Cas s to Cal; N Amer to n Mex.

Golden eagle, *Aquila chrysaetos.* L 30"–40". Large; uniformly dk color. Rare-com res, rough, open country, mostly E Cas, BC to Cal; widespread in N Amer; Eurasia.

Bald eagle, *Haliateetus leucocephalus.* L 33"–43". Large; white head and tail in adult; patches of white in young. Rare or locally com res near water, BC to Cal; com win vis to lowl rivers, lakes, bays; rare post-nesting wanderers in Cas; N Amer s to s US.

OSPREY FAMILY (PANDIONIDAE)

Osprey, *Pandion haliatus.* L 21"–24½". White underparts, white head with blk through cheek. Local, rare-com res near lakes, BC to Cal; widespread in N Amer; worldwide.

FALCON FAMILY (FALCONIDAE)

Peregrine falcon, *Falco peregrinus.* L 15"–21". Gray back, blk and white head, long pointed wings, no blk patches in wingpits during flt. Rare and local res or vis, in all our mtns; widespread but rare (endangered) in N Amer; worldwide. Prairie falcon, *F. mexicanus,* is sandy colored, with blk wingpits; casual or rare vis. Gyrfalcon, *F. rusticolus,* much larger, grayer, less distinctly marked; casual win vis.

American kestrel (sparrow hawk), *Falco sparverius.* L 9"–12". Small; pointed wings; rusty color; F similar but wings rusty and tail banded. Fairly com sum res, open places, mostly E Cas, but also w to coast, BC to Cal; most of N and S Amer.

Northern Goshawk

Cooper's Hawk

Red-tailed Hawk

Swainson's Hawk

Golden Eagle

Bald Eagle

Osprey

Peregrine Falcon

American Kestrel

PLATE 80

GROUSE AND PTARMIGAN FAMILY (PHASIANIDAE)

Blue (dusky, sooty) grouse, *Dendragapus obscurus.* L 15½"–21". M has dk gray plumage, paler band at tip of tail; F brownish with dk tail. Com res, forest, BC to Cal; Alas, n Can, s to Cal, Ariz, NMex.

Spruce (Franklin's) grouse, *Falcipennis canadensis.* L 15"–17". M has blkish plumage with white spots on sides and tail; F rusty brown, barred, with tail like M's. Fairly com res, forest, esp mont-subalp, CMtns, Cas, BC and n Wn; Alas, Can, n US.

Ruffed grouse, *Bonasa umbellus.* L 16"–19". Barred breast and sides, barred tail with blk band. Most birds rusty brown, some gray-brown. Com, lowl-mont forest in all our mtns, s to s Ore; Alas, most of Can, s in mtns of US.

White-tailed ptarmigan, *Lagopus leucurus.* L 12"–13". Short white tail; no blk eye mark in win. Com res, alp, Alas s in mtns to Wn, e to RM. Rock ptarmigan, *L. mutus,* has short blk tail, dker sum plumage, blk eye mark in win; uncom res in CMtns of s BC n to Alas, n Can.

NEW WORLD QUAIL FAMILY (ODONTOPHORIDAE)

Mountain quail, *Oreortyx pictus.* L ca 11". Long, erect head plume; chestnut throat, sides, and belly; vertical white streaks on sides. Rare-com local res, brushy places, OMtns, Cas, n Wn to Cal. California quail, *Callipepla californica,* has comma-shaped head plume, blk throat, golden-scaled belly, horizontal side streaks; lowl–low mtns only. Northern bobwhite, *Colinus virginianus,* has white throat and eye line; E Cas foothills.

PIGEON FAMILY (COLUMBIDAE)

Band-tailed pigeon, *Columba fasciata.* L ca 15". Similar to domestic pigeon (rock dove), but slimmer; white crescent on nape of neck, light band on tail. Com sum res, woods and forest, low-mid el, in all our mtns s to Cal. Mourning dove, *Zenaida macroura,* is much slimmer, has long, pointed tail bordered in white; rare res and vis, mostly lower el, E Cas.

Blue Grouse

Spruce Grouse

Ruffed Grouse

winter

summer

White-tailed Ptarmigan

Mountain Quail

Band-tailed Pigeon

PLATE 81

OWL FAMILY (STRIGIDAE)

Western screech owl, *Otus kennicottii.* L 8"–10". Small; prominent ear tufts; gray, brown, and rusty phases. Nocturnal. Call a series of rapid, descending hoots. Open forest, oft near water, gen low-mid el, in all our mtns s to Cal; coastal BC throughout all of US to cen Mex.

Flammulated owl, *Otus flammeolus.* L 6"–7". Small; dk eyes, tiny ear tufts. Nocturnal. Call a series of hollow-sounding hoots, often in pairs. Uncom res, dry forest, E Cas s to Cal; extreme s BC s in mtns of w US to Cen Amer.

Great horned owl, *Bubo virginianus.* L 18"–25". Large; prominent ear tufts, barred underparts. Nocturnal. Call a loud series of 3–8 hoots, 2nd and 3rd often short and rapid, last hoots spaced apart. Fairly com res, various habitats in all our mtns s to Cal; widespread in w hemis.

Northern saw-whet owl, *Aegolius acadicus.* L 7"–8½". Songbird size; no ear tufts; streaked underparts; white **V** over eyes in young. Nocturnal. Call a series of same note repeated, sometimes sounding mechanical. Com-uncom res, forest in all our mtns s to Cal; se Alas s through most of Can and US to cen Mex.

Northern pygmy owl, *Glaucidium gnoma.* L ca 7". Songbird size; blk patches at nape of neck, streaked sides. Nocturnal/diurnal. Call a repeated series of evenly spaced, high-pitched hoots. Rare-uncom res, forest, Vanc I, CMtns, Cas s to Cal; Alas s in w Can and w US to cen Mex.

Barred owl, *Strix varia.* L 18"–21". Large; dk eyes, no ear tufts, heavily streaked undersides. Nocturnal. Call a series of loud hoots, usu 6–8, last one extended: *who cooks for youuuuu.* Only owl likely to call during daylight. Com res, forest in all our mtns, BC, Cas s to Cal, e states. Spotted owl, *S. occidentalis,* L 16½"–19", similar but smaller, spotted and streaked undersides; nocturnal; call a set of doglike barks; rare res, forest in all our mtns s to Cal, Pac coast, BC to Cal, e to s RM.

GOATSUCKER FAMILY (CAPRIMULGIDAE)

Common poorwill, *Phalaenoptilus nuttallii.* L 7"–8½". Rounded wings without white bars, short rounded tail with white outer corners. Nocturnal. Seldom noticed. Rare res, mostly E Cas, Wn s to Cal; e to mid US, s to cen Mex.

Common nighthawk, *Chordeiles minor.* L 8½"–10". Pointed, swept-back wings with white crossbar on ea. Gen seen flying at twilight. Utters a distinctive metallic-sounding call during flt. Com-rare res, open areas, pine forest, in all our mtns s to Cal; widespread in N Amer in sum; win S Amer.

Western Screech Owl

Flammulated Owl

Great Horned Owl

Northern Saw-whet Owl

Northern Pygmy Owl

Barred Owl

Common Poorwill

Common Nighthawk

PLATE 82

WOODPECKER FAMILY (PICIDAE)

Northern flicker, *Colaptes auratus.* L 12½"–14". Orange on underside of wings and tail, heavily spotted breast and belly; M has red streak on gray cheek (lacking in F). Com res, open forest, clearings, in all our mtns s to Cal. Yellow-shafted race, with yellow on underside of wings and tail, uncom-irreg win vis in our area, widespread in N Amer.

Pileated woodpecker, *Dryocopus pileatus.* L 16"–19½". Large; red crest, white wing patches in flt. Uncom res, forest, in all our mtns s to Cal; Can s to nw and e US.

Lewis' woodpecker, *Melanerpes lewis.* L ca 11". Red face, pink underparts, green head and back. Uncom res, open woods, clearings, in all our mtns s to Cal; breeds cen Can s in w US to s Cal, NMex; win widely.

Red-naped sapsucker, *Spyrapicus nuchalis.* L 7"–8½". Red on crown and chin, blk and white pattern on face, yellow underparts, barred back. Com res, forest, riparian woods, in all our mtns, BC to Cal.

Red-breasted sapsucker, *Sphyrapicus ruber.* L 8"–9". Bright red head and breast, lemon yellow belly. Com res, mixed conif and decid forest, in all our mtns, se Alas to Cal.

Williamson's sapsucker, *Sphyrapicus thyroideus.* L 8¼"–9½". M has blk back and breast, blk crown and red chin, white wing patch; F has brown head, barred back and wings, yellow belly. Uncom res, open forest, mostly mid-high el, gen E Cas, s BC to Cal; widespread in mtns of w US.

Hairy woodpecker, *Picoides villosus.* L 8½"–10½". Clear white back, large blk bill; F lacks red on head. Com res, forest, in all our mtns s to Cal; widespread in US, s to Cen Amer.

Downy woodpecker, *Picoides pubescens.* L 6"–7". Very similar to above sp but noticeably smaller in most cases, slimmer bill; F lacks red on head. Com res, decid woods, in all our mtns s to Cal; Alas s in w and se Can through most of US.

White-headed woodpecker, *Picoides albolarvatus.* L 7¾"–9". White head; red nape absent in F. Uncom res, dry forest, E Cas, Wn to Cal; s in SNev.

Black-backed woodpecker, *Picoides arcticus.* L 9"–10". Blk back, barred sides, yellow cap. Rare res, open forest, mont-subalp, mostly E Cas, BC s to Cal; Alas s in mtns of Pac states, e to n RM, ne US.

Three-toed woodpecker, *Picoides tridactylus.* L 8"–9½". Barred back and sides; yellow cap. Uncom-rare res, forest, upper mont–subalp, in all our mtns s to Cal; widespread in Can and n US.

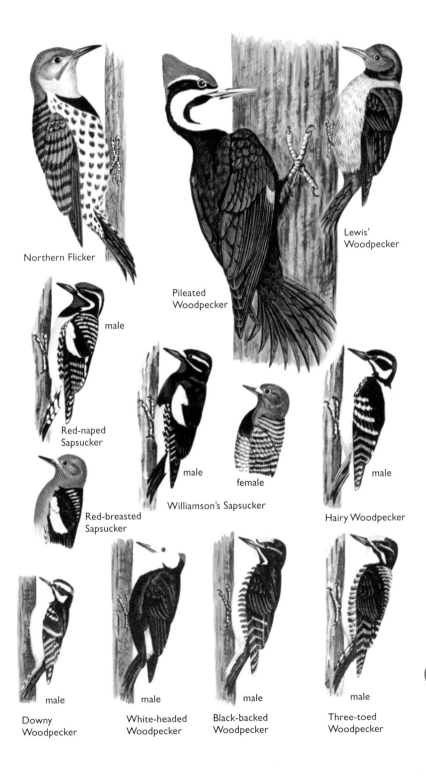

Northern Flicker

Lewis'
Woodpecker

Pileated
Woodpecker

Red-naped
Sapsucker

male

male

female

Williamson's Sapsucker

Red-breasted
Sapsucker

male

Hairy Woodpecker

male

Downy
Woodpecker

male

White-headed
Woodpecker

male

Black-backed
Woodpecker

male

Three-toed
Woodpecker

PLATE 83

HUMMINGBIRD FAMILY (TROCHILIDAE)

Calliope hummingbird, *Stellula calliope.* L 2¾"–3½". M has green head, back, and tail, reddish- to purple-streaked throat; F smaller than but nearly identical to F rufous (cf sp below). Local, occas com sum res, clearings, mdws, mostly E CMtns–Cas s to Cal; breeds cen BC s to Colo and s Cal; win Mex.

Rufous hummingbird, *Selasphorus rufus.* L 3¼"–4". M has rusty head, back, sides, and tail, metallic red throat; F green above, ± white below, buffy on sides, with rust in tail. Cf sp above. Com sum res, mdws, clearings, low-high el, in all our mtns s to Cal; breeds se Alas to nw Cal, e to n RM; win Mex.

SWIFT FAMILY (APODIDAE)

Vaux's swift, *Chaetura vauxi.* L 4"–4½". Dk but not blk underparts, stubby tail, narrow swept-back wings. Sum res, forest, se Alas s in BC and Pac states to Mex.

Black swift, *Cypseloides niger.* L ca 7¼". Narrow swept-back wings, blk underparts, forked tail; larger than following sp. Local sum res, near waterfalls, se Alas s in mtns to Mex, e to RM.

SWALLOW FAMILY (HIRUNDINIDAE)

Violet-green swallow, *Tachycineta thalassina.* L 5"–5½". White rump patches and eye patch, green head and back; purple at nape and tail. Com sum res, various habitats, in all our mtns s to Cal; breeds Alas s in BC and w US to Mex; win Mex and Cen Amer.

Tree swallow, *Tachycineta bicolor.* L 5"–6". Solid blue-green head and back, white underparts, no purple or white near eye or on rump. Com sum res, forest, oft near water, in all our mtns s to Cal; breeds widely N Amer; win s US to Cen Amer.

Northern rough-winged swallow, *Stelgidopteryx serripennis.* L 5"–5¾". Brown back and white underparts without dk band. Com sum res near water, mostly lowl, but also mont, in all our mtns s to Cal; breeds s Can through all of US to n Mex; win s of US. Bank swallow, *Riparia riparia,* similar but brown band across breast; sum vis and res, low-mid el.

Barn swallow, *Hirundo rustica.* L 5¾"–7¾". Blue back, orange underparts, forked tail. Com sum res near habitations, in all our mtns s to Cal; widespread sum res, N Amer and Eurasia; win s hemis.

Cliff swallow, *Petrochelidon pyrrhonota.* L 5"–6". Rusty throat and rump, pale underparts, unforked tail. Com, irreg sum res near cliffs and water, low-mid el in all our mtns s to Cal; widespread sum res N Amer; win S Amer.

male

Calliope Hummingbird

male

Rufous Hummingbird

Black Swift

Vaux's Swift

Violet-green Swallow

Tree Swallow

Northern Rough-winged Swallow

Barn Swallow

Cliff Swallow

PLATE 84

TYRANT FLYCATCHER FAMILY (TYRANNIDAE)

Eastern kingbird, *Tyrannus tyrannus.* L 8"–9". White underparts, blk head and back, blk tail with white band at tip. Rare-com sum res, open woods, gen near water, low el, CMtns, Cas s to n Ore; breeds s Can, nw and e US; win S Amer. Western kingbird, *T. verticalis,* similar with light gray head, yellow belly; lowl, E Cas.

Empidonax flycatcher, *Empidonax* spp. L 5"–6¾". Dk green, olive, or gray back; white to yellowish underparts; 2 white wingbars; light eye ring. In our area 6 spp, very difficult to distinguish, esp during migr; all distinguished from kinglets and vireos by habit of repeatedly sallying forth from same perch to catch flying insects. Hammond's flycatcher, *E. hammondii,* is the most com in mtns. Dusky flycatcher, *E. oberholseri,* E Cas.

Western wood-pewee, *Contopus sordidulus.* L 6"–6½". Similar to *Empidonax* flycatchers but gen larger, lacks eye ring, wings much longer. Uncom-com sum res, forest, decid woods, esp near water, low-mid el, in all our mtns s to Cal; breeds Alas s to n Mex, e to RM; win Cen and S Amer.

Olive-sided flycatcher, *Contopus cooperi.* L 7"–8". Olive vest, no wingbars. Distinctive *hic-three-beers* call. Uncom-com sum res, forest, lowl-subalp in all our mtns, s to Cal; breeds Alas s to n Mex, e to RM and ne US; win S Amer.

KINGLET FAMILY (REGULIDAE)

Golden-crowned kinglet, *Regulus satrapa.* L 3¼"–4". Blk and yellow (and red in M) crown and white eye stripe. Com res, forest; com win vis, woods; in all our mtns s to Cal; breeds widely Can, n US, mtns of W; win widely s Can to Mex.

Ruby-crowned kinglet, *Regulus calendula.* L 3¾"–4½". M has red crown patch (oft not seen); both M and F have broken eye ring, habit of continually fluttering wings. Com sum res, forest; win vis other wooded areas; Vanc I, CMtns, Cas s to Cal; widespread in N Amer.

VIREO FAMILY (VIREONIDAE)

Cassin's vireo, *Vireo cassinii.* L 5"–6". White "spectacles," 2 white wingbars, white throat. Sum res, gen forest, low-mid el, in all our mtns s to Cal; breeds Can, w US, ne US s in Appalachians; win from s US south.

Red-eyed vireo, *Vireo olivaceus.* L 5½"–6½". Blk and white eyebrow stripes, red eye, no spectacles or wingbars. Com sum res, decid woods, low-mid el, CMtns, OMtns, Cas s to n Ore; breeds Can, n and e US; win S Amer.

Warbling vireo, *Vireo gilvus.* L 4½"–5½". Plain, unmarked, dull greenish plumage. Com sum res, decid woods, low-mid el, in all our mtns s to Cal; widespread sum res in N Amer; win Mex and Cen Amer.

Empidonax Flycatcher

Western Wood-pewee

Eastern Kingbird

Olive-sided Flycatcher

Cassin's Vireo

male

female

Golden-crowned Kinglet

Red-eyed Vireo

male

Ruby-crowned Kinglet

Warbling Vireo

PLATE 85

CROW FAMILY (CORVIDAE)

Gray jay, *Perisoreus canadensis.* L 10"–13". Fluffy gray plumage, white forehead, blk across back of head. Young are slate gray. Com res, forest, lowl-subalp, in all our mtns to Mt. Shasta; Alas across Can to ne US, s in RM and Pac mtns.

Steller's jay, *Cyanocitta stelleri.* L 12"–13½". Dk blue body; blk, crested head. Com res, conif forest, lowl-subalp, in all our mtns s to Cal; Alas s in mtns and forests w of RM to Cen Amer. Two other blue jay spp occas range into Cas of Ore, s Wn; both lack crests. Western scrub jay, *Aphelocoma californica,* res of oak woodland and chaparral, may range upslope into pine-fir forests. Pinyon jay, *Gymnorhinus cyanocephalus,* inhabits juniper woods e of Cas from s Ore to Cal.

Clark's nutcracker, *Nucifraga columbiana.* L 12"–13". Blk and white wings and tail, gray body; long, blk, awl-shaped bill. Com res, subalp forest where pines, esp whitebark pine, occur, CMtns, OMtns, Cas s to Cal.

Common raven, *Corvus corax.* L 21½"–27". Large; thick bill, shaggy throat feathers, wedge-shaped tail. Deep, harsh, croaklike call. Com res, forest, woodland, in all our mtns s to Cal; widespread in n hemis.

American crow, *Corvus brachyrhynchos.* L 17"–21". Smaller than raven, thinner bill, no shaggy throat feathers, fan-shaped tail (in flt), higher-pitched call. Com res, various habitats, low-mid el, in all our mtns s to Cal; widespread in Can and US.

Steller's Jay

Gray Jay

Clark's Nutcracker

Common Raven

American Crow

PLATE 86

CHICKADEE (TIT) FAMILY (PARIDAE)

Black-capped chickadee, *Poecile atricapillus.* L 4¾"–5¾". Solid blk cap, gray back, buffy sides. Com res, decid and mixed woods, low-mid el, CMtns, OMtns, Cas s to n Cal; widespread, Alas, Can, n US.

Mountain chickadee, *Poecile gambeli.* L 5"–5¾". White eyebrow, blk line through eye. Com res, open-semiopen forest, gen upper mont–subalp, CMtns, OMtns, Cas s to Cal; mtns of w US and Can.

Boreal chickadee, *Poecile hudsonicus.* L 5"–5½". Dull brown cap, rich brown sides. Com-rare res, open-semiopen forest, CMtns, Cas of BC and extreme n Wn; Alas, Can, ne US.

Chestnut-backed chickadee, *Poecile rufescens.* L 4½"–5". Reddish brown back and sides. Com res, moist coastal forest, lowl-mont, in all our mtns s to Ore; along coast s to Cal, n to Alas.

NUTHATCH FAMILY (SITTADAE)

White-breasted nuthatch, *Sitta carolinensis.* L 5"–6". Blk cap, gray back, white face and underparts. Com-rare res, open forest, mostly E Cas (uncom W Cas), lowl-subalp, BC to Cal; res much of US.

Red-breasted nuthatch, *Sitta canadensis.* L 4½"–4¾". Reddish underparts, white eyebrow stripe, blk line through eye. Com res, conif forest, mostly mont-subalp, lower in win, in all our mtns s to Cal; widespread in s Can, US.

Pygmy nuthatch, *Sitta pygmaea.* L 3¾"–4½". White underparts, blk eyestripe, gray head and back. Com res, pine forests, E Cas, BC to s Ore; both sides Cas in s Ore and Cal; western US s into Mex, n just barely into BC.

CREEPER FAMILY (CERTHIIDAE)

Brown creeper, *Certhia familiaris.* L 5"–5¾". Curved bill; rusty, pointed tail; streaked brown back; habit of spiraling up tree trunks. Easily overlooked but com res, forest, in all our mtns s to Cal; widespread in w and s Can and in US s to Mex.

Black-capped Chickadee

Mountain Chickadee

Boreal Chickadee

Chestnut-backed Chickadee

White-breasted Nuthatch

Red-breasted Nuthatch

Pygmy Nuthatch

Brown Creeper

PLATE 87

LARK FAMILY (ALAUDIDAE)
Horned lark, *Eremophila alpestris.* L 7"–8". Blk bib, face patch, "horns," yellow face, pale underparts. Young lack horns, show little or no blk. Rare-com sum res, dry mdws, subalp-alp, lower in win, CMtns, OMtns, Cas s to Cal; widespread in N Amer s to S Amer.

DIPPER FAMILY (CINCLIDAE)
Dipper (water ouzel), *Cinclus mexicanus.* L 7"–8½". Bobbing motion, chunky build, uniform slate gray color, short tail, habit of entering water. Com res, mtn streams, less oft near lakes, in all our mtns s to Cal; Alas to Mex w of RM.

WREN FAMILY (TROGLODYTIDAE)
Winter wren, *Troglodytes troglodytes.* L 4"–4½". Small; short tail, faint eyestripe, heavily barred flanks. Com res, lowl-mont, moist coastal forest, decid woods, Alas s in all our mtns to Cal; e US, Eurasia.

House wren, *Troglodytes aedon.* L 4½"–5¼". Plain gray-brown plumage; dusky, faintly barred underparts. Rare-uncom res or vis, CMtns, OMtns, Cas s to Cal; widespread in US, n to s Can; win s US, Mex. Bewick's wren, *Thryomanes bewickii,* occas vis from lowl, has white underparts, prominent white eyestripe.

Rock wren, *Salpinctes obsoletus.* L 5"–6¼". Buffy corners of tail, lightly streaked breast, faint white stripe over eye. Uncom–fairly com res, rocky places, Cas, BC to Cal; sum res in nw US and extreme sw BC; res in sw US s to Cen Amer.

WAGTAIL FAMILY (MOTACILLIDAE)
American pipit, *Anthus rubescens.* L 6"–7". Sparrowlike but slimmer, with more slender bill; streaked, buffy underparts, white outer tail feathers. Com sum res, alp and arctic tundra, N Amer, Eurasia; win along shores and in fields, s US to Cen Amer, N Africa, s Asia.

WAXWING FAMILY (BOMBYCILLIDAE)
Cedar waxwing, *Bombycilla cedrorum.* L 6½"–8". Crest, fawn color, blk mask and chin, yellow band on tail. Com sum res, decid and riparian woods, low-mid el, fall vis at higher el; breeds across s Can and n US; win widely in s US s to Cen Amer. Bohemian waxwing, *B. garrulus,* very similar but with white and yellow marking on wings, rusty under-tail coverts, no yellow tint on belly.

Horned Lark

Winter Wren

House Wren

Rock Wren

Dipper

American Pipit

Cedar Waxwing

PLATE 88

MIMIC-THRUSH FAMILY (MIMIDAE)

Catbird, *Dumetella carolinensis.* L 8"–9¼". Blk cap, long tail, rusty under-tail coverts. Uncom–rare sum res, riparian woods, low el, E Cas, Wn; breeds s Can, n and e US; win s US to Cen Amer.

THRUSH FAMILY (TURDIDAE)

American robin, *Turdus migratorius.* L 9"–11". Rusty breast, dk grayish blk back. Com res, areas with grassy openings for feeding, trees for nesting, in all our mtns s to Cal; widespread in N Amer.

Hermit thrush, *Catharus guttatus.* L 6½"–7¾". Spotted and rusty tail. Com sum res, upper mont–subalp forest, in all our mtns s to Cal; breeds Alas, Can, n US; win along Pac coast, in s US, s to Cen Amer.

Varied thrush, *Ixoreus naevius.* L 9"–10". Robinlike, but with blk breast band, rusty eyebrow stripe and wing markings. Com res, forest, in all our mtns (gen W CMtns–Cas), BC to Ore; breeds n to Alas; win s to s Cal.

Swainson's thrush, *Catharus ustulatus.* L 6½"–7¾". Spotted breast, dull brown back and head, buffy cheek and eye ring. Com res, forest and decid woods, lowl-mont, in all our mtns s to Cal; breeds widely in n US, Can, Alas; win Mex s to Peru.

Veery, *Catharus fuscescens.* L 6½"–7¾". Uniformly warm brown upper parts, buffy spotted breast, white (not buffy) eye ring. Fairly com sum res, riparian woods, low-mid el, E CMtns–Cas, BC and Wn; breeds n US, s Can, s in RM; win S Amer.

Western bluebird, *Sialia mexicana.* L 6½"–7". M has bright blue head, wings, tail; rusty back and breast, white belly; F gen similar but paler. Com res, dry conif forest, pine-oak woods, mostly E Cas in BC, Wn; both sides Cas, Ore and Cal.

Mountain bluebird, *Sialia currucoides.* L 6½"–7¾". M has uniform turquoise color; F resembles F western bluebird but has gray (not rusty) breast. Com sum res, upper mont–subalp forest near mdws, clearings, lower in win, CMtns, OMtns, Cas, BC to Cal; breeds Alas s in mtns of w Can and US; win widely in lowl s to Mex.

Townsend's solitaire, *Myadestes townsendi.* L 8"–9½". White eye ring, white tail margins, buffy wing patches. Com sum res, pine-fir forest, E CMtns–Cas s to Cal; breeds Alas s in mtns of w Can, US to Mex; win in lowl.

Catbird

American Robin

Hermit Thrush

Varied Thrush

Swainson's Thrush

Veery

Western
Bluebird

Mountain Bluebird

Townsend's Solitaire

PLATE 89

WOOD WARBLER FAMILY (PARULIDAE)

Orange-crowned warbler, *Vermivora celata*. L 4½"–5½". Olive green above, yellow-green beneath, lack of distinctive markings; orange crown patch oft not apparent. Com-uncom sum res, brushy slopes, lowl-subalp, in all our mtns s to Cal; widespread sum res, w N Amer; win s US to Cen Amer.

Nashville warbler, *Vermivora ruficapilla*. L 4"–5". White eye ring, blue-gray head, yellow throat, no wingbars. Com sum res, pine forest, gen E Cas, BC to Cal; breeds s Can, w and n US; win s US to Cen Amer.

Yellow warbler, *Dendroica petechia*. L 4½"–5¼". M has yellow breast with faint rusty streaks (oft not apparent), yellow in tail, no white markings; F similar but paler, oft without rusty streaks. Com sum res, riparian woods, wet thickets, low el in all our mtns s to Cal; widespread sum res in N Amer; win from Mex to S Amer.

Yellow-rumped (Audubon's) warbler, *Dendroica coronata*. L 5"–5½". Yellow throat and rump, blk breast, white wing patches; F brown with 2 white wingbars; win birds brownish, streaked, white below with yellow throats. Com res or sum res, forest, low-high el, in all our mtns s to Cal; breeds widely in w N Amer; win s to Cen Amer. Myrtle race, uncom migr in mtns and win vis in lowl w of mtns, is similar but has a white throat.

Black-throated gray warbler, *Dendroica nigrescens*. L 4½"–5". M has blk crown, cheeks, throat; F duller, lacks blk throat. Com-uncom sum res, forest, in all our mtns, gen W CMtns–Cas, BC to Cal; breeds widely w US; win sw US, Mex.

Townsend's warbler, *Dendroica townsendi*. L 4½"–5". Blk and yellow head, yellow underparts, striped sides; F lacks blk throat. Com sum res, conif forest, in all our mtns (W CMtns–Cas) s to Cal; breeds s Alas to Wn, Idaho, Wyo; win Ore s to Cen Amer.

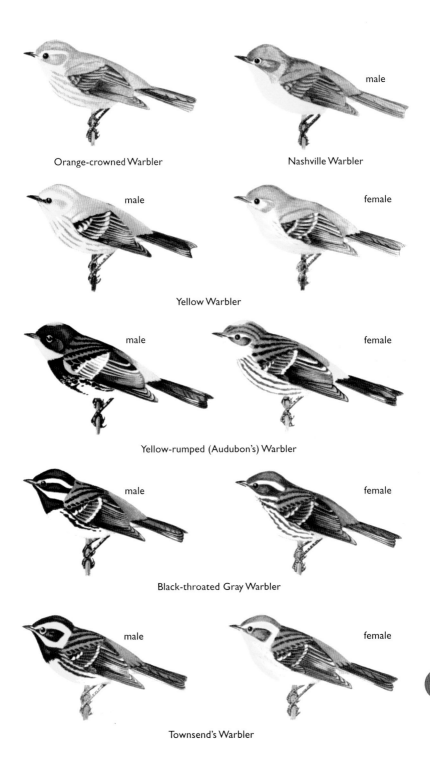

Orange-crowned Warbler

Nashville Warbler — male

Yellow Warbler — male, female

Yellow-rumped (Audubon's) Warbler — male, female

Black-throated Gray Warbler — male, female

Townsend's Warbler — male, female

PLATE 90

WOOD WARBLER FAMILY (PARULIDAE)

Hermit warbler, *Dendroica occidentalis.* L 4½"–4¾". Yellow head, white breast and belly; M has blk throat. Uncom-com sum res, forest, Cas, s Wn to Cal; also breeds s in Coast Ranges to nw Cal and SNev; win Mex, Cen Amer.

Northern waterthrush, *Seiurus noveboracensis.* L 5½"–6½". Brown back, streaked underparts, white eyebrow stripe. Uncom sum res, riparian woods, bogs, E CMtns–Cas to n Wn; breeds Alas s in Can and n US; win Cen and S Amer.

MacGillivray's warbler, *Oporornis tolmiei.* L 4¾"–5½". Olive back, gray head, blk and gray throat, yellow belly. F lacks blk on throat. Com sum res, damp, dense brush, lowl-subalp, in all our mtns s to Cal; breeds w US, BC mtns; win Mex to S Amer.

Common yellowthroat, *Geothlypis trichas.* L 4½"–5¾". M has blk mask, yellow throat; F has white belly, buffy sides. Com sum res, freshwater marshes, low el, in all our mtns s to Cal; widespread in N Amer; win s US to Cen Amer.

Wilson's warbler, *Wilsonia pusilla.* L 4¼"–5". M has blk cap; F has yellow eyebrow, no wingbars. Com sum res, decid or mixed forest, thickets, low-mid el, in all our mtns s to Cal; breeds widely w and n N Amer; win Mex to Cen Amer.

American redstart, *Setophaga ruticilla.* L 4½"–5¾". M has bold blk and orange pattern; F has white underparts, yellow patches in wings and tail. Mixed woods with willows, alders, E CMtns–Cas to n Ore; breeds widely n and e N Amer; win Mex to S Amer.

male

female

Hermit Warbler

Northern Waterthrush

male

MacGillivray's Warbler

male

female

Common Yellowthroat

male

female

Wilson's Warbler

male

female

American Redstart

PLATE 91

BLACKBIRD FAMILY (ICTERIDAE)

Red-winged blackbird, *Agelaius phoeniceus.* L 7"–9½". M has red shoulder patches; F has streaked underparts. Com-uncom sum res, mtn marshes; res in lowl, in all our mtns s to Cal; widespread N Amer.

Brewer's blackbird, *Euphagus cyanocephalus.* L 8"–10". M has iridescent blk plumage, yellow eye; F has gray plumage, dk eye; win M ± browner, lacks iridescence. Occas vis, mtns of BC, Wn (res in lowl); com sum res, mdws, Cas, Ore-Cal; widespread w US, sw Can.

Bullock's oriole, *Icterus bullockii.* L 7"–8½". M has blk and orange plumage, white wing patch, long pointed bill; F dull olive above, paler, buffy beneath. Local sum res, riparian woods, low-el valleys, Cas, Wn to Cal; breeds widely w US; win Mex to Cen Amer.

TANAGER FAMILY (THRAUPIDAE)

Western tanager, *Piranga ludoviciana.* L 6¼"–7½". M has red head, yellow breast and belly, blk back, wings, and tail; F has green back, yellow breast and belly, blk wings and tail. Com sum res, forest, in all our mtns s to Cal; breeds widely in forests sw Can and w US; win Mex to Cen Amer.

CARDINAL FAMILY (CARDINALIDAE)

Black-headed grosbeak, *Pheucticus melanocephalus.* L 6½"–7¾". M has blk head, ocher breast, white wing spots; F has striped head, thick bill, tan breast. Uncom-com sum res, pine forest, decid woods, low-mid el, in all our mtns s to Cal; breeds widely s Can, w US; win mainly in Mex.

FINCH FAMILY (FRINGILLIDAE)

Evening grosbeak, *Coccothraustes vespertina.* L 7"–8½". Very large, pale, conical bill; M has yellow brow, blk back and belly, blk and white wings; F has gray plumage, white wingbars. Com res mont-subalp forest, in all our mtns s to Cal; breeds widely Can and n US, s in mtns; win widely in lowl in all but se US.

SPARROW FAMILY (EMBERIZIDAE)

Spotted towhee, *Pipilo maculatus.* L 7"–8½". White underparts, rusty sides, blk head, breast, white-spotted back, tail; F very similar but head and back dk brown. Com res, mixed or decid woods, mostly lowl, but also low el, in all our mtns (mostly W CMtns–Cas) s to Cal; widespread N Amer.

Green-tailed towhee, *Pipilo chlorurus.* L 6¼"–7". Rusty cap and white throat. Local sum res, mtn brush, mostly E Cas of Ore and Cal, sum res w US, win Mex.

female

male

Red-winged
Blackbird

female

male

Brewer's Blackbird

female

male

Western Tanager

male

Bullock's Oriole

Black-headed
Grosbeak

male

male

Evening Grosbeak

male

Spotted Towhee

Green-tailed Towhee

PLATE 92

CARDINAL FAMILY (CARDINALIDAE)

Lazuli bunting, *Passerina amoena*. L 5"–5½". M has rusty breast, white belly, white wingbars, bright turquoise head and back; F has unstreaked underparts, white wingbars. Com sum res, woods, thickets, esp E Cas, BC to Cal, mostly low-mid el; breeds sw Can, s in w and mid US; win Ariz, Mex.

FINCH FAMILY (FRINGILLIDAE)

Purple finch, *Carpodacus purpureus*. L 5½"–6¼". M has rosy head, breast, and rump, white belly, unstreaked flanks; F much streaked beneath, very similar to F Cassin's finch (cf next sp). Com res, coastal forest, riparian woods, lowl–low mont, mostly W Cas, in all our mtns s to Cal; widespread in N Amer. The familiar house finch, *C. mexicanus*, of parks and gardens, very similar but more red than rose and has streaked flanks, square tail; rarely in mtns.

Cassin's finch, *Carpodacus cassinii*. L 6"–6½". Very similar to purple finch (cf above sp), but M has paler pink breast and contrast between rosy crown and brown nape of neck; F very similar to F purple finch. Com sum vis (res at lower el), forest to timberline, mostly E CMtns, Cas s to Cal; widespread in mtns of w US.

Pine grosbeak, *Pinicola enucleator*. L 8"–10". Large; M has dull rosy color; F has yellow-green color; both M and F have blk wings with white wingbars. Uncom-rare res, mont-subalp forest, in all our mtns s to Cal; breeds Alas s in mtns of w Can, US, e in Can to ne US; win widely lowl Can and US.

American goldfinch, *Carduelis tristis*. L 4½"–5½". M has blk cap, wings, and tail, yellow body; win birds buffy to pale yellow, without blk cap. Com res, decid woods, open brushy areas, mostly lowl, also low mtn, in all our mtns s to Cal; widespread in s Can, US.

Pine siskin, *Carduelis pinus*. L 4½"–5¼". Heavy streaking and yellow in wings and at base of tail. Very com res, forest, lowl–subalp, in all our mtns s to Cal; breeds Can, n US, s in mtns of w N Amer; win widely in lowl in large flocks.

Gray-crowned rosy finch, *Leucosticte tephrocotis*. L 5¾"–6¾". Pinkish wash on wings and rump, gray patch on back of head. Com sum res, alp, lower in win, in all our mtns s to Cal; Alas s in mtns to SNev, n RM.

Red crossbill, *Loxia curvirostra*. L 5¼"–6½". Crossed bill. M has brick red color; F has olive-gray color. Fairly com but irreg res, forest, in all our mtns s to Cal; widespread in conif forests N Amer.

White-winged crossbill, *Loxia leucoptera*. L 6"–6¾". Crossed bill. M has rosy pink color; M and F have 2 white wingbars. Rare res, conif forest, mont-subalp, in all our mtns s to Wn; conif forests of Can, n US.

female

male

Purple Finch

Lazuli Bunting

female

male

female

male

Cassin's Finch

Pine Grosbeak

female

male

American Goldfinch

male

Pine Siskin

Gray-crowned Rosy Finch

female

male

male

White-winged Crossbill

Red Crossbill

PLATE 93

SPARROW FAMILY (EMBERIZIDAE)

Lark sparrow, *Chondestes grammacus.* L 5½"–6¾". Bold head stripes, blk spot on pale breast. Sum res, uncom in pine forest, com in brushy open areas, E Cas, BC to Cal; breeds widely US; win s US to Cen Amer.

Dark-eyed (Oregon) junco, *Junco hyemalis.* L 5"–6". M has blk head, rusty back, pink or buffy sides; F similar but paler; young have gray head. Com res, forest, lowl-subalp, in all our mtns s to Cal; breeds Alas to Baja, e to RM; win lowl. Slate-colored race rare win vis, gen in lowl.

Chipping sparrow, *Spizella passerina.* L 5"–5¾". Rusty crown, white eyebrow stripe. Com sum res, forest, woods, lowl-subalp, in all our mtns s to Cal; breeds widely N Amer; win s US and s.

White-crowned sparrow, *Zonotrichia leucophrys.* L 5½"–7". Blk and white stripes on head, gray throat, pink bill; young have gray- and brown-striped crowns. Rare-com sum res, conif forest, brushy places, near mdws, lowl-subalp, in all our mtns s to Cal; breeds Alas, Can, s in US to Cal, cen RM; win w US s to Cen Amer.

Golden-crowned sparrow, *Zonotrichia atricapilla.* L 6"–7". Dull yellow crown bordered with blk. Res, thickets, subalp-alp, CMtns; com migr and win vis s; breeds Alas to BC; win s BC to s Cal, Baja.

Fox sparrow, *Passerella iliaca.* L 6¼"–7¼". Dk or rusty brown back, pale, blotchy underparts, rusty tail. Uncom-com sum res, brushy thickets, lowl-subalp, in all our mtns s to Cal; breeds widely Alas, n Can, w US; win coastal and s US.

Lincoln's sparrow, *Melospiza lincolnii.* L 5"–6". Streaked, buffy breast. Com sum res, moist thickets, mid-high el, CMtns, Cas s to Cal; breeds widely Alas, Can, mtns w US; win Ore, s US and s.

Song sparrow, *Melospiza melodia.* L 5"–6". Heavily streaked breast with central spot. Com res or sum res (higher el), riparian woods, moist thickets, in all our mtns s to Cal; breeds widely N Amer; win s US and s.

Lark Sparrow

Dark-eyed (Oregon) Junco

Chipping Sparrow

White-crowned Sparrow

Golden-crowned Sparrow

Fox Sparrow

Lincoln's Sparrow

Song Sparrow

14

mammals

Mammals are four-legged, fur-bearing animals that suckle their young. Body temperature is regulated internally, but protection from extreme cold is provided by their fur, or *pelage,* which consists of durable outer guard hairs and short, soft inner fur for insulation. The young are born live and are thereafter nourished by milk secreted from the mother's mammary glands. The young of some species, notably rodents and carnivores, are born naked, blind, and helpless. Young deer, elk, mountain goats, and snowshoe hares, however, are fully active and alert shortly after birth. Most mammals have acute senses of smell, hearing, and vision. Many also possess sensitive facial whiskers that convey information through touch. Bats possess a type of sonar that enables them to locate flying insects at night.

Small mammals tend to be nocturnal, active at a time when they are least conspicuous to predators. In response, however, most predators are at least partly nocturnal as well. Large mammals such as deer, elk, mountain goats, bears, coyotes, and others are abroad both day and night. Among the smaller mammals that are active during the day are squirrels, marmots, pikas, and hares.

During the winter, mammals must contend with food shortages occasioned by cold weather and deep snow. Though some of the larger species—notably deer and elk, along with their predators—migrate downslope in the fall, the great majority of mammals remain in the mountains all year long. Of these, only marmots truly hibernate. Chipmunks and bears sleep soundly for much of the season but awaken from time to time and may even be seen abroad. They do not experience the deep coma of true hibernation, and their body temperatures and metabolisms do not reach extremes of depression. Most carnivores are active throughout the winter, though some migrate downslope if food becomes too scarce. Even at higher elevations, however, many small mammals and birds remain active throughout the winter, holing up only during nasty weather. Some small mammals, such as voles and pocket gophers, spend the winter foraging under the protective insulation of the snow cover. They generally encounter difficulty only when extreme cold combined with a lack of snow cover prevents them from foraging without expending a great deal of energy. Tree squirrels cope with winter food shortages by living off caches of seeds stored up during the summer. Many small rodents subsist largely on bark during the winter months, as does the larger porcupine.

Approximately seventy-five species of mammals occur in our mountains. These include typically northern species, such as the wolverine, fisher, and bog lemming; southern species, such as the western gray squirrel and western jumping mouse; and numerous species of widespread distribution, such as the mule deer, black bear, coyote, and mountain lion. The Coast Mountains–Cascade crest, separating the humid coastal region from the drier interior, has formed a geographic barrier to some species. The mountain beaver, hoary marmot, and Townsend's chipmunk, for example, occur mainly west of the crest, while the yellow-bellied marmot, least chipmunk, and badger occur mainly on the east. A number of species—the California ground squirrel, for example—that are found on both sides of the Cascades in Oregon and California are restricted to the east slope of the range in Washington and British Columbia. Water has also presented a barrier to many animals that might otherwise occur on Vancouver Island but do not. These include moles, pikas, snowshoe hares, mountain beavers, pocket-gophers, chipmunks, Douglas squirrels, northern flying squirrels, and porcupines. The Olympic Mountains also lack several species that occur or once occurred in the nearby Cascades—the pika and grizzly bear, for example.

The more than fifty species of mammals depicted in this chapter include all those that one is likely to see, as well as a few of the rarer and more reclusive types. A few groups of mammals, such as the shrews, bats, and voles, which are extremely difficult or impossible for most people to distinguish by species in the field, are treated generically.

FINDING MAMMALS

Because mammals have much keener senses than ours, often they make themselves scarce as we approach. One of the best strategies for observing mammals is to find a likely spot and sit quietly. Large, loud groups charging down the trail in full conversation seldom see much wildlife. With a bit of practice, it is possible to move along a trail aware and quiet. As you hike, keep your eyes moving and scout ahead, looking for movement that will alert you to the presence of animals. A pair of binoculars are an essential tool for wildlife watching. The most likely places to encounter mammals are near water sources, in open areas, or near nesting sites. An observer who waits patiently and quietly downwind from a prospective observation area stands the best chance of success.

If you encounter an animal while on the trail, move slowly and, if possible, sit down. By reducing your size, you may become less noticeable and certainly less threatening. While some animals do not see colors, all animals can distinguish tones, so it is best to wear muted colors, especially those that blend into the background to make you less visible. If you should see an animal of interest and it runs out of view, sit patiently for a little while. Often animals take to cover and then may return to what they were doing previously once they are assured the threat is gone.

The animals in our national parks are not hunted, and so in many popular areas the animals have become accustomed to humans and are more tolerant. Remember, though, even these seemingly tame animals are wild and will defend themselves if you approach too closely. Never feed wild animals; it almost certainly will lead to their death.

The best times to see mammals are at dawn and dusk, when both nocturnal and diurnal types may be abroad. The worst time is midday, when even diurnal mammals may be resting. More often than not, however, one sees not the mammal itself but only signs of the beast, such as tracks, scat, and nests. In this revised edition, tracks are shown with the animal's illustration. Distinctive signs and voice are mentioned in the species descriptions. Some species of wildlife follow specific corridors and trails, and so tracks are an excellent indicator of good places to wait and watch.

Common and scientific names conform to the *Revised Checklist of North American Mammals North of Mexico* (J. K. Jones Jr., R. S. Hoffman, D. W. Rice, C. Jones, R. J. Baker, and M. D. Engstom, 1992, *Occasional Papers, Museum of Texas Tech University*, vol. 146, pp. 1–23). Alternate common names in wide use are sometimes given in parentheses. For information on the use of the species descriptions and illustrations, as well as for a list of the abbreviations used in the accounts, see the Introduction.

PLATE 94

SHREW FAMILY (SORIEIDAE)

Shrew, *Sorex* spp. H/B 2"–3¾"; T 1¼"–3¼". In our range, 7 spp, all very difficult to separate; 2 spp partly aquatic. Tiny mouselike insectivores, pale brown or gray to nearly blk; narrow, pointed snout; inconspicuous, beady eyes. Nocturnal/diurnal. Gen moist places in all our mtns.

MOLE FAMILY (TALPIDAE)

Mole, *Scapuous* spp. H/B 5"–7"; T 1¼"–2". In our range, 3 spp, all very difficult to separate. Small, tunneling insectivores with dk brown or blk fur (our spp); naked, pointed snout; large out-turned foreclaws for digging. Sign: soil ridges. Nocturnal/diurnal; mostly subterranean. Rich, workable soils, in all our mtns but Vanc I.

Shrew mole, *Neurotrichus gibbsii.* H/B 2½"–3"; T 1"–1½". Tiny shrewlike mole with gray fur, scaly hairy tail. Nocturnal/diurnal; oft aboveground. Moist, dense forest undergrowth, W Cas to coast, s BC (not Vanc I) to Cal.

POCKET-GOPHER FAMILY (GEOMYIDAE)

Pocket-gopher, *Thomomys* spp. H/B ca 5"–6½"; T ca 2½". In our range, 2 spp, both very similar. Tunneling rodents with long incisors and foreclaws; brown to gray or nearly blk. Nocturnal/diurnal; mostly subterranean. Mdws, grassy places in all our mtns but Vanc I.

BAT FAMILY (VESPERTILIONIDAE)

Bat, several genera. L 3"–5½". Flying mammals with hands formed into wings, digits elongated and connected by membranous skin, thumbs exposed and clawed. Ca 12 spp in our range, all difficult to separate when in flt. Nocturnal; roost by day gen in caves or trees. Most habitats, gen seen overhead at dusk or night.

MOUNTAIN BEAVER FAMILY (APLODONTIDAE)

Mountain beaver, *Aplodontia rufo.* H/B 12"–17"; T ca 1". Dk brown, stocky; not a true beaver (cf plate 96). Sign: large burrow openings, runways; "haystacks"; earth cores to 6" diam. Mostly nocturnal; reclusive. Moist woods, thickets, oft near water, W Cas to coast, s BC (not Vanc I) to Cal.

PIKA FAMILY (OCHOTONIDAE)

Pika, *Ochotona princeps.* H/B 6¼"–8½"; no visible tail. Grayish to buffy brown; large, rounded ears. Sign: blk pelletlike scat; "haystacks" of vegetation left in sun to cure. Voice: shrill whistle or squeak. Diurnal; hibernates. Rockslides, subalp-alp, CMtns s in Cas to SNev, e to RM.

HARE FAMILY (LEPORIDAE)

Snowshoe hare, *Lepus americanus.* H/B 13"–18". In sum brown above, white or buffy beneath; in win white with blk-tipped ears. Nocturnal; rests beneath brush during day. Forest, thickets, in all our mtns but Vanc I; Alas, Can, s in mtns of US.

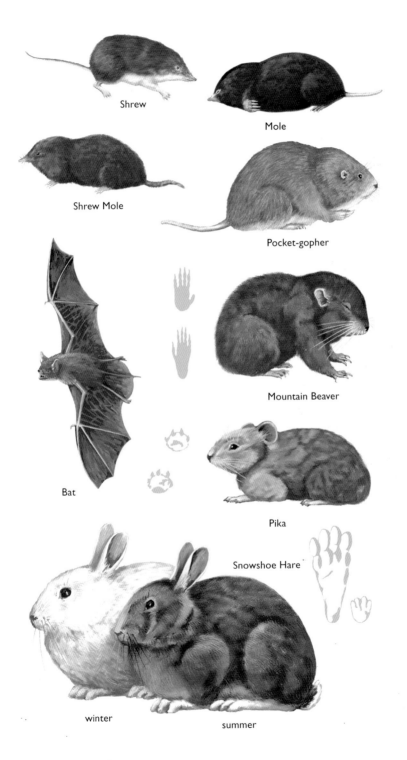

Shrew

Mole

Shrew Mole

Pocket-gopher

Bat

Mountain Beaver

Pika

Snowshoe Hare

winter   summer

PLATE 95

SQUIRREL FAMILY (SCIURIDAE)

Least chipmunk, *Tamias minimus.* H/B 3"–4½"; T 3"–4½". Yellowish gray above with distinct blk and white stripes. Diurnal; hibernates. Sagebrush, dry forest, E Cas, s Wn to Cal; widespread Can, w US.

Yellow-pine chipmunk, *Tamias amoenus.* H/B 4½"–5½"; T 3"–4½". Bright golden or reddish brown above with distinct blk and white stripes. Diurnal; hibernates. Forest (esp pine), CMtns, Cas s to n Cal, also RM.

Townsend's chipmunk, *Tamias townsendi.* H/B 5¼"–6½"; T 3"–4½". Dk brown above with ± indistinct blk and creamy or grayish stripes; distinctly larger than preceding spp. Diurnal; hibernates. Dense woods, forest, Cas to coast, extreme s BC (not Vanc I) to SNev, nw Cal.

Golden-mantled ground squirrel, *Spermophilus lateralis.* H/B 6"–8"; T 2½"–4¾". Distinguished from chipmunks by larger size and lack of facial stripes; head and shoulders ("mantle") bright reddish or golden brown. Diurnal; hibernates. Open forest, rocky places, brush, mont-subalp, Cas, s Wn to Cal, e to RM. Cascade golden-mantled ground squirrel, *S. saturatus,* very similar but duller, with fainter stripes; diurnal; hibernates; Cas of BC and n Wn.

Beechey ground squirrel, *Spermophilus beecheyi.* H/B 9"–11"; T 5"–9". Brown grizzled with white or buff, neck and shoulders whitish, dk V between shoulders, buffy beneath. Diurnal; hibernates. Open forest, rocky places, mdws, Cas, s Wn to Cal.

Douglas squirrel (chickaree), *Tamiasciurus douglasii.* H/B 6"–7"; T 4¾"–5". Reddish olive above (grayer in win), yellowish or rusty beneath. Sign: dismantled cones, nests in trees. Voice: scolding chatter, trilling whistle. Diurnal. Forest, in all our mtns but Vanc I, s BC to Cal. Red squirrel, *T. hudsonicus,* very similar but white beneath; forest, E CMtns–Cas to n Wn; Vanc I; Alas s to Wn, e to RM, ne US, e Can.

Northern flying squirrel, *Glaucomys sabrinus.* H/B 5½"–6½"; T 4¼"–5½". Brown above, white beneath; loose fold of skin between legs forms a "cape" for gliding from tree to tree. Sign: nut caches. Voice: birdlike chirps. Nocturnal; seldom seen but fairly com. Forest in all our mtns but VancI; Alas e across Can to ne US, s in mtns of w US.

Western gray squirrel, *Sciurus griseus.* H/B 9"–12"; T 10"–12". Gray above, white beneath, very bushy tail. Sign: gnawed nuts, large twiggy nests in trees. Diurnal. Oak woods, pine forest, low-mid el Cas, s Wn to Cal.

Least Chipmunk

Yellow-pine Chipmunk

Townsend's Chipmunk

Golden-mantled
Ground Squirrel

Douglas Squirrel

Beechey Ground Squirrel

Northern Flying Squirrel

Western Gray Squirrel

PLATE 96

SQUIRREL FAMILY (SCIURIDAE)

Yellow-bellied marmot, *Marmota flaviventris.* H/B 14"–19"; T 4½"–9". Frosted golden brown above, yellowish beneath; dk brown—not blk—feet; dk head, white between eyes. Voice: loud chirps or whistles. Diurnal; hibernates. Rocky places, gen subalp, Cas, BC to Cal, e to RM.

Hoary marmot, *Marmota caligata.* H/B 18"–21"; T 7"–10". Silvery gray above, white beneath; brown rump and tail; blk feet; blk and silver head. Voice: similar to above sp. Diurnal; hibernates. Rocky places, gen subalp, CMtns–Cas; Alas s to Wn.

Olympic marmot, *Marmota olympus.* H/B 18"–21"; T 7"–10". Grizzled brown; brown feet, white muzzle. Voice: similar to above spp. Diurnal; hibernates. Rocky places, mdws, subalp-alp, OMtns only (and only marmot in OMtns).

BEAVER FAMILY (CASTORIDAE)

Beaver, *Castor canadensis.* H/B 25"–30"; T 9"–10". Large; rich brown fur; naked, scaly, paddlelike tail; huge incisors; webbed hind feet. Sign: dammed streams, beaver lodges, gnawed and cut trees, sound of tail slapping on water, 1"-long oval pellets in which woody materials are apparent. Diurnal/nocturnal. Streams and beaver ponds, gen near aspen or alder, in all our mtns; widespread in N Amer.

MOUSE FAMILY (MURIDAE)

Muskrat, *Ondatra zibethicus.* H/B 17"–22"; T 7"–11". Rich brown fur on back; flanks and sides lighter brown. Underside gray. Tail blk, flattened from side to side. Hind feet webbed. Sign: clipped cattails, lodge 3'–4' tall of cattails, usually at edge of lake. Diurnal/nocturnal. Ponds and lakes, gen with cattails, lowl, in all our mtns; widespread.

PORCUPINE FAMILY (ERETHIZONTIDAE)

Porcupine, *Erethizon dorsatum.* H/B 18"–22"; T 7"–9". Yellowish brown; long guard hairs near shoulders and sharp quills on rump and tail. Diurnal/nocturnal. Forest in all our mtns but Vanc I; widespread in Alas, Can to ne US, mtns of w US.

Yellow-bellied Marmot

all marmots

Hoary Marmot

Olympic Marmot

Beaver

Muskrat

Porcupine

PLATE 97

MOUSE FAMILY (MURIDAE)

Bushy-tailed wood rat, *Neotoma cinerea.* H/B 7"–9¾"; T 5¼"–7½". Gray-brown above, white beneath; bushy, squirrel-like tail. Sign: stick nests in rock crevices. Nocturnal. Rocky places, in all our mtns but Vanc I; widespread in w N Amer.

Deer mouse, *Peromyscus maniculatus.* H/B 2¾"–3¾"; T 2"–5". Brown above, white beneath, bicolored tail. Nocturnal. Most habitats, in all our mtns; widespread N Amer. Forest deer mouse, *P. keeni* of some authorities, treated here as larger, darker race of *P. maniculatus.* Western harvest mouse, *Reithrodontomys megalotis.* H/B ca 3"; T 2¼"–3¼". Brownish above, white beneath, buffy on sides. Nocturnal. Gen dense vegetation near water, low el, E Cas, s Ore to Cal; widespread in w US.

Southern red-backed vole, *Clethrionomys gapperi.* H/B 3¾"–4¾"; T 1¼"–1¾". Reddish on back, buffy to gray on sides, gray or whitish beneath; short tail. Sign: runways, perhaps littered with vegetation. Diurnal/nocturnal. Damp, wooded areas, C Mtns–Cas, BC to Wn; widespread Can, s to n US, RM, Appalachians. Western red-backed vole, *C. occidentalis,* dk brown above, back not contrasting sharply with sides; O Mtns, s W C Mtns.

Meadow voles (mice), *Microtus* spp, **heather vole,** *Phenacomys intermedius,* **water vole,** *Arvicola richardsonii.* H/B ca 3½"–6½"; T ca 1"–3½". All these spp very difficult to separate without in-hand specimens. Stout bodies, blunt snouts, small, + obscure ears, beady eyes. Fur thick, gray or brown to blk. Sign: runways, oft littered with vegetation. Diurnal. Mdw voles most com in wet mdws or grassy places near water; heather vole, in subalp heather mdws; water vole, near water; in all our mtns.

Northern bog-lemming, *Synaptomys borealis.* H/B 4"–4¾"; T ¾"–1". Brown above, gray beneath; short bicolored tail. Diurnal/nocturnal. Mtn bogs, wet mdws, heather mdws, C Mtns, Cas of BC and extreme n Wn; Alas, Can, s to n US.

JUMPING MOUSE FAMILY (DIPODIDAE)

Pacific jumping mouse, *Zapus trinotatus.* H/B 3⅝"–3¾"; T 5"–6"+. Back dusky, sides yellowish, underparts white; long tail, large hind feet. Nocturnal; hibernates. Marshes, mdws, moist woods, in all our mtns but Vanc I, BC to s Ore, s along coast to cen Cal. Western jumping mouse, *Z. princeps,* very similar; replaces preceding sp in n C Mtns, Cas of s Ore and Cal.

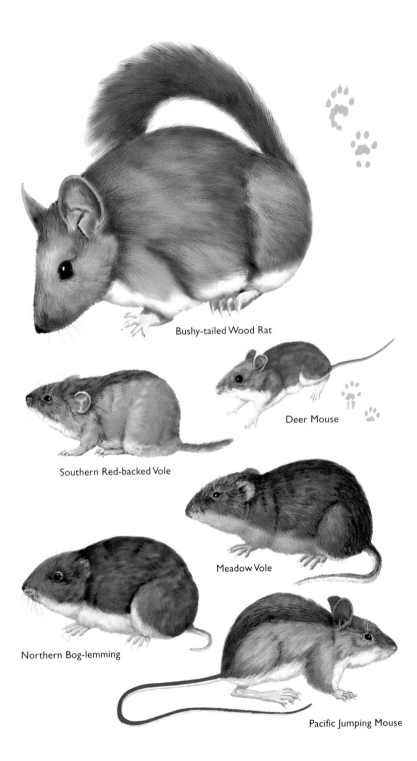

Bushy-tailed Wood Rat

Deer Mouse

Southern Red-backed Vole

Meadow Vole

Northern Bog-lemming

Pacific Jumping Mouse

PLATE 98

DOG FAMILY (CANIDAE)

Gray wolf, *Canis lupis.* H/B 43"–48"; T 12"–19". Color varied but gen grizzled gray to blkish above, lighter on sides and belly. Like coyote but larger, carries tail high while running. Diurnal/nocturnal. All habitats, BC and NCas, Idaho.

Coyote, *Canis latrans.* H/B 32"–37"; T 11"–16". Grizzled gray above, buffy beneath, legs reddish, tail blk tipped. Like wolf but carries tail low while running. Sign: doglike scat, large dens. Voice: howls, barks. Diurnal/nocturnal. All habitats in all our mtns but Vanc I; widespread in N Amer.

Red fox, *Vulpes vulpes.* H/B 22–25"; T 14"–16". Color variable: rusty red; blk grizzled with silver; reddish with dk cross on shoulders and back; blk (most com in our range). Nocturnal. Most habitats, CMtns, Cas s to Cal; widespread in N Amer.

Gray fox, *Urocyon cinereoargenteus.* H/B 21"–29"; T 11"–16". Forehead, back, upper sides, top of tail all grizzled gray; rusty around head, throat, lower sides, legs, underside of tail; throat and belly white. Mostly nocturnal. Most habitats, Cas, Ore to Cal; widespread in s US, Mex.

RACCOON FAMILY (PROCYONIDAE)

Raccoon, *Procyon lotor.* H/B 18"–28"; T 8"–12". Grizzled gray with blk and white rings on tail, blk mask on whitish face. Mostly nocturnal. Brushy or wooded areas near water, gen lowl–lower mont, sw CMtns, Vanc I, OMtns, Cas s to Cal; widespread in N Amer.

WEASEL FAMILY (MUSTELIDAE)

Western spotted skunk, *Spilogale gracilis.* H/B 9"–13½"; T 4½"–9". Blk with irreg white spots and stripes. Nocturnal. Brushy or rocky places, open woods, oft near water, low-mid el, CMtns, OMtns, Cas, s BC to Cal; widespread in w US s to Mex.

Striped skunk, *Mephitis mephitis.* H/B 13"–18"; T 7"–10". Blk with white cap and 2 broad white stripes down back. Mostly nocturnal. Open woods, brush, oft near water, lowl–low mtn, all our mtns but Vanc I; widespread in N Amer.

Raccoon

Gray Wolf

Western Spotted Skunk

Coyote

Red Fox

Gray Fox

Striped Skunk

PLATE 99

WEASEL FAMILY (MUSTELIDAE)

Pine marten, *Martes americana.* H/B 16"–17"; T 8"–9"; F slightly smaller. Various shades of brown above, paler beneath and on head, darker on legs; throat orange or buffy. Nocturnal/diurnal. Forest, oft near talus in sum, mid-high el, in all our mtns; widespread Alas, Can, n US, s in mtns.

Short-tailed weasel (ermine), *Mustela erminea.* H/B 6"–9"; T 2½"–4"; F slightly smaller. In sum, dk brown above, white beneath, feet white; in win, white with tail blk tipped. Diurnal/nocturnal. Wooded or open places, oft near water, in all our mtns; widespread Alas, Can, n US, mtns of w US. Long-tailed weasel, *M. frenata,* very similar but slightly larger and feet brown, not white; in all our mtns but Vanc I.

Mink, *Mustela vision.* H/B 13"–17"; T 7"–9"; F slightly smaller. Dk brown to blk, white chin patch. Mostly nocturnal. Near and in water in all our mtns; widespread in N Amer except sw US.

Badger, *Taxidea taxus.* H/B 18"–22"; T 4"–6". Body + flattened, grizzled gray to brown, face blk and white, tail yellowish, legs short with long foreclaws. Nocturnal/diurnal. Grassy places, mdws, mostly foothills E CMtns–Cas, BC to Cal; widespread in w N Amer.

River otter, *Lutra canadensis.* H/B 26"–30"; T 12"–17". Dk brown above, pale beneath, oft silvery at throat; feet webbed, tail long and pointed. Nocturnal/diurnal. Near or in water in all our mtns; widespread in N Amer.

BEAR FAMILY (URSIDAE)

Black bear, *Ursus americanus.* L 5'–6'; ht 3'–3½' at shoulders. Color variable, gen blk or brown in our mtns. Sign: clawed or chewed "bear trees," various feeding signs, large doglike scat. Nocturnal/diurnal; hibernates. Most habitats in all our mtns; widespread in N Amer.

Grizzly bear, *Ursus arctos.* L 6'–7'; ht 3'–4½' at shoulders. Color variable, yellowish brown to blk, oft grizzled with white hairs; hump over shoulders, face dished. Sign: remains of a kill, excavated areas, same signs as for black bear. Nocturnal/diurnal; hibernates. Unpredictable, can be dangerous. Most habitats, mtns of BC; rare straggler NCas; Alas, Can, s in US to Wyo; formerly widespread in N Amer.

Pine Marten

winter

summer

Short-tailed Weasel

Mink

Badger

River Otter

Black Bear

Grizzly Bear

PLATE 100

CAT FAMILY (FELIDAE)

Mountain lion, *Puma concolor.* H/B 42"–54"; T 30"–36". Tawny with dark-tipped tail. Sign: scratching trees, remains of a kill, copious catlike scat. Nocturnal/diurnal. Various habitats in all our mtns; formerly widespread in N Amer, range now much reduced.

Bobcat, *Lynx rufus.* H/B 25"–30"; T 5". Tawny or grayish above, indistinctly spotted, cheek ruffs short, tail stubby and only partly tipped in blk. Nocturnal/diurnal. Various habitats in all our mtns but Vanc I; widespread in N Amer.

Lynx, *Lynx canadensis.* H/B 32"–36"; T 4". Buffy or tawny, mixed with darker hairs above, rusty beneath; long, blk ear tufts, long cheek ruffs, stubby tail entirely tipped with blk. Nocturnal. Forest, CMtns–Cas s to n Ore; Alas, Can, s in mtns of US.

DEER FAMILY (CERVIDAE)

Mule deer (including black-tailed deer), *Odocoileus hemionus.* L 3¾'–6½'; ht 3'–3½' at shoulders. In sum, reddish to golden brown; in win, grayish above, throat, rump, insides of legs and ears white; tail either white above and tipped in blk (mule deer) or blk above (black-tailed deer). Nocturnal/diurnal. Most habitats in all our mtns; widespread in w N Amer.

Elk (wapiti), *Cervus elaphus.* L 6¾'–9¾'; ht 4½'–5' at shoulders. Brown or reddish brown, darker beneath and on neck, head; yellowish on rump, tail; large many-tined antlers to 5' long on M. Voice: a bugling call. Most active mornings and evenings. In sum, subalp mdws; in win, lowl, esp r valleys; in all our mtns s to Cal, also RM, Can.

CATTLE FAMILY (BOVIDAE)

Mountain goat, *Oreamnos americanus.* L 4'–5¾'; ht 3'–3½' at shoulders. White, shaggy, goatlike; smooth, blk, curved horns. Nocturnal/diurnal. Rocky slopes, cliffs, gen subalp-alp, in all our mtns s to Wn; se Alas to Wn and RM.

Bighorn sheep, *Ovis canadensis.* L 5¼'–6'; ht 2½'–3½' at shoulders. Brown to grayish, rump white; horns of M massive and coiled; F's horns shorter, not coiled. Sign: bell-shaped scat; day beds littered with scat. Diurnal. Rough, rocky terrain, high mdws, cliffs; local bands in CMtns, e NCas; mtns of w N Amer.

Mountain Lion

Bobcat

Lynx

Black-tailed Deer

female

Mule Deer

Mountain Goat

male

Elk

male

Bighorn Sheep

selected references

GENERAL ECOLOGY AND NATURAL HISTORY

Arno, Stephen F., and R. P. Hammerly. 1984. *Timberline: Mountain and Arctic Forest Frontiers.* Seattle: The Mountaineers Books.

Cannings, Richard, and Sydney Cannings. 1996. *British Columbia: A Natural History.* Vancouver, B.C.: Greystone Books.

Franklin, Jerry F., and C. T. Dyrness. 1973. *Natural Vegetation of Oregon and Washington.* Portland, Ore: U. S. Forest and Range Experiment Station, USDA.

Kirk, Ruth, and Jerry F. Franklin. 1992. *The Olympic Rain Forest: An Ecological Web.* Seattle: University of Washington Press.

Kozloff, Eugene N. 1976. *Plants and Animals of the Pacific Northwest.* Seattle: University of Washington Press.

Kruckeberg, Arthur R. 1991. *The Natural History of Puget Sound Country.* Seattle: University of Washington Press.

Luoma, Jon R. 1999. *The Hidden Forest: The Biography of an Ecosystem.* New York: Henry Holt and Company.

Maser, Chris. 1989. *Forest Primeval: The Natural History of an Ancient Forest.* San Francisco: Sierra Club Books.

McNulty, Tim. 1996. *Olympic National Park: A Natural History Guide.* Boston: Houghton Mifflin Company.

Whitney, Stephen. 1989. *A Sierra Club Naturalist's Guide to the Pacific Northwest.* San Francisco: Sierra Club Books.

Zwinger, Ann H., and Beatrice E. Willard. 1977. *Land Above the Trees: A Guide to American Alpine Tundra.* New York: Harper and Row.

CLIMATE

Reifsnyder, William F. 1980. *Weathering the Wilderness: The Sierra Club Guide to Practical Meteorology.* San Francisco: Sierra Club Books.

Renner, Jeff. 1992. *Northwest Mountain Weather: Understanding and Forecasting for the Backcountry User.* Seattle: The Mountaineers Books.

Rue, Walter. 1978. *Weather of the Pacific Coast: Washington, Oregon, British Columbia.* Mercer Island, Wash.: The Writing Works.

Schaefer, Vincent J., and John A. Day. 1981. *A Field Guide to the Atmosphere.* Boston: Houghton Mifflin Company.

GEOLOGY

Alt, David, and Donald W. Hyndman. 1981. *Roadside Geology of Oregon.* Missoula,
    Mont.: Mountain Press Publishing.
————. 1984. *Roadside Geology of Washington.* Missoula, Mont.: Mountain Press
    Publishing.
————. 1995. *Northwest Exposures: A Geologic Story of the Northwest.* Missoula,
    Mont.: Mountain Press Publishing.
Babcock, Scott, and Bob Carson. 2000. *Hiking Washington's Geology.* Seattle: The
    Mountaineers Books.
Bishop, Ellen M. 2003. *Hiking Oregon's Geology, second edition.* Seattle: The
    Mountaineers Books.
Cvancara, Alan M. 1995. *A Field Manual for the Amateur Geologist: Tools and Activities
    for Exploring Our Planet.* New York: John Wiley and Sons Inc.
Easterbrook, Don J., and David A. Rahm. 1970. *Landforms of Washington: The
    Geologic Environment.* Bellingham, Wash.: Union Printing Company.
Harris, Stephen L. 1988. *Fire Mountains of the West: The Cascade and Mono Lake
    Volcanoes.* Missoula, Mont.: Mountain Press Publishing.
Orr, Elizabeth, and William Orr. 2000. *Geology of Oregon.* Dubuque, Iowa: Kendall
    Hunt Publishing Company.
Tabor, Rowland W. 1975. *Guide to the Geology of Olympic National Park.* Seattle:
    University of Washington Press.
Tabor, Rowland, and Ralph Haugerud. 1999. *Geology of the North Cascades.* Seattle:
    The Mountaineers Books.

MUSHROOMS

Arora, David. 1986. *Mushrooms Demystified: A Comprehensive Guide to the Fleshy
    Fungi.* Berkeley, Calif.: Ten Speed Press.
————. 1991. *All That the Rain Promises and More: A Hip Pocket Guide to Western
    Mushrooms.* Berkeley, Calif.: Ten Speed Press.
Lincoff, Gary H. 1981. *The Audubon Society Field Guide to North American
    Mushrooms.* New York: Alfred A. Knopf.
McKenny, Margaret, and Daniel E. Stuntz. 1987. *The New Savory Wild Mushroom.* Revised
    and enlarged by Joseph F. Ammirati. Seattle: University of Washington Press.

GENERAL FLORAS

Biek, David. 2000. *Flora of Mount Rainier National Park.* Corvallis, Ore.: Oregon
    State University Press.
Buckingham, Nelsa M., et al. 1995. *Flora of the Olympic Peninsula.* Seattle:
    Northwest Interpretive Association.
Gilkey, H. M, L. D. Johnson, and L. R. J. Dennis. 2001. *Handbook of Northwestern
    Plants.* Corvallis, Ore.: Oregon State University Press.
Hitchcock, C. Leo, and Arthur Cronquist. 1973. *Flora of the Pacific Northwest.* Seattle:
    University of Washington Press.

Hitchcock, C. Leo, Arthur Cronquist, Marion Ownbey, and J. W. Thompson. 1955–
    1969. *Vascular Plants of the Pacific Northwest,* 5 vols. Seattle: University of
    Washington Press.
Pojar, Jim, and Andy MacKinnon, eds. 1994. *Plants of the Pacific Northwest Coast:
    Washington, Oregon, British Columbia and Alaska.* Edmonton, Alb.: Lone Pine
    Publishing.
Taylor, Ronald J., and George W. Douglas. 1995. *Mountain Plants of the Pacific
    Northwest.* Missoula, Mont.: Mountain Press Publishing.
Varner, Collin. 2003. *Plants of Vancouver and the Lower Mainland.* Vancouver, B.C.:
    Raincoast Book Distribution.

WILDFLOWERS

Clark, Lewis J. 1976. *Wildflowers of the Pacific Northwest from Alaska to Northern
    California.* Sidney, B.C.: Grays Publishing, Ltd.
Lamb, Susan, and Larry Ulrich. 1999. *Wildflowers of the Pacific Northwest.* Santa
    Barbara, Calif.: Companion Press.
Lyons, C. P. 2002. *Wildflowers of Washington.* Edmonton, Alb.: Lone Pine Publishing.
Niehaus, Theodore F., and Charles L. Ripper. 1997. *A Field Guide to Pacific States
    Wildflowers: Washington, Oregon, California and Adjacent Areas.* Boston:
    Houghton Mifflin Company.
Ross, Robert A., Henrietta Chambers, and Shirley A. Stevenson. 1988. *Wildflowers
    of the Western Cascades.* Portland, Ore.: Timber Press.
Stewart, Charles. 1994. *Wildflowers of the Olympics and Cascades.* San Francisco:
    Nature Education Enterprises.
Strickland, Dee. 1993. *Wayside Wildflowers of the Pacific Northwest.* Columbia Falls,
    Mont.: Flower Press.
Taylor, Ronald J., and George W. Douglas. 1975. *Mountain Wild Flowers of the Pacific
    Northwest.* Portland, Ore.: Binford and Mort, Publishers.

TREES AND SHRUBS

Arno, Stephen F., and Ramona Hammerly. 1977. *Northwest Trees.* Seattle: The
    Mountaineers Books.
Brayshaw, T. C. 1996. *Trees and Shrubs of British Columbia.* Vancouver, B.C.:
    University of British Columbia Press.
Derig, Betty R., and Margaret C. Fuller. 2001. *Wild Berries of the West.* Missoula,
    Mont.: Mountain Press Publishing.
Krumm, Bob. 1998. *The Pacific Northwest Berry Book.* Helena, Mont.: Falcon
    Publications.
Little, Elbert J. 1998. *The Audubon Society Field Guide to North American Trees: Western
    Region.* New York: Alfred A. Knopf.
McMinn, Howard E., and Evelyn Maino. 1967. *An Illustrated Manual of Pacific Coast
    Trees.* Berkeley: University of California Press.

Peattie, Donald C. 1991. *A Natural History of Western Trees*. Boston: Houghton Mifflin Company.

Petrides, George A., and Olivia Petrides. 1998. *A Field Guide to Western Trees*. Boston: Houghton Mifflin Company.

INSECTS

Acorn, John, and Ian Sheldon. 2001. *Bugs of Washington and Oregon*. Edmonton, Alb.: Lone Pine Publishing.

Arnett, Ross H., N. M. Downie, and H. E. Jaques. 1980. *How to Know the Beetles*. Boston: WCB McGraw Hill.

Bland, Roger G., and H. E. Jaques. 1978. *How to Know the Insects*. Boston: WCB McGraw Hill.

Borror, Donald J., Dwight M. Delong, and Charles A. Triplehorn. 1989. *An Introduction to the Study of Insects*. New York: Holt, Rinehart & Winston.

Borror, Donald J., and Richard E. White. 1970. *A Field Guide to the Insects of America North of Mexico*. Boston: Houghton Mifflin Company.

Furniss, R. L., and V. M Collin. 1977. *Western Forest Insects*. Washington, D.C.: U.S. Department of Agriculture, Miscellaneous Publication #1339, U.S. Government Printing Office.

Milne, Lorus, and Margery Milne. 1980. *The Audubon Society Field Guide to North American Insects and Spiders*. New York: Alfred A. Knopf.

White, Richard E. 1983. *A Field Guide to the Beetles of North America*. Boston: Houghton Mifflin Company.

BUTTERFLIES

Glassberg, Jeffrey. 2001. *Butterflies Through Binoculars: A Field Guide to the Butterflies of Western North America*. Oxford, U.K.: Oxford University Press.

Pyle, Robert Michael. 1981. *The Audubon Society Field Guide to North American Butterflies*. New York: Alfred A. Knopf.

———. 2002. *The Butterflies of Cascadia: A Field Guide to All the Species of Washington, Oregon, and Surrounding Territories*. Seattle: Seattle Audubon Society.

Scott, James A. 1992. *The Butterflies of North America: A Natural History*. Palo Alto, Calif.: Stanford University Press.

Tilden, J. W., and Arthur C. Smith. 1986. *A Field Guide to Western Butterflies*. Boston: Houghton Mifflin Company.

TROUT AND SALMON

Behnke, Robert J., et al. 2002. *Trout and Salmon of North America*. New York: Free Press.

Bond, C. E. 1973. *Key to Oregon Freshwater Fishes*. Rev. ed. N.p.: Oregon Agriculture Experiment Station, Technical Bulletin 58.

McAllister, D. E., and E. J. Crossman. 1973. *A Guide to the Freshwater Sport Fishes of Canada*. Ottawa, Ont.: National Museum of Natural Sciences.

Wydoski, Richard S., and Richard R. Whitney. 2003. *Inland Fishes of Washington*. Seattle: University of Washington Press.

AMPHIBIANS AND REPTILES

Bechler, John L. 1979. *The Audubon Society Field Guide to North American Reptiles and Amphibians*. New York: Alfred A. Knopf.

Corkran, Charlotte C., and C. R. Thoms. 1996. *Amphibians of Oregon, Washington and British Columbia*. Edmonton, Alb.: Lone Pine Publishing.

Nussbaum, Ronald A., E. D. Brodie Jr, and R. M. Storm. 1983. *Amphibians and Reptiles of the Pacific Northwest*. Moscow, Idaho: University Press of Idaho.

St. John, Alan. 2002. *Reptiles of the Northwest*. Edmonton, Alb.: Lone Pine Publishing.

Stebbins, Robert C. 2003. *A Field Guide to Western Reptiles and Amphibians*. Boston: Houghton Mifflin Company.

Storm, Robert M., and W. P. Leonard. 1995. *Reptiles of Washington and Oregon*. Seattle: Seattle Audubon Society.

BIRDS

Ehrlich, Paul R., D. S. Dobkin, and D. Wheye. 1988. *The Birder's Handbook: A Field Guide to the Natural History of North American Birds*. New York: Simon & Schuster.

National Geographic Society. 2002. *Field Guide to the Birds of North America*. Washington, D.C.: National Geographic Society.

Nehls, Harry B., and R. B. Horsfal. 1990. *Familiar Birds of the Pacific Northwest*. Portland, Ore.: Audubon Society of Portland.

Peterson, Roger T. 1998. *A Field Guide to Western Birds: A Completely New Guide to Field Marks of All Species Found in North America West of the 100th Meridian and North of Mexico*. Boston: Houghton Mifflin Company.

Sibley, David Allen. 2001. *The Sibley Guide to Bird Life and Behavior*. New York: Alfred A. Knopf.

———. 2002. *Sibley's Birding Basics*. New York: Alfred A. Knopf.

———. 2003. *The Sibley Field Guide to Birds of Western North America*. New York: Alfred A. Knopf.

Stokes, Donald W. 1979. *A Guide to the Behavior of Common Birds*. 3 vols. Boston: Little, Brown & Company.

Uvardy, M. D. F., and John Farrand. 1997. *The Audubon Society Field Guide to North American Birds: Western Region*. New York: Alfred A. Knopf.

Wassink, Jan L., and Kathleen Ort. 1995. *Birds of the Pacific Northwest Mountains: The Cascade Range, the Olympic Mountains, Vancouver Island, and the Coast Mountains*. Missoula, Mont.: Mountain Press Publishing.

MAMMALS

Banfield, Alexander W. F. 1974. *The Mammals of Canada*. Toronto, Ont.: University of Toronto Press.

Burt, William H., and Richard P. Grossenheider. 1998. *A Field Guide to the Mammals: North America North of Mexico*. 3rd ed. Boston: Houghton Mifflin Company.

Chapman, Joseph A., and G. A. Feldhamer, eds. 1982. *Wild Mammals of North America: Biology, Management, Economics*. Baltimore: Johns Hopkins University Press.

Eder, Tamara. 2002. *Mammals of Washington and Oregon*. Edmonton, Alb.: Lone Pine Publishing.

Ingles, Lloyd. 1965. *Mammals of the Pacific States*. Stanford, Calif.: Stanford University Press.

Maser, Chris. 1998. *Mammals of the Pacific Northwest: From the Coast to the High Cascades*. Corvallis, Ore.: Oregon State University Press.

Murie, Olaus, and R. P. Grossenheider. 1996. *Animal Tracks*. Boston: Houghton Mifflin Company.

Sheldon, Ian, and Gary Ross. 1997. *Animal Tracks of Washington and Oregon*. Edmonton, Alb.: Lone Pine Publishing.

Whitaker, John O. Jr. 1996. *The Audubon Society Field Guide to North American Mammals*. New York: Alfred A. Knopf.

index

about the authors

Stephen R. Whitney is the author of six books on natural history, including *Western Forests* (Knopf) and *A Field Guide to the Grand Canyon* (The Mountaineers Books). He is a former managing editor of the *Sierra Club Bulletin,* now *Sierra,* associate editor of *The Mother Earth News,* and contributing editor of *Backpacker* magazine. In addition, he was editorial manager of The Mountaineers Books for six years. A resident of Washington State since 1978, he and his wife live alongside a lovely river a few miles outside of Seattle.

Rob Sandelin is a naturalist and environmental educator who has since childhood spent much of his life observing and studying nature in the mountains of the Northwest. He has served as a park naturalist at Yosemite National Park, Olympic National Park, and Denali National Park. Currently he teaches field skills to student naturalists at the Environmental Education School of the Sky Valley Education Center in Monroe, Washington. He is the author of This Week in the Woods, a series of natural history essays; the *Cohousing Resource Guide;* and the Intentional Communities Resource Pages website. He lives with family and friends in the Sharingwood Cohousing Community in Snohomish County.

THE MOUNTAINEERS, founded in 1906, is a nonprofit outdoor activity and conservation club, whose mission is "to explore, study, preserve, and enjoy the natural beauty of the outdoors. . . . " Based in Seattle, Washington, the club is now one of the largest such organizations in the United States, with seven branches throughout Washington State.

The Mountaineers sponsors both classes and year-round outdoor activities in the Pacific Northwest, which include hiking, mountain climbing, ski-touring, snowshoeing, bicycling, camping, kayaking and canoeing, nature study, sailing, and adventure travel. The club's conservation division supports environmental causes through educational activities, sponsoring legislation, and presenting informational programs. All club activities are led by skilled, experienced volunteers, who are dedicated to promoting safe and responsible enjoyment and preservation of the outdoors.

If you would like to participate in these organized outdoor activities or the club's programs, consider a membership in The Mountaineers. For information and an application, write or call The Mountaineers, Club Headquarters, 7700 Sand Point Way NE, Seattle, Washington 98115; 206-521-6001.

The Mountaineers Books, an active, nonprofit publishing program of the club, produces guidebooks, instructional texts, historical works, natural history guides, and works on environmental conservation. All books produced by The Mountaineers Books fulfill the club's mission.

Send or call for our catalog of more than 500 outdoor titles:

The Mountaineers Books
1001 SW Klickitat Way, Suite 201
Seattle, WA 98134
800-553-4453
mbooks@mountaineersbooks.org
www.mountaineersbooks.org

The Mountaineers Books is proud to be a corporate sponsor of Leave No Trace, whose mission is to promote and inspire responsible outdoor recreation through education, research, and partnerships. The Leave No Trace program is focused specifically on human-powered (nonmotorized) recreation.

Leave No Trace strives to educate visitors about the nature of their recreational impacts, as well as offer techniques to prevent and minimize such impacts. Leave No Trace is best understood as an educational and ethical program, not as a set of rules and regulations.

For more information, visit *www.LNT.org,* or call 800-332-4100.

OTHER TITLES YOU MIGHT ENJOY FROM THE MOUNTAINEERS BOOKS:

BEST WILDFLOWER HIKES
Washington
Art Kruckeberg, Ira Spring, Karen Sykes, and Craig Romano
A noted botanist, local hiking columnists, and a renowned outdoor photographer lead 50 field trips to the best native wildflower fields in the state.

BIRDSONGS OF THE PACIFIC NORTHWEST:
A Field Guide and Audio CD
A great field guide set—hear the songs, see the illustrations.

NATURE IN THE CITY
Seattle
Kathryn True & Maria Dolan
The best places to experience wildlife and wild surroundings in the city.

DAY HIKING SERIES
The Mountaineers Books' newest hiking guides provide hikers with accurate hiking information in attractive, high-quality packaging and are infused with the environmental ethic that distinguishes The Mountaineers Books from other outdoor publishers.

DAY HIKING: Olympic Peninsula
Craig Romano
DAY HIKING: South Cascades
Dan Nelson, Photographs by Alan Bauer
DAY HIKING: Snoqualmie Region
Dan Nelson, Photographs by Alan Bauer
DAY HIKING: North Cascades
Craig Romano
DAY HIKING: Mount Rainier
Dan Nelson, Photographs by Alan Bauer
DAY HIKING: Central Cascades
Craig Romano